Bill Harvill

PLAIN
TALK
ON
Matthew

PLAIN
TALK
ON
Matthew

MANFORD GEORGE GUTZKE
PH.D.

**Lamplighter
Books** Grand Rapids,
Michigan
Zondervan Publishing House

PLAIN TALK ON MATTHEW
Copyright 1966 by Zondervan Publishing House
Grand Rapids, Michigan

Lamplighter Books are published by Zondervan
Publishing House, 1415 Lake Drive, S.E.,
Grand Rapids, Michigan 49506

Library of Congress Catalog Card No. 66-13689

ISBN 0-310-25601-1

Printed in the United States of America

84   85   86   87   88 / 24   23   22   21   20

CONTENTS

PLAIN
TALK
ON
Matthew

Chapter 1

THE BABY THAT SHOOK THE WORLD

How to Get to Know Jesus

What do you know about Jesus Christ? Who was He? What did He do? For what is He famous?

You may not have realized it before, but Jesus Christ received no notice in the world while He was here for anything He did as a man. He painted no pictures, invented no machine, led no army.

Yet He is cherished, revered, honored and worshiped by millions of people all around the world.

Who then is He? How could anyone get to know Him?

Men cannot know anything about Jesus Christ by looking at His portrait, for there are no real pictures of Him. We have likenesses of George Washington, Napoleon and even Julius Caesar, but even in the Bible there is no physical description of Jesus Christ (with the possible exception of Isaiah 53:2).

You could read the gospels of Matthew, Mark, Luke and John, but you wouldn't find anything about His appearance. Nor would you find any description of His occupation. Some people talk about Jesus working in Joseph's carpenter shop, but that is only inference. The Bible says nothing about it.

The Bible says nothing about what He did as a boy. There is a brief glimpse of Jesus at the age of twelve in the temple at Jerusalem, but then you hear no more of Him until He is about thirty years old and His public ministry begins. So the Bible says virtually nothing of what Jesus did for about ninety per cent of His life.

You may ask, "Does the Bible say anything at all about Jesus?"

This is what we are going to talk about in this book. We will look at what the Bible has to say about Jesus of Nazareth by studying the gospel of Matthew. Actually, all that the world knows about Jesus of Nazareth is what is written in the Bible. There is no other source. Each of the four gospels tells us about Jesus of

Nazareth in a special way, but they do not contradict each other.
Ever since the Lord Jesus Christ lived on earth, some people
have confessed they believed He was the Son of God, the Saviour
of the world. Some who lived with Him wrote in the Bible of what
they saw and heard. What Christians believed about Him in the
history of the church is to be found in the creeds of the church.
But all the great creeds of the church are based on the Bible, and
so we turn to the Bible to find out what they knew about Him.

Great theologians discuss aspects of what is believed about
the Lord Jesus Christ, of His nature and work. But when you read
the books these great theologians write, you find that when they
talk about Jesus Christ they too start with the Bible. So we say
again, what you have in your Bible is the only actual information
anyone has about Jesus Christ.

Someone may say, "But not everyone accepts the Bible!" Quite
true. But keep in mind that when the Lord was here on earth,
not everyone accepted Him either, yet that did not change one
fact about Him. He lived in Palestine, walked the streets of Jerusalem, stood in the open court and was examined by the crowds.
It is a fact that thousands saw Him even though few believed in
Him. So it is not strange that many people read the Bible today
and then say, "I can't believe it." This does not change anything
in the Bible. It only shows us something about the person who
says it.

There is a way in which a person could be convinced that what
is written in the Bible is true. Actually, no man would have to
take my word for it; there is a better way for him to find out
for sure.

If a man were to tell me that the tea in a certain cup is sweet,
I could look at it forever, but I could never know simply by looking whether it is sweet or not. I might even argue, "Tea as dark
as that can't be sweet," but my argument wouldn't help me to
know and it would not affect the tea. There is one way to find
out for sure! A very simple way: taste it. If I were to sip a bit
of it, I would know whether or not it was sweet.

So it is with the Scriptures: "Taste and see," and you will
know.

In this book we are going to study the gospel of Matthew to
find out about Jesus of Nazareth. As we think about what is written, we may keep in mind that if we want to understand about
Jesus Christ, there are some basic ideas we must accept first.

1. We must accept the idea of the reality of another world. Sometimes it is called a "heavenly" world; sometimes it is called a
"spiritual" world. We live in a world we can see, but there is
another world we cannot see. Both worlds are real. Both worlds

were made by God and are under His control, but the way things happen in one is different from the other. In this world men dominate; in the other world God dominates. The world in which God dominates (the "spiritual") is just as real as the world in which man dominates (the "natural"). Not only is God's world a real world, but God is real too, just as real as your neighbor, just as real as your family and just as real as you are.

2. We must accept the idea that God has a plan for each of us. God knows the trouble we are in, and He has set up a plan of salvation for us. This salvation is made possible in Jesus Christ.

3. We must also accept the idea that God can show His plan of salvation to us. It would be of no help to us for God to have a plan for us to follow unless He can somehow show us who live in this world what that plan is. Only then can we follow it.

God reveals Himself to man in various ways. You can look at nature and see the work of God. The sky above, the earth around you, the grass, the flowers, the birds, the beasts, everything on the face of the earth – God made all these things. We call all these things "Nature," and as we look at them we learn about God.

Almost everyone has some faith in nature's revelation of God. A farmer plants grain in the field, expecting the sun to shine, the rain to fall, and that in time he will harvest his crop. Perhaps the farmer needs a certain kind of faith to plant the seed, but this is not the kind of faith of which the Bible speaks, when it says a man is saved by faith.

If a man has faith in the God of nature *and only that,* he will reap the rewards of such faith *and only that.* But if he wants to know God in a deeper way, in a way which goes beyond nature, in a way that will discover God's plan of eternal salvation, he must find a further revelation of God than what can be seen in nature.

When we think, we use words. We can have feelings without words, but we do not think without words. If anyone wants to share some idea with you, he must put it in words. He must speak and you must listen.

This is the way it is with God and you. When God wants to share with you His plan of salvation, He expresses it in words, and His words are in the Bible which He has addressed to you. In the Bible God explains His plan of salvation. Through the Scriptures God speaks to your heart. When He speaks, we must listen. In just this way, when God reveals Himself in this gospel of Matthew, we may see Him, hear Him, understand Him and respond to Him as He shows Himself to be.

4. We must accept the idea that Jesus Christ in Himself is the true Word of God. The Bible is called the written Word of

God, but Jesus Christ is the living Word of God. The outstanding revelation of God is in the person of Jesus Christ. If we ever want to understand Jesus Christ, we must accept the idea that in Him God is working out His plan of salvation. Therefore it is in Jesus Christ, not in nature, that God has accomplished His greatest work. In Jesus Christ, God is reconciling the world to Himself.

Each of these four ideas is to be accepted in faith. Accepting any idea in faith means to hold as true and real something that cannot be seen just now. A man can't see God; he can't see Jesus Christ; he can't see heaven. To take these as real is to exercise faith.

Some years ago, I was eating lunch with two university professors and talking about this matter of exercising faith in what is not seen. They asked me, "Isn't your faith so personal and so subjective that you could not share it with anyone else?"

I thought about that for a moment. Then I asked, "When a scientist looks through a microscope and sees something, can he tell you what he saw?"

They said, "Certainly."

I replied, "You would not know what he saw. You would only know what he said he saw. You would not know if he were telling the truth or not."

"But we could test it," they answered.

"Just so! And don't you think you could test the Gospel?" I replied.

Actually this is the way it works. Persons who believe in Jesus Christ testify to others of Him. Anyone who hears can test the evidence for himself. The common conclusion of everyone who has ever tested for himself what the witnesses tell, is that Jesus Christ of whom they speak is exactly what they say He claims to be.

And this is how anyone gets to know about Jesus Christ. You read in the Bible, or you listen to someone who teaches what is in the Bible, until you hear what has been written in the Word of God about Him. You think about it and consider all the evidence reported to you by persons who put the promises in the Scriptures to the test, and in that way you arrive at your own conclusion.

"Faith cometh by hearing, and hearing by the word of God" (Romans 10:17).

WHY ARE THERE FOUR GOSPELS?

The New Testament begins with Matthew, Mark, Luke and John, known as the four gospels. Each presents a different account of what happened when Jesus Christ was on earth. Not one of these is a biography since there are long periods in the life of Jesus of Nazareth about which nothing is recorded. Two of the four tell something about His birth, and one reports an event when he was twelve years old. Nothing else is mentioned until He began to preach at about thirty years of age. It seems clear the four gospels were not written to give a complete story of the life of Jesus, but rather to tell about the "good news" that is in Christ Jesus: that God has provided a way of salvation for sinful man through Christ Jesus.

While Matthew, Mark, Luke and John are each different, yet they all agree. They agree that God cares about sinners. In each gospel, as you read about the Lord Jesus you find troubled people coming to Him for help. The blind came to Jesus and were made to see; the sick were brought to Him and were made well; the lame were brought to Him and were made to walk.

You read this in each of the four gospels. They all show how much Jesus cared for the helpless and the hopeless. In fact, the four gospels are each a message of hope. Since Jesus came to earth, the sinner who recognizes that he is spiritually blind, spiritually sick and spiritually lame, can have hope.

The "good news" of all four gospels is this: Jesus Christ came to save sinners.

Yet, you might ask, "Why did there have to be four gospels? Wouldn't one have been enough?"

Have you ever been at the scene of an accident? If there are four witnesses to it, and each one told exactly what he saw, would you get the same story? No, you would not. Each witness would tell the story the way he saw it. Each would see things the others did not see; some would mention details the others would omit. Yet, if they were reliable witnesses, they would all agree on the main facts. And if four told about it, you would have a more complete report. The four gospels agree on the main facts. And the most significant fact of all is simply this: Jesus Christ came into the world to save sinners.

The Family Tree

The book of the generation of Jesus Christ, the son of David, the son of Abraham. Abraham begat Isaac; and Isaac begat Jacob; and Jacob begat Judas and his brethren; And Judas begat Phares and Zara of Thamar; and Phares begat Esrom; and Esrom begat Aram; And Aram begat Aminadab; and Aminadab begat Naasson; and Naasson begat Salmon; And Salmon begat Booz of Rachab; and Booz begat Obed of Ruth; and Obed begat Jesse; And Jesse begat David the king; and David the king begat Solomon of her that had been the wife of Urias; And Solomon begat Roboam; and Roboam begat Abia; and Abia begat Asa; And Asa begat Josaphat; and Josaphat begat Joram; and Joram begat Ozias; And Ozias begat Joatham; and Joatham begat Achaz; and Achaz begat Ezekias; And Ezekias begat Manasses; and Manasses begat Amon; and Amon begat Josias; And Josias begat Jechonias and his brethren, about the time they were carried away to Babylon: And after they were brought to Babylon, Jechonias begat Salathiel; and Salathiel begat Zorobabel; And Zorobabel begat Abiud; and Abiud begat Eliakim; and Eliakim begat Azor; And Azor begat Sadoc; and Sadoc begat Achim; and Achim begat Eliud; And Eliud begat Eleazar; and Eleazar begat Matthan; and Matthan begat Jacob; And Jacob begat Joseph the husband of Mary, of whom was born Jesus, who is called Christ. So all the generations from Abraham to David are fourteen generations; and from David until the carrying away into Babylon are fourteen generations; and from the carrying away into Babylon unto Christ are fourteen generations (Matthew 1:1-17).

If you were a little Jewish boy named Samuel, you would bring your genealogy with you on the first day you came to a Jewish school. It would say something like this: "The book of the generation of Samuel, the son of Levi, the Son of Solomon, the son of Abraham."

And it is in this way, very familiar to the Jews, that the gospel of Matthew begins. Among the Jews, a genealogy indicated who the person was and where he stood in his community.

To a somewhat lesser extent a genealogy serves the same purpose for all of us.

Suppose you ask a friend of yours, "Who is that young fellow across the street?"

"Tom Jones," your friend replies.

"Tom Jones? That name isn't familiar; I don't think I know him," you say.

Then your friend says, "Tom is the son of Banker Jones."

Immediately you know not only who he is but also his status in the community. His status in the community, in your opinion, is considerably raised because Banker Jones is his father. Even if your friend knew the young man was an adopted son, or a stepson, he might well say simply that he is the "son of Banker Jones."

Notice the great names included in the genealogy of Jesus Christ. Abraham was a great name in the Old Testament, and his name is still great. Three world religions point back to this great patriarch—Judaism, Mohammedanism and Christianity. Not only in the Old Testament, but in the New Testament as well, Abraham is considered to be the great pioneer of faith.

Abraham received blessing from God simply by believing in

Him: "Abraham believed God, and it was counted unto him for righteousness" (Romans 4:3). In the epistle of James, he is called "the Friend of God" (James 2:23).

God promised Abraham, "And in thy seed shall all the nations of the earth be blessed" (Genesis 22:18). In other words, Abraham was to be the channel through whom God would bless mankind. It was because of Abraham's faith and not his good works that God promised to bless him. This blessing was also promised to Abraham's seed or descendants, who would also receive the blessing of God by believing.

So as you begin the gospel of Matthew and read, "The book of the generation of Jesus Christ, the son of Abraham," you know that Jesus Christ is the promised seed of Abraham who carries on the blessing. It is in Jesus Christ, the Seed of Abraham, that all nations would be blessed.

Jesus was also "the son of David," the greatest king in Israel's history. Like Abraham, David too received a promise from God. Just as Abraham was promised that he would receive God's blessing, so David was promised that one of his seed would sit on the throne forever. To Abraham, God promised that He would bless anyone who would believe in Him and obey Him. To David, God promised that He would bless by bringing order and peace to the world (through one of his seed) to replace chaos and confusion.

Later on, Matthew quotes the prophecy that refers to Jesus Christ as a governor that would rule the people of Israel. Jesus Christ was the One who would fulfill the promise to David and would be on the throne in control of the activities of the people of God, and through them would affect all men everywhere.

The long genealogy in verses 2 to 17 identifies Jesus Christ as belonging to the family of Joseph, who was a direct descendant of David and of Abraham.

But now there may be a question in your mind: Since Jesus was born of a virgin and Joseph was not His natural father, how then can He be counted as a child of Joseph so that He can inherit the right to the throne? Did you know that even today any child born in wedlock takes the name of the husband of the mother, is counted as his child, and has all the rights and privileges his child would have?

So when Jesus was born of Mary, He inherited all the rights and privileges of a child of Joseph, who was then Mary's husband. And thus it appears that Matthew presents the genealogy which gives Jesus of Nazareth the legal right to be counted the son of David, and to sit on the throne.

Whenever you see, as you read through the gospel of Matthew, the phrase "the kingdom of heaven," you can always remember the first verse in the book which says that Jesus of Nazareth was the son of David. And whenever you think about being saved by grace through faith, you can remember that Jesus was also the son of Abraham.

THE VIRGIN BIRTH

Now the birth of Jesus Christ was on this wise: When as his mother Mary was espoused to Joseph, before they came together, she was found with child of the Holy Ghost. Then Joseph her husband, being a just man, and not willing to make her a public example, was minded to put her away privily. But while he thought on these things, behold, the angel of the Lord appeared unto him in a dream, saying, Joseph, thou son of David, fear not to take unto thee Mary thy wife: for that which is conceived in her is of the Holy Ghost. And she shall bring forth a son, and thou shalt call his name JESUS: for he shall save his people from their sins. Now all this was done, that it might be fulfilled which was spoken of the Lord by the prophet, saying, Behold, a virgin shall be with child, and shall bring forth a son, and they shall call his name Emmanuel, which being interpreted is, God with us. Then Joseph being raised from sleep did as the angel of the Lord had bidden him, and took unto him his wife: And knew her not till she had brought forth her firstborn son: and he called his name JESUS (Matthew 1:18-25).

Reading Matthew 1:18-25 will show plainly that the record states Jesus of Nazareth was born of a virgin. Some men may not believe it, but let us not be surprised about that. Many people don't believe the Bible at all. However, no one can possibly deny that the Bible says Jesus Christ was born of a virgin. And nothing is written anywhere else in Scripture which contradicts this plain teaching.

The virgin birth was the belief of the early Christian church. In the Apostles' Creed we say, "I believe in Jesus Christ . . . who was conceived of the Holy Ghost, born of the Virgin Mary." Apparently in this, the early church, by common consent, made it a matter of record that the apostles believed the virgin birth.

Though Jesus Christ was *legally* the son of Joseph according to Jewish custom, He was *not actually* the son of Joseph. He was really the Son of God who was His true Father. Someone may say, "But I am also a son of God." In a sense, that is true. According to the Bible, when you believe in the Lord Jesus Christ you become a child of God. Paul says in Romans that believers are adopted into God's family. In this way as a believer, you are an "adopted" son. But there is only one "begotten" Son of God: the Lord Jesus Christ.

Shortly before His crucifixion, Jesus prayed, "Father, glorify thou me with thine own self with the glory which I had with thee before the world was" (John 17:5). This means that before He was born in Bethlehem, the Lord Jesus Christ had lived in glory with God. After His death He arose and now He lives in glory again. I certainly wouldn't claim that I lived before I was born. But this is what Jesus claimed. When He was born in Bethlehem, He was the Son of God become incarnate: that is, He became flesh and bones. And this was possible because of the virgin birth. As the begotten Son of God, He did not have the sin of Adam in Him, but rather the holiness of God. The virgin birth makes the whole story of Jesus Christ, as the only begotten Son of God, consistent with His pre-existence, and shows Him to be not sinful as Adam, but holy as God.

It is quite true that when the Lord Jesus Christ came into this world He was given a human body just as any other man has, with this one exception, he was "yet without sin." In this birth He "took upon him the form of a servant" but He was always the Son of God. Since He was eternally the Son of God, He could not be born the way you and I were born. You were born of father and mother, because you are a child of man. But when Jesus of Nazareth was born with a nature that had no sin in it, He was in Himself not the child of human parents, but the child of God.

In the accounts of the birth of Jesus of Nazareth the Bible is not giving an "opinion" regarding the virgin birth; it is giving a straightforward account of an event that actually occurred, just as it is written.

The Wise Men From the East

Now when Jesus was born in Bethlehem of Judea in the days of Herod the king, behold, there came wise men from the east to Jerusalem, Saying, Where is he that is born King of the Jews? for we have seen his star in the east, and are come to worship him. When Herod the king had heard these things, he was troubled, and all Jerusalem with him. And when he had gathered all the chief priests and scribes of the people together, he demanded of them where Christ should be born. And they said unto him, In Bethlehem of Judea: for thus it is written by the prophet, And thou Bethlehem, in the land of Juda, art not the least among the princes of Juda: for out of thee shall come a Governor, that shall rule my people Israel. Then Herod, when he had privily called the wise men, enquired of them diligently what time the star appeared. And he sent them to Bethlehem, and said, Go and search diligently for the young child; and when ye have found him, bring me word again, that I may come and worship him also. When they had heard the king, they departed; and, lo, the star, which they saw in the east, went before them, till it came and stood over where the young child was. When they saw the star, they rejoiced with exceeding great joy. And when they were come into the house, they saw the young child with Mary his mother, and fell down, and worshipped him: and when they had opened their treasures, they presented unto him gifts; gold, and frankincense, and myrrh. And being warned of God in a dream that they should not return to Herod, they departed into their own country another way (Matthew 2:1-12).

Everyone knows the story about the wise men coming to Bethlehem to see the One who was born King of the Jews. It is a simple story, but there are things in it not nearly as simple as they look.

For instance, no one knows who these wise men were, nor how many there were. You may feel quite sure that there were three, but the Bible doesn't say so. Perhaps because they brought three different kinds of gifts some may think that there were three wise men, but there may have been two, or eight, or a dozen. As "wise men" they may have been scholars or scientists in their day, but this does not say they were "three kings" as we often sing. We can be sure of one thing: they came "from the East." Yet this does not say very much. East of Palestine could be Arabia, Persia or India. No one knows which country they came from.

When they arrived in Jerusalem, they asked a definite question: "Where is he that is born King of the Jews?"

The key word in that question is "born." This was the word that troubled King Herod. Herod, after all, had been "appointed" king; he was not "born" king. To make matters worse, as far as the Jews were concerned, Herod had been appointed by the Roman government. The Jews resented having such a puppet king, because they knew that the throne really belonged to a descendant of David. King Herod knew how the Jews felt about it, and this naturally made him uneasy. If these visitors from the East had been poor beggars, shepherds, or even merchants, Herod might have ignored their question. But obviously they were important persons. It is no wonder Herod was troubled.

Herod asked the Jewish scholars where Christ was to be born. "Christ" is the Greek word for "Messiah," which means "Anointed One." The scholars pointed out to him the passage in the Scriptures by the prophet Micah which says the Messiah would be born in Bethlehem.

When Herod returned to the wise men with this information, he asked them questions about the strange star they were following.

For 2,000 years since Herod, people have been asking about that star.

Some try to explain it as a meteor, but the meteors we know about do not last that long. Others say it may have been a bright light that simply looked like a star. Actually no one knows what that star really was. Nor does anyone understand how the wise men were able to follow it. It is another of the simple things in this story that no one can explain.

We do know, however, that this star led them to the house where the young child was. In the gospel of Luke, we read that when the Lord Jesus was born He was laid in a manger. Some people think the wise men came to Bethlehem on Christmas Eve, but this does not seem possible. We read the wise men came to the young child with Mary, His mother. This sounds very much as if Mary were sitting there holding the young child on her knee. Shortly afterward, Joseph was warned by God in a dream to take Mary and the baby and flee to Egypt, which he did. This would seem to indicate the child was old enough to travel.

When Herod decided to kill all the boy babies in the Bethlehem area, he ordered the death of all who were two years old and younger. Since he had previously asked the wise men when the star had first appeared, it may mean that they had been seeing this phenomenon in the heavens for some time.

In any case it seems quite probable the wise men didn't come on Christmas Eve. In fact, they may not have arrived in Bethlehem until as much as two years later.

These matters may not be so very important and yet they are interesting. They do help us to get a more accurate picture of this remarkable event, which has meant so much to the whole world.

Step by Step With God

And when they were departed, behold, the angel of the Lord appeareth to Joseph in a dream, saying, Arise, and take the young child and his mother and flee into Egypt; and be thou there until I bring thee word: for Herod will seek the young child to destroy him. When he arose, he took the young child and his mother by night, and departed into Egypt: And was there until the death of Herod: that it might be fulfilled which was spoken of the Lord by the prophet, saying, Out of Egypt have I called my son. Then Herod, when he saw that he was mocked of the wise men, was exceeding wroth, and sent forth, and slew all the children that were in Bethlehem, and in all the coasts thereof, from two years old and under, according to the time which he had diligently enquired of the wise men. Then was fulfilled that which was spoken by Jeremy, the prophet, saying, In Rama was there a voice heard, lamentation, and weeping, and great mourning, Rachel weeping for her children, and would not be comforted, because they are not. But when Herod was dead, behold, an angel of the Lord appeareth in a dream to Joseph in Egypt, Saying, Arise, and take the young child and his mother, and go into the land of Israel: for they are dead which sought the young child's life. And he arose, and took the young child and his mother, and came into the land of Israel. But when he heard that Archelaus did reign in Judea in the room of his father Herod, he was afraid to go thither: notwithstanding, being warned of God in a dream, he turned aside into the parts of Galilee: And he came and dwelt in a city called Nazareth: that it might be fulfilled which was spoken by the prophets, He shall be called a Nazarene. (Matthew 2:13-23).

When the only begotten Son of God was born as a child of a humble virgin, everything that happened to Him was controlled by the hand of God. His coming was not made known to the Roman rulers, nor to the Jewish religious leaders. Even the people in Bethlehem did not realize who He was. In fact, when Joseph and Mary were led to flee for safety with the young child they were directed to go to Egypt, a pagan country. As far as God was concerned Egypt could be as safe as Judea. He made both countries and both peoples. They were all under His control.

Another unusual aspect of this chapter is the way God directed men. He led the wise men to Bethlehem. He directed Joseph to take Mary to be his wife. He guided Joseph with Mary and the baby Jesus to safety in Egypt, and after Herod was dead He led them back again and guided them to Nazareth.

God wants to guide you, too, and He will if you get in close contact with Him through Jesus Christ. He will make known His will to you and you can follow Him step by step.

Through all the events relating to the birth of Jesus Christ, the touch of God's hand is felt. The record shows that Almighty God is overruling in all things to bring His will to pass. With all confidence you can expect God will lay His hands on you and guide you, if you are willing to follow His guidance.

Chapter 2

BEFORE HIS MINISTRY BEGAN

The gospel of Matthew tells how God the Father sent the message of salvation to men through His Son Jesus Christ. But men, being what they are, have minds of their own and are naturally not ready to receive God's salvation in Jesus Christ. Human beings are naturally self-centered. From the time a baby is born, it refers everything to itself. Everything it gets hold of it takes for itself. The same disposition that causes your baby to go after a rattle is the urge you will find in a businessman who tries to purchase another piece of property.

The first necessary step for anyone who is going to let the work of Christ be done in him is to deny himself. The Lord Jesus said, "If any man will come after me, let him deny himself, and take up his cross, and follow me" (Matthew 16:24). When you deny yourself, you deny the "I" that is naturally always in first place in your mind.

In other words, a man must admit he just hasn't got what it takes. Such a person, judging himself to be unfit, would be willing to receive the life of God through Jesus Christ, which comes in place of his own life. You see, the Lord Jesus Christ was sent down from God to be a "substitute" *in* you, *for* you. The Lord Himself will take over inside you and live out the life of God in you.

But just as long as you think you can manage your own life by yourself, you will want to run it independently of God. You will need to be ready to give up on yourself, before you can receive Jesus Christ as Saviour and Lord.

Have you ever seen a little boy walking across the street with his mother, all the while fussing because she is holding his hand? He wants to walk across the street all by himself, without any help. Many people are that way spiritually. As long as a man has confidence in himself, he will not let God take charge of his life.

In preparation for the work of Christ, a man must "repent." John the Baptist was the great preparer for the Lord Jesus Christ. He went before Him, preparing the people for Christ's coming. He preached about judging oneself in the sight of God as unworthy.

This was an important preparation, but it was not all that was needed. It has the same relation to the Gospel that scouring a pot has to cooking a meal. If you were going to cook a kettle of soup, you would first cleanse the kettle. Washing the kettle is certainly not making the soup, but it is very important in the whole process.

To be ready for the work of Christ in your heart, you must first of all repent. The heart that knows its need is the heart that is ready to receive God's help.

The second important step in preparing to receive Jesus Christ is to see this world as Jesus of Nazareth looked at it when He came. It seems clear that He did not see anything in this world which He would seek to have for His own, for which He would be willing to serve. He certainly did not come to advance Himself in this world. He did not come to build up a fortune. He did not come to reorganize the political structure of the world. He did not come to write books nor to paint pictures. Nor did He come to help men make the most of themselves. He never encouraged a man to go out and see what he could make of himself. And He did not come into the world to fix the world up.

He came into the world *to bring man into a right relationship with God.* He came to bring man into relationship with another world which is different from this one. Jesus came to tell us about the spiritual world, which has a different set of values than this world.

The natural world, which comes to me through my senses, attracts me and intrigues me. But there is a certain blight upon everything that is natural. The consequences of sin have ruined the natural. Everything in the natural world leads to death.

The Lord Jesus always confronted the reality of the natural world with the reality of the spiritual world. Over and over again He won the victory over the natural world by exercising His spiritual power.

This is seen especially in the temptation in the wilderness. After He had fasted forty days, and the temptation came that He should turn the stones into bread, His answer was not based on whether He could do it or not, but on whether or not this was God's will for Him to do. Bread would feed the body in the natural world, but the Word of God feeds the spirit in God's world.

Although Jesus lived in this world in the body, He did all

things in this world with His body to please His Father. In other words, the deciding principle in His life was the will of the Father. To be sure, at the last it brought about His death, but God raised Him from the dead.

So we find in the Lord Jesus the pattern of godly living in this world, denying the flesh and walking in the ways of the Spirit. In this way Jesus showed how He rates this natural world to be less important than the Spiritual world.

And so to prepare yourself for the work of the Lord Jesus Christ in your heart, there are two things you can do:

1. Make a judgment concerning yourself. Realize you are not worthy because of sinfulness. Repent.

2. Make a judgment concerning this world. It is second-rate. Put it in second place. Then you can use it, manage it, control it for the benefit of others, in such a way as to "lay up treasure in heaven."

The Man Who Prepared the Way

In those days came John the Baptist, preaching in the wilderness of Judea, And saying, Repent ye: for the kingdom of heaven is at hand. For this is he that was spoken of by the prophet Esaias, saying, The voice of one crying in the wilderness, Prepare ye the way of the Lord, make his paths straight. And the same John had his raiment of camel's hair, and a leathern girdle about his loins; and his meat was locusts and wild honey. Then went out to him Jerusalem, and all Judea, and all the region round about Jordan, And were baptized of him in Jordan, confessing their sins (Matthew 3:1-6).

Who was this young preacher, John the Baptist? What do we know about him?

We know something about his age, for he was just six months older than Jesus of Nazareth. Since Jesus began to preach at about thirty years of age, John must have been about thirty or thirty-one years old at this time.

We also know that his mother was Elisabeth, a cousin and close friend of Mary, the mother of the Lord Jesus. And, we know that his father was Zacharias, a priest.

But the most striking thing we know about John the Baptist is that he was filled with the Holy Spirit from his birth. As a result, we can think he grew to be a man who was unusually sensitive in spiritual things.

An Old Testament prophecy predicted he would come. Isaiah (40:3) said that before Messiah came, there would be a forerunner, a herald who would come to prepare the way.

In old times, when a king traveled anywhere, an advance agent always went before him to prepare the community into which he would journey. They had no telephones, telegraphs or radios to alert the citizens of the community that the king was coming. So if such a trip were planned, a herald was sent ahead to open up the roads, to make arrangements for food and lodging, and to prepare the people for his coming. He tried to make sure that everything would be ready when the king came. In this way John the Baptist came as a herald of the King of kings, the Lord Jesus Christ.

He certainly seems to us to have been a strange herald for such a divine king. His raiment was of camel's hair. He wore a leather girdle around his loins. He ate locusts and wild honey. For many years I thought John must have been a freak. Only recently have I come to realize that the Bible is simply giving a description of a poor man's dress and a poor man's diet of that day. In our day, John's camel's hair clothing would be something like blue denim overalls. He was dressed in the clothing of the average working man.

There was nothing strange about the record: "His meat was locusts and wild honey." In our own day college students have made a fad out of swallowing goldfish and you might imagine that John was a similar attention-seeker or at best a health food faddist. But just recently I read in a letter from some missionary friends in the Congo, who had been visiting with Congolese natives, and they had dined on fried ants. This does not sound very appetizing to me, but those people apparently liked them.

When I was a professor in college, I had a student who grew up in the Congo. Once I asked him if it were true that the natives ate locusts.

He replied, "Oh, yes."

"What do they taste like?" I asked.

Without realizing what he was saying, he answered, "Oh, just like other grasshoppers." Of course, he had eaten them himself.

To say that John the Baptist lived on locusts and wild honey is not much different from saying today that a man lives on oatmeal and cornbread. It was a poor man's diet. Far from making a spectacle of himself, John the Baptist, by his clothing and diet, was showing that he was only an ordinary, everyday man.

There is one other thing to note about John. He was a powerful preacher. Although he was only a young man preaching out in the country, all Jerusalem went out to hear him preach.

In the days of D. L. Moody, thousands would flock to hear that great evangelist preach. Wherever Billy Sunday went, practically the entire city would come to hear him. And in our day, as many as 100,000 people at a time throng into a stadium to hear Billy Graham.

This young John the Baptist was the Billy Graham of the day. As he preached, people went out to him, "and were baptized of him in Jordan, confessing their sins."

Baptizing by John the Baptist was very much the same as when a modern-day evangelist gives an invitation. Often an evangelist invites anyone who wants to make a confession of faith to come to the front. Or perhaps you have heard the evangelist say, "If anyone here really believes what I am holding out before you, come down here and shake my hand. I will talk with you afterward." When a person steps out and walks down the aisle in full view of the whole congregation, this can be very meaningful. I don't think there is anything magical about it, but it can be extremely meaningful. It is a sign that the person really means to receive the message.

John's baptism was something like that. In those days John the Baptist was not the only person who baptized. His disciples baptized and so did the disciples of Jesus, although Jesus Himself did not. They used baptism as a public procedure to get people to commit themselves; in other words, after the preacher had preached a message that deeply moved his audience, the people were invited to step out and be baptized.

What was John's message all about? He was asking these people to repent, and in repenting they would be confessing their sins.

Perhaps you have noticed that the Bible never talks about what happens to people who never sin. There aren't any such people. On the other hand, the Bible says, "There is none righteous, no, not one" (Romans 3:10); "For all have sinned, and come short of the glory of God" (Romans 3:23).

The wonderful message of the Bible is that it tells you what to do about your sins. You can't erase them; you can't ignore them. You can only admit that they are there, all out in the open before a mighty God. And you can confess them. In the presence of God, you can acknowledge your sins. The first step in getting right with God is to be honest with God about yourself. Admitting the truth about your sin is a vital part of repentance.

Since Jesus Christ came to save people from their sins, it was important that people should confess their sins and repent to be ready to receive Him. This is what John the Baptist preached in preparing the people to hear and to receive Jesus Christ.

If a man is to be ready to let a doctor help him, he must be ready to admit that he is sick and needs help. A man who thinks there is nothing the matter with him does not want to go to a doctor.

John the Baptist helped men to realize they were sinners and needed to be saved.

What Is Repentance?

But when he saw many of the Pharisees and Sadducees come to his baptism, he said unto them, O generation of vipers, who hath warned you to flee from the wrath to come? Bring forth therefore fruits meet for repentance: And think not to say within yourselves, We have Abraham to our father: for I say unto you, that God is able of these stones to raise up children unto Abraham. And now also the ax is laid unto the root of the trees: therefore every tree which bringeth not forth good fruit is hewn down, and cast into the fire. I indeed baptize you with water unto repentance: but he that cometh after me is mightier than I, whose shoes I am not worthy to bear: he shall baptize you with the Holy Ghost, and with fire: Whose fan is in his hand, and he will throughly purge his floor, and gather his wheat into the garner; but he will burn up the chaff with unquenchable fire (Matthew 3:7-12).

You will hear much about the Pharisees and Sadducees in the gospel of Matthew. The Pharisees put great emphasis upon the Scriptures and tried to hold them exactly as they were written. They prided themselves upon their outward conformity to God's law, even though they did not keep the spirit of it in their hearts. Scrupulously they read the Scriptures, prayed, tithed and attended public worship.

The Sadducees, however, were quite different. Although they claimed to have the blessing of God, they did not believe in the spiritual world. They did not believe in the reality of the soul, nor in the reality of heaven. They denied the supernatural in everything. They denied miracles, a resurrection and life after death. In fact, they seemed to deny everything they could not see.

But, you may ask, how in the world could they call themselves religious?

To be sure, they knew how God had helped the children of Israel in the past, and somehow, though vaguely and inconsistently, they wanted divine blessing. They denied that God could work in a spiritual realm and yet they wanted His help. It doesn't make sense, but there are many people who hold the same position today.

It is true we have both Pharisees and Sadducees in our churches today. Some people, like Pharisees, depend on outward form. They do what is required of them, and often nothing more. Others, like Sadducees, do not want to believe anything supernatural, but they still want the blessing of God. If a man were to speak of love, joy and peace, the Sadducees would say, "Yes, that is just what we want." But if he then spoke of heaven, the Holy Spirit or regeneration, they would say, "Well now, we can't believe in that old-fashioned stuff."

When John the Baptist recognized these two prominent groups of religious leaders coming to him, he challenged them, "Don't come out here to merely put on an outward show; show some actual evidence that you have repented, if you expect the blessing of God."

There were also other people not willing to respond to John's preaching who felt that they personally did not need to do anything to qualify to receive the blessing of God.

Have you ever heard a person say, "This matter of being converted is all right for people who are not Christians, but I am a Christian"? "What makes one a Christian?" you might ask.

"My father was one and my grandfather was one. In fact, our whole family is Christian. We have always belonged to the church, we always go to church and we always give to church."

This was the attitude of the Pharisees and Sadducees in that day. But just as John the Baptist said, "Simply because you are a descendant of Abraham doesn't mean that you are holy," so you could say to their modern counterparts, "Just because your father is a good Christian, that doesn't mean that you are a Christian." Every man must come to God himself, repent of his sins and believe in the Lord Jesus Christ.

What does it mean to repent?

There are two things it does not mean:

1. To repent does not mean to be sorry for your sins. Certainly we might well be sorry for our sins, but that is not what "repent" means. It is not a matter of crying over spilt milk. If you have done wrong, you should confess it to God. But to spend your time lamenting that you did wrong is not repentance.

2. To repent does not mean to promise to do better. When someone says to me, "I'm just going to do better than I have," I always feel like asking, "You, and who else?" You see, if he yielded to a certain temptation today, he will probably yield to the same temptation tomorrow.

Then, what *is* repentance?

Repentance is a judgment on yourself. When you repent, you admit that you are not what you ought to be and you judge yourself as unfit and unworthy.

Someone might ask, "What is the point in doing that?"

This prepares a frame of mind to accept Christ. You honestly admit that you are not what you ought to be. In the sight of God you are a sinner. This will incline you to let the Lord Jesus Christ come in and make you what you ought to be. This makes repentance an important prerequisite to becoming a Christian.

If you want to come to God, the first thing you need to do is to repent – to judge yourself.

Isaiah said, "Woe is me! for I am undone; because I am a man of unclean lips, and I dwell in the midst of a people of unclean lips." Job said, "I have heard of thee by the hearing of the ear: but now mine eye seeth thee. Wherefore I abhor myself, and repent in dust and ashes." Paul said, "I know that in me (that is, in my flesh) dwelleth no good thing."

When you admit you are weak, it seems easy to look to Jesus, who is strong. When you admit you are sinful, you can always look to Jesus, who is holy.

When I was a boy, I sometimes had to bring in a pail of milk. Suppose I found a pail that had some water in it. What would I do? I would empty out the water, so I could fill the pail full of milk.

The way in which we receive Jesus Christ is to empty ourselves by repenting. As long as we are full of ourselves in our self-righteousness, Jesus Christ can't come in.

THE BAPTISM OF JESUS

Then cometh Jesus from Galilee to Jordan unto John, to be baptized of him. But John forbad him, saying, I have need to be baptized of thee, and comest thou to me? And Jesus answering said unto him, Suffer it to be so now: for thus it becometh us to fulfil all righteousness. Then he suffered him. And Jesus, when he was baptized, went up straightway out of the water: and, lo, the heavens were opened unto him, and he saw the Spirit of God descending like a dove, and lighting upon him: And lo a voice from heaven, saying, This is my beloved Son, in whom I am well pleased (Matthew 3:13-17).

John's reluctance to baptize the Lord Jesus is probably the most outstanding tribute we have concerning the life Jesus lived in His first thirty years.

John the Baptist, filled with the Holy Spirit and consequently especially sensitive to spiritual things, was quite aware of the significance of a man's conduct. Since John and Jesus were second cousins, they no doubt had been boyhood friends. Now when John saw his cousin coming to him to be baptized, he was reluctant to do it.

Why?

Remember John was preaching repentance for the remission of sins. When he saw Jesus coming to be baptized, he protested because he knew Jesus had not sinned in all his acquaintance with Him.

John said, "I have need to be baptized of thee," or in other words, "What you've got is greater than what I've got."

The Lord Jesus did not say that John was wrong. Rather, He replied, "Suffer it to be so now," as if to say, "Even though you do not understand exactly what I am doing, trust me in this and let's go through with it."

Why would Jesus come to be baptized? John's message was known throughout the land. While many people accepted his message, many others did not. Many refused even to hear him. But when a man was baptized by John, it showed to the entire community that he believed what John was saying.

Some people today wonder why it is necessary for them to join the church. The answer is simply this: When you are going to fulfill all righteousness, you should do not only what is right in the sight of God, but also what is right in the sight of man. It always seems right to the community for a professing Christian to join a local church.

In any church you will find some things with which you cannot agree. Perhaps in your community there may not be a single church to which you would like to belong. But if you do not join, what impression does your community gain from that? The community assumes that you are against what the churches stand for. You may know and God will know that the reason you have not joined any church is because you see something in every church in the community which is not as it ought to be. But what does the community think? They would say it was because you did not stand for what the church claims to stand for.

The Lord Jesus would say that in fulfilling all righteousness, if there is a Christian house of worship in your community, the thing for you to do is to go to that church. This is a modern-day application of Christ's words, "It becometh us to fulfill all righteousness."

Jesus Christ came to be baptized by John, not because He needed to repent, but because He wanted to show that He endorsed the message of John the Baptist.

At the baptism two things happened that John had not anticipated:

1. The heavens opened and the Holy Spirit came down "in the form of a dove." I am not certain that an actual dove came down. It says, "He saw the Spirit of God descending 'like a dove' and lighting upon him." But the Spirit actually came down in some visible fashion.

2. A voice from heaven said, "This is my beloved Son, in whom I am well pleased."

In the gospel of John you will see that John the Baptist said he did not know at this time who "the Christ" was going to be. His whole ministry was to prepare the way for the Messiah, yet he did not know who the Messiah would be.

When John saw Jesus on this day of His baptism, he did not at first know that this was the Christ. He knew Him only as Jesus of Nazareth. When he said he did not want to baptize Him, it was not that he knew this was the Christ; it was because he knew the life of Jesus was more godly than his own.

But when the heavens opened and the Spirit of God descended upon Jesus then John knew, because he had been told that "Upon whom thou shalt see the Spirit descending, and remaining on him, the same is he which baptizeth with the Holy Ghost" (John 1:33).

How Jesus Resisted Temptation

Then was Jesus led up of the spirit into the wilderness to be tempted of the devil. And when he had fasted forty days and forty nights, he was afterward an hungred. And when the tempter came to him, he said, If thou be the Son of God, command that these stones be made bread. But he answered and said, It is written, Man shall not live by bread alone, but by every word that proceedeth out of the mouth of God. Then the devil taketh him up into the holy city, and setteth him on a pinnacle of the temple. And saith unto him, If thou be the Son of God, cast thyself down: for it is written, He shall give his angels charge concerning thee: and in their hands they shall bear thee up, lest at any time thou dash thy foot against a stone. Jesus said unto him, It is written again, Thou shalt not tempt the Lord thy God. Again, the devil taketh him up into an exceeding high mountain, and sheweth him all the kingdoms of the world, and the glory of them; And saith unto him, All these things will I give thee, if thou wilt fall down and worship me. Then saith Jesus unto him, Get thee hence, Satan: for it is written, Thou shalt worship the Lord thy God, and him only shalt thou serve. Then the devil leaveth him, and, behold, angels came and ministered unto him (Matthew 4:1-11).

Immediately after He had been baptized when He received the Holy Spirit and heard the voice from heaven, the Lord Jesus was led of the Spirit into a situation where He would be tempted. He followed the leading of the Spirit as an obedient person, subject to the will of God, going out into the wilderness.

After Jesus had fasted for forty days, Satan came with the words, "*If* thou be the Son of God." What a contrast this would be to the voice from heaven, which could still be ringing in the ears of Jesus!

This will remind us that when Satan came to Eve in the Garden of Eden, he said, "Yea, hath God said, Ye shall not eat of every tree of the garden?" In each instance, Satan was simply repeating what God had said, yet doing it in such a way as to imply doubt as to the meaning.

Take notice of that. When Satan comes to test you, he is far too smart to show you something out of the will of God. The first thing he does is to loosen your simple commitment in your obedience to the revelation of God's will by questioning your understanding of what God meant. If Satan can get you to the place where you are not sure what God wants, you will be open to suggestions from him as to possible meanings different than you had in mind.

Here Satan raised the question, "*If* thou be the Son of God, command these stones be made bread." Put Your idea that You are the beloved Son of God to the test, he suggests.

Putting an idea to the test might seem innocent enough to a superficial look, but it isn't. If I test my friend to find out if he really is my friend, I concede the possibility that he might not be. If you and I are in business together and you hire a private detective to shadow me, you are at least conceding the possibility that I am unreliable, and this would certainly damage our further mutual affairs.

When you begin to look for flaws in the Bible, you have already moved away from it. You have already conceded that it is open to question. When a man trusts the Bible as God's Word he does not act that way.

So when Satan suggested to the Lord Jesus, "Put your ideas to the test," he was proposing a procedure to test the integrity of God's Word. This, Jesus of Nazareth would never do; He trusted God implicitly.

In response to this suggestion, Jesus replied, "It is written, man shall not live by bread alone, but by every word that proceedeth out of the mouth of God." For that word "alone," you can use the word "only." Man does live by bread *surely*, but not "only." Man has a soul as well as a body. Man is a spiritual being as well as a natural being. The natural man feeds on bread, that is true, but the spiritual man feeds on the Word of God.

The interests of the flesh, which can be satisfied with bread, and the interests of the soul, which can be satisfied with the Word of God, are not the same. There will be times in your life when you will either have to reach for bread or seek the will of God. For Jesus, this was one of those times. And though He had fasted physically for forty days, the interests of His soul were still more important to Him. This truth is of profound importance throughout all spiritual experience.

After the first temptation had failed to gain the consent of Jesus, Satan took Him up into a high pinnacle and said, "If thou be the Son of God, cast thyself down, for it is written . . . "

This is frightening. Satan can actually quote the Bible. If you have only a pat answer from the Bible when you are faced with some question, remember that someone else may be able to match your pat answer with another pat answer, which will leave you helpless in bewilderment.

The Scripture which Satan quoted was quite applicable to Jesus: "He shall give his angels charge concerning thee." This quotation from Psalm 91 really does belong to Jesus. But Jesus replied with another reference to the Old Testament Scriptures, thereby resisting the temptation successfully.

Whenever you interpret the Bible at any one passage, have the whole Scripture in mind and not just that one passage. When you find a passage which seems to mean a certain thing, look to see what the Bible says elsewhere about the same subject. Don't try to make a creed out of a single verse. No, take that verse which is truly the Word of God, and see what the Bible makes of it, comparing Scripture with Scripture.

In this way we can have victory over the temptations of the devil. Safety and deliverance from temptation is by means of the Scriptures. The Lord Jesus defeated Satan by His skillful handling of the Word of God, and He is our example.

If any man ever could have withstood Satan in His own strength and holiness, surely that would be Jesus of Nazareth! Yet He did not resist Satan that way – He used Scripture, a wide, true grasp of Scripture, to resist the temptations of Satan. What an example for us!

THE CALLING OF THE DISCIPLES

Now when Jesus had heard that John was cast into prison, he departed into Galilee; And leaving Nazareth, he came and dwelt in Capernaum, which is upon the sea coast, in the borders of Zabulon and Nephthalim: That it might be fulfilled which was spoken by Esaias, the prophet, saying, The land of Zabulon, and the land of Nephthalim, by the way of the sea, beyond Jordan, Galilee of the Gentiles; The people which sat in darkness saw great light; and to them which sat in the region and shadow of death light is sprung up. From that time Jesus began to preach, and to say, Repent: for the kingdom of heaven is at hand. And Jesus, walking by the sea of Galilee, saw two brethren, Simon called Peter, and Andrew his brother, casting a net into the sea: for they were fishers. And he saith unto them, Follow me, and I will make you fishers of men. And they straightway left their nets, and followed him. And going on from thence, he saw other two brethren, James the son of Zebedee, and John his brother, in a ship with Zebedee their father, mending their nets; and he called them. And they immediately left the ship and their father, and followed him. And Jesus went about all Galilee, teaching in their synagogues, and preaching the gospel of the kingdom, and healing all manner of sickness and all manner of disease among the people. And his fame went throughout all Syria: and they brought unto him all sick people that were taken with divers diseases and torments, and those which were possessed with devils, and those which were lunatick, and those that had the palsy: and he healed them. And there followed him great multitudes of people from Galilee, and from Decapolis, and from Jerusalem, and from Judea, and from beyond Jordan (Matthew 4:12-25).

When Jesus heard that John the Baptist was cast into prison, He entered Galilee where John had been, and began preaching John's message: "Repent: for the kingdom of heaven is at hand." Leaving His home in Nazareth, He went to Capernaum to preach. The message which called for repentance was still the message of preparation for the coming of the Christ. It was a message of spiritual housecleaning before the Guest should arrive.

The meaning was simply: "Take an honest look at yourself and see your own need. Look in your own heart and see how unfit you are for God. Judge yourself in the sight of God as being unworthy, for the kingdom of heaven is at hand. You will have an opportunity to enter into the blessing if you are humble in repentance."

The kingdom of heaven is a state in which God will bless men. When God rules in your heart, when He directs your affairs, you are in the kingdom of God. In other words, He is king of your soul.

It has not been made clear at this point in the account just how a soul can enter the kingdom. This will come later. Repentance is prerequisite, and we shall see that receiving Jesus Christ as Lord is the way.

After He began public preaching, Jesus called several persons to follow Him as disciples. Thus He called Peter, Andrew, James and John. Thus he called the brothers, Peter and Andrew, when He came upon them while they were fishing. Their response was immediate. They left their nets and followed Him. Later He saw the two brothers James and John mending their nets, for they were also fishermen. When He called them, they immediately left what they were doing and followed Him.

Need we think this was the first time He had seen these men, or that He spoke no other words than the simple command, "Follow Me"?

Is it not likely these fishermen had heard John the Baptist preach, perhaps many times? The story as told by John (1:40-42) may well be the account of the first meeting Andrew and Peter had with Jesus of Nazareth. Luke tells us in more detail what happened when Peter was called (Luke 5:1-11). But the account in Matthew shows us how simply the call was given: they were to follow Him personally. Just that – without any persuasive argument or any specific promises.

Here we can learn much for our own understanding of His call to us.

When you hear the Gospel and are asked to let Christ come into your life, your heart will not be empty. It will be full of other things. You see, the Gospel of Jesus Christ comes to human beings who are already involved in this world. It comes to be received as a substitute for what men already are doing.

Peter and Andrew were busy fishermen. When Jesus called them, He called them away from something they were doing. Just so when He called two other brothers, James and John. They, too, may have known about the Lord Jesus for some time, but this was the day when they felt an urgent call to commit their lives to Jesus Christ. "And they immediately left the ship and their father, and followed him." Jesus called these four men away from what they were doing naturally, into a life in which God would tell them what to do. This is an important aspect of our responding to His call.

At this time Jesus was teaching in the synagogues, preaching the Gospel of the kingdom, healing all kinds of diseases and gaining widespread popularity.

What does "teaching in the synagogues" mean? It means taking the Old Testament Scriptures and showing their meaning. The major difference between teaching and preaching is that in teaching you show what the truth is; in preaching you urge a man to follow it. The teacher wants you to understand something; the preacher wants you to do it. Teaching usually comes first. Preaching normally follows to urge us to do what we now know to do.

Chapter 3

THE SERMON ON THE MOUNT

WHAT IS GOD'S LAW?

Many people are confused about "the law of God." The Bible refers to it so often and in so many ways that it is important to your understanding of Biblical teaching to know what it means. Basically, "the law of God" refers to "the Ten Commandments." At times, the phrase refers to the Bible as a whole and especially the Old Testament. More particularly, it refers to the first five books of the Bible, the Pentateuch. For instance, when you read that the Lord Jesus, "beginning at the law and in the psalms and in the prophets expounded the things concerning himself," the word *law* refers to the first five books of the Bible. Still, at other times, when you use the phrase "the law of God," you might mean the general pattern of God's dealings with man. In this sense, the law of God is His characteristic way of dealing with man. It will help to remember that the law of God is not some rule that He made up in an arbitrary fashion.

"The Law of the Harvest" is a good example. The Bible says, "Whatsoever a man soweth, that shall he also reap." This is not a rule God added to the world of nature. Rather this is a law that was built into the universe. So, if a man sows wheat in the field, he will reap wheat. If he sows barley, he will reap barley. "Whatsoever a man soweth, that shall he also reap" is a law of God that is true in every situation, including moral and spiritual situations.

On the other hand, at the time of Christ the Jewish religious leaders had set up a list of rules of conduct that they felt were based on the revealed law of God. These rules were designed to bring a man into conformity with God's law.

But what they didn't realize was this: You can't make a man become acceptable in God's sight by a set of rules. Rules can be helpful. They can lead you along the right way if you want to do the right thing anyway. But unless you are minded to do what is right, the Ten Commandments won't be of any help to you.

Suppose my neighbor and I respect each other's property. I don't trespass on his property and he doesn't trespass on mine. In order to determine where our property lines are, we put up a marker which shows clearly where my yard ends and his yard begins. This does not mean that I have no further interest in my neighbor, nor does it mean that I cannot go into his yard to visit him. No, it is just a handy reference so that when I am going about my ordinary activity, I won't inadvertently trespass upon his territory. A marker can be useful to two good neighbors who do not want to impose on each other.

In this way you could accept such guidance as "Thou shalt not kill." But the godly heart has a far greater interest in the other person than just not killing him. The godly heart goes on to watch over the other person's welfare.

This can be seen in the parable of the Good Samaritan. A man was beset by thieves and was left in a ditch half-dead. A priest saw him, and went by on the other side. He did not steal anything from the poor man in the ditch. He did not hurt him in any way. But did he keep the law of God?

A Levite looked at the man and also passed by on the other side. He did not take anything from the unfortunate man either. He did not break the law that said, "Thou shalt not kill," or "Thou shalt not steal," but did he do right? Did he really keep the law of God?

When the Good Samaritan came and saw the man's condition, he did not steal anything either. But what did he do? He went down into the ditch and shared with him. He took of his own and gave it to the poor man. He put the man on his own beast, took him to a hotel, ministered to him as long as he was with him, and when he had to leave the next day, he left money to pay for the man's bill and told the innkeeper to take care of the man as long as he needed it, and when he, the Samaritan, came back he would settle the bill. This is a classic example of keeping the law of God.

Here you can see that the law of God is far more than simply "Thou shalt not kill." It is far more than simply "Thou shalt not steal." It is better phrased in "Thou shalt love thy neighbor."

This is what the Lord Jesus is pointing out in Matthew 5. As you read the Sermon on the Mount, you will discover the righteousness which is acceptable to God. The way of living that God will accept, Jesus says, must be better than the righteousness of the scribes and the Pharisees.

The scribes and Pharisees drew up regulations of external conduct. By obeying these regulations, they held you would be doing right in the sense that you would not be doing wrong. But the

Lord Jesus said that even if you live your life in such a way that you are not doing wrong, this is not enough. It is not true only that we must not do wrong. The whole truth is that we must do what is right. The law was given to show you where you do wrong, but the Lord Jesus wants you to know what God really expects: not only outward conformity to a pattern, but an inward conformity to the will of God so that you do right.

In Matthew 5, as Jesus discussed the commandment, "Thou shalt not kill," He said that if you are angry with your brother without a cause, you are in danger of judgment. When you despise other people, when you belittle them, when you shove them away or when you wish they weren't around, you are not like God. When you act in such a way, you have actually violated the law of God, because the positive law of God is "Thou shalt love thy neighbor as thyself."

When Jesus discussed the commandment, "Thou shalt not commit adultery," He pointed out that the physical act of adultery is certainly wrong, but it is also wrong to cherish the thoughts, to let the thought of adultery occupy your mind. In other words, you are not like God when you think that way.

The judgments of Moses (in Exodus, Leviticus and Numbers) not only informed the people of certain things they should not do, but also made the worship of God and charity toward man required practices for Israel. They described certain actions which would be in God's will for them.

Since the people of Israel wanted to walk in the ways of God, Moses spelled out for them how they could do God's will. If they wanted to please God, they should remember the Sabbath day, they should tithe their income, they should lend their coat to a man in need, they should walk a mile to escort a man to his home.

As Jesus rehearsed these things, He reminded the people that outward conformity to the law was not as important as the inner spirit of a man. If a man had the right attitude, he would desire to please God rather than simply measure up to some regulation.

What is this attitude? It is the way a man wants to do when he is moved by love. Love is never satisfied with what it does. If you love a person, you never feel that you give enough. Love is infinite in its demands upon us to share with the other person.

If you truly love, you will not only give a coat because the regulations require it, you will give a sweater too, because you want the man to be warm. If you truly love, you will want to go not just one mile with the traveler on his way at night because the regulations require this, but you will go the second mile because you really want to help the traveler in his need.

In other words, Jesus taught that the real meaning of the law

which had been spelled out in the judgments of Moses based on
the "Ten Words" at Sinai actually was love toward God and love
toward man. This is the real thrust of the Sermon on the Mount.

BLESSINGS ON YOU

And seeing the multitudes, he went up into a mountain: and when
he was set, his disciples came unto him: And he opened his
mouth, and taught them, saying, Blessed are the poor in spirit:
for theirs is the kingdom of heaven. Blessed are they that mourn:
for they shall be comforted. Blessed are the meek: for they shall
inherit the earth. Blessed are they which do hunger and thirst
after righteousness: for they shall be filled. Blessed are the merciful: for they shall obtain mercy. Blessed are the pure in heart:
for they shall see God. Blessed are the peacemakers: for they
shall be called the children of God. Blessed are they which are
persecuted for righteousness' sake: for theirs is the kingdom of
heaven. Blessed are ye, when men shall revile you, and persecute you, and shall say all manner of evil against you falsely,
for my sake. Rejoice, and be exceeding glad: for great is your
reward in heaven: for so persecuted they the prophets which
were before you (Matthew 5:1-12).

In chapter four of Matthew's gospel you will read that Jesus
preached the Gospel of the kingdom. The Sermon on the Mount,
contained in Matthew 5 through 7, shows the kind of preaching
He did.

This sample sermon begins with a section called the Beatitudes. These Beatitudes point out the benefits and blessings of
letting the will of God be done in your life.

"Blessed are the poor in spirit" was not written to urge you
to go out and try to be poor in spirit; rather it is saying that if
you are a person who believes in God you will be conscious of
your own weakness, and this will make you poor in spirit. In
other words, you will feel poor in the sight of God. After all, this
is really what happens in you when you repent. And when this
is true in you, you are fortunate in that now you are being blessed
of God.

"Blessed are they that mourn" may seem to say there is virtue
in feeling morbid. But this is not the meaning here. The Lord
Jesus is saying that people who mourn because of their sins are
being blessed of God. Isaiah cried, "Woe is me! for I am undone"
(6:5). Paul wrote, "I know that in me dwelleth no good thing."
Blessed are they, Jesus was saying, who mourn because of their
own conduct for they shall be comforted in that God is being
gracious to the contrite heart.

"Blessed are the meek" refers to a person who does not retaliate when some injustice is done. This expression, "They shall inherit the earth," does not mean that they will inherit all the real estate in the world. No, this is a promise quoted from the Old Testament, when the Israelites were traveling toward the land of Canaan. "The earth" can be translated "the land." Israel was being called to obey His guidance, since God promised that He would lead them into the Promised Land. This passage here means that if you fight for yourself you are not trusting God. But if you trust your case to God, you are the kind of person to whom God gives the promise: you shall inherit what He had promised you.

"Blessed are they which do hunger and thirst after righteousness" means that the man in whom the will of God is being done wants to be and to do what is right in the sight of God. A hunger for righteousness is a sign that shows God is at work affecting that man.

"Blessed are the merciful, for they shall obtain mercy" reminds you of "Forgive us out debts, as we forgive our debtors." If I have the right to demand the payment of a debt but I do not insist when I see the debtor is unable to pay, I would be showing mercy; and this shows God is working in me. Mercy shows the grace of God to be operating in my heart, for God Himself is merciful. To have God working in me is truly fortunate for me.

"Blessed are the pure in heart." This is understood when you think of a person who is single-minded having just one idea in heart and mind. If you had only this one thought in your mind, that you wanted to please God, you would not think of engaging in sinful conduct. However, you know only too well that your heart is not naturally pure. In itself this could cause you to despair – except for one thing: every time you see the word "pure" you can think of the word "purified," because by the grace of God your heart can be purified. "The blood of Jesus Christ cleanseth us from all sin." And so when your heart has been "purified" by the Lord Jesus Christ so that you have just one purpose – to please God – you shall "see God": you shall be conscious of God's presence and of His blessing.

"Blessed are the peacemakers." You don't make peace by talking peace nor by telling everyone: "Let's quit fighting." If two boys were quarreling about riding a bicycle, which one would be the peacemaker? The one who would give the bicycle to the other boy. A third person cannot make peace between two fighting forces. The only person who can make peace is one who is involved in the dispute.

"Blessed are they which are persecuted for righteousness' sake." The servant is not greater than his master, and the Master, the Lord Jesus Christ, even though He lived a perfect life, was killed. So the servant should not expect to avoid trouble. To the man so persecuted belongs the kingdom of heaven. Persecution for righteousness' sake is a sign that a man truly does belong to the Lord who was also persecuted.

All these characteristics appear in your heart when the will of God is being done there. The Beatitudes are not given for you to imitate, but that you may see the blessings in store for you when you belong to God and His will is operative in you.

Only one person ever did the will of God perfectly. That was the Lord Jesus Christ. But He wants to give you His righteousness to replace your sinfulness, so that you can have all these blessings through faith in Him.

Only one person ever lived who had the characteristics described in the Beatitudes. This was Jesus Christ, in whom God was "well pleased." When you receive Him as Saviour and Lord, He will give His righteousness to replace your natural sinfulness. Then you can receive the blessings listed in the Beatitudes.

Don't Keep It Secret

> Ye are the salt of the earth: but if the salt have lost his savour, wherewith shall it be salted? it is thenceforth good for nothing, but to be cast out, and to be trodden under foot of men. Ye are the light of the world. A city that is set on an hill cannot be hid. Neither do men light a candle, and put it under a bushel, but on a candlestick; and it giveth light unto all that are in the house. Let your light so shine before men, that they may see your good works, and glorify your Father which is in heaven (Matthew 5:13-16).

If you lived on a farm before the days of refrigeration, you will remember that you did not have any way of keeping meat chilled unless you had an icehouse to put it in. If you had to preserve the meat any other way you used salt. Pork was put in barrels with brine. The reason for having salt pork was certainly not because anyone liked salt that well, but because the salt kept the pork fresh.

Back in the time of Christ, preserving meat was also a great problem. In the warm climate of the Holy Land meat spoiled easily. So salt was relied on as a preservative.

However, their salt was not as pure as our salt. Salt today is highly refined. Mixed with sand or earth, as it was then, salt loses some of its pungency and consequently its effectiveness.

So, "when salt has lost its savour" is a way of saying that the salt is not strong enough anymore. When the salt once lost its effectiveness as a preservative, it was absolutely no good. You couldn't use it for any other purpose. It was good for nothing else, but to be thrown out and trodden under foot.

The Lord Jesus used the illustration of salt to teach a lesson. People in whom the will of God is being done are like salt in this world. The presence of a Christian keeps society from spoiling so quickly. Any community that has a strong church is a better community. Any group that has one or two strong Christians will be a better group of people. You as a Christian can have a tremendous effect on your entire environment. With this in mind, Jesus told His disciples that they should so conduct themselves openly that their influence upon others would be significant.

Jesus' next illustration is about light. What does light do? Light illuminates. Light shows up things the way they are. When you turn on the light in a room, you see things as they really are.

Even so, a godly life in any community helps the entire area to see things better. As light shows everything up for what it really is, so does a Christian in his community. As he lives in obedience to the will of God, anyone else can see what his conduct really means.

When the Lord Jesus said, "Let your light so shine," He meant that as a Christian you should let your conduct be seen. You may be inclined to worship God in secret or to read the Bible in secret or to pray in secret. But Jesus urged that you should not hide your light under a bushel.

The truth of the matter is that you do have an influence on others. If you do what is right, that is always commendable. But if you do the right thing and do it openly, that is even better.

It is good for your neighbors to know that you are going to church. There is value for young people to be seen with Bibles in their hands. It is good when men carry Testaments in their pockets and read them in their spare time. You certainly don't want to "wear your religion on your sleeve," but neither is there any virtue in keeping it a secret.

Of course, there are other good works besides church attendance and Bible reading, but whatever they may be when they are done openly in the name of the Lord, they always have a special significance. It is a good thing to let people see your good works, that they may glorify your Father who is in heaven.

THE HIGH STANDARD

Think not that I am come to destroy the law, or the prophets: I am not come to destroy, but to fulfil. For verily I say unto you, Till heaven and earth pass, one jot or one tittle shall in no wise pass from the law, till all be fulfilled. Whosoever therefore shall break one of these least commandments, and shall teach men so, he shall be called the least in the kingdom of heaven: but whosoever shall do and teach them, the same shall be called great in the kingdom of heaven. For I say unto you, That except your righteousness shall exceed the righteousness of the scribes and Pharisees, ye shall in no case enter into the kingdom of heaven. Ye have heard that it was said by them of old time, Thou shalt not kill; and whosoever shall kill shall be in danger of the judgment: But I say unto you, That whosoever is angry with his brother without a cause shall be in danger of the judgment: and whosoever shall say to his brother, Raca, shall be in danger of the council: but whosoever shall say, Thou fool, shall be in danger of hell fire. Therefore if thou bring thy gift to the altar, and there rememberest that thy brother hath ought against thee; Leave there thy gift before the altar, and go thy way; first be reconciled to thy brother, and then come and offer thy gift. Agree with thine adversary quickly, whiles thou art in the way with him; lest at any time the adversary deliver thee to the judge, and the judge deliver thee to the officer, and thou be cast into prison. Verily I say unto thee, Thou shalt by no means come out thence, till thou hast paid the uttermost farthing (Matthew 5:17-26).

Jesus set a high standard when He said, "Except your righteousness shall exceed the righteousness of the scribes and Pharisees, ye shall in no case enter into the kingdom of heaven." The scribes were the scholars and the interpreters of the Bible. They were also well acquainted with the opinions of the Jewish rabbis who had written comments on the Old Testament law.

What would be the righteousness of the scribes? Perhaps it would be a kind of book learning, something you would write as a theme in school or something which would be argued in a debate.

The Pharisees emphasized outward conformity to the regulations of the Bible. They stressed external conduct. In fact, they were so concerned about the letter of the law that they neglected the spirit of the law.

The attitudes of the scribes and Pharisees naturally influenced all the Jewish people to whom Jesus was preaching. Everyone would realize the difference in the teaching of Jesus of Nazareth when He would say about these customary religious ideas, "This is not really the truth."

It is not so much what your conduct looks like on the outside. It is what you are inside. It is not only what you do; it is also what you think.

Because Jesus' preaching seemed so different, many of the people might have wondered if He were discarding the entire law of Moses. So He had to explain, "I am not come to destroy, but to fulfil" the law. Jesus emphasized that obedience to God goes beyond negative rules and regulations. It is true you should not do wrong, but it is just as true that you should do right. It is true that you should not steal, but God is not fully satisfied until you learn to give. It is true that you should not kill, but God is not fully satisfied until you learn to save people. You can check through all the Ten Commandments and see the same thing. This is how your righteousness could exceed that of the scribes and the Pharisees.

In the final verses of this section, Jesus began to explain the meaning behind some of the Ten Commandments. For instance, "Thou shalt not kill" not only meant that you should not commit murder, but it also meant that if there was hate in your heart you were guilty of breaking this commandment.

Actually, the Christian is to avoid quarrels, because the man who carries on quarrels, soon begins to hate, and hate breeds the disposition to kill.

In I John it says that if any man hate his brother, he is a murderer. This is what the Lord Jesus is teaching here. You should not only keep the law of Moses; you should go far beyond it.

A Matter of the Heart

Ye have heard that it was said by them of old time, Thou shalt not commit adultery: But I say unto you, That whosoever looketh on a woman to lust after her hath committed adultery with her already in his heart. And if thy right eye offend thee, pluck it out, and cast it from thee: for it is profitable for thee that one of thy members should perish, and not that thy whole body should be cast into hell. And if thy right hand offend thee, cut it off, and cast it from thee; for it is profitable for thee that one of thy members should perish, and not that thy whole body should be cast into hell. It hath been said, Whosoever shall put away his wife, let him give her a writing of divorcement: But I say unto you, That whosoever shall put away his wife, saving for the cause of fornication, causeth her to commit adultery: and whosoever shall marry her that is divorced committeth adultery. Again, ye have heard that it hath been said by them of old time, Thou shalt not forswear thyself, but shalt perform unto the Lord thine oaths: But I say unto you, Swear not at all; neither by heaven; for it is God's throne: Nor by the earth; for it is his footstool: neither by Jerusalem; for it is the city of the great King. Neither shalt thou swear by thy head, because thou canst not make one hair white or black. But let your communication be, Yea, yea; Nay, nay: for whatsoever is more than these cometh of evil (Matthew 5:27-37).

Real godliness involves more than outward conformity to a pattern of conduct.

For instance, a school teacher who wants to protect school

property might make a rule that you are not to break any windows. But this would not mean that you could smash the front door or scribble on the walls. To abide only by the letter of the law is not enough.

In this part of the Sermon on the Mount, Jesus is talking about adultery as forbidden in the law of Moses. Jesus said it would be adultery in God's sight when a man "looketh upon a woman to lust after her." It is possible a casual thought may go through a man's mind suggesting an evil possibility, but this is not particularly what the Lord Jesus is referring to. We are not responsible for every thought that passes through our minds, but we are responsible for the thoughts we cherish. We are responsible for the thoughts we welcome and keep there.

So Jesus said, "If thy right eye offend thee, pluck it out." Some people with more zeal than understanding have actually put out their eyes in an effort to stop certain thoughts from coming to their minds. But they found out too late that this does not help. Actually the expression, "thy eye offend thee" refers not just to the physical eye. It refers to thoughts or to the eye of the mind. In other words, if your customary practices are such that they actually bring harm to yourself and to others, cut them off and cast them from you. In the language of the Apostle Paul, "mortify them."

The world will encourage you to strive for a well-rounded personality. But this passage in the Sermon on the Mount says differently. In your life there may be certain tendencies which need to be cut out. One of the first lessons in a course "How to Cultivate and Nurture a Godly Life" would be a lesson on amputation, cutting some things out.

Referring to the commandment "Thou shalt not take the name of the Lord thy God in vain," Jesus said this does not primarily mean profanity. The real meaning refers to your manner of speech with others: as when you try to impress them with your honesty by swearing on the Bible, or when you try to impress others with your spirituality by constantly dropping references to God in your conversation for its affect.

People in Bible times used to do that. They would call upon God to witness that they were telling the truth. "As sure as there is a God in heaven, this is the truth," they would say. The people who heard them were to think that because they referred to God the statement was absolutely true.

The Lord Jesus pointed out it is not what you say, no matter how pious you sound: it is not all the various references to God that you offer; it is personal integrity that counts. True godliness is a matter of the heart, not a matter of outward speech.

Of course, outward conduct is important, for it does make a difference what we say, where we go and how we act. But what is most important is the way we are in our hearts.

GOING BEYOND JUSTICE

Ye have heard that it hath been said, An eye for an eye, and a tooth for a tooth: But I say unto you, That ye resist not evil: but whosoever shall smite thee on thy right cheek, turn to him the other also. And if any man will sue thee at the law, and take away thy coat, let him have thy cloke also. And whosoever shall compel thee to go a mile, go with him twain. Give to him that asketh thee, and from him that would borrow of thee turn not thou away. Ye have heard that it hath been said, Thou shalt love thy neighbour, and hate thine enemy. But I say unto you, Love your enemies, bless them that curse you, do good to them that hate you, and pray for them which despitefully use you, and persecute you; That ye may be the children of your Father which is in heaven: for he maketh his sun to rise on the evil and on the good, and sendeth rain on the just and on the unjust. For if ye love them which love you, what reward have ye? do not even the publicans the same? And if ye salute your brethren only, what do ye more than others? do not even the publicans so? Be ye therefore perfect, even as your Father which is in heaven is perfect (Matthew 5:38-48).

"An eye for an eye and a tooth for a tooth" is justice, and justice is fair. That already goes far beyond human nature. But the Lord Jesus said that true righteousness goes beyond justice.

"Whosoever shall smite thee on thy right cheek, turn to him the other also," is much more reasonable than it sounds to many people. But this is not the kind of thing human nature can do. It is the kind of thing that only God can do in you when He has complete control of your life. If the will of God is being done in your heart, then when others harm you, you will not repay them with harm.

The Lord Jesus went on to say: "If any man will sue thee at the law and take away thy coat, let him have thy cloke also." Now you might wonder, how in the world could a man sue me for my coat?

Under the law of Moses, if a man were working in a field a long way from home and the weather changed suddenly so that at night he did not have sufficient garments for his long walk home, he could go to any Israelite home and ask for a coat. The Israelite would be required to give the coat to him.

The Lord Jesus said, "Don't give him only the coat because

you have to, but give him a sweater as well." In other words, in helping others, do more than you have to do.

We often speak of going "the second mile." Have you ever wondered how anyone could compel you to go even one mile? If you were an Israelite, this could be done.

If a man were working in a field and at night when he was finished he were four or five miles from home, he could go into any Israelite home and ask for an escort, and the law of Moses required they would have to escort him one mile. They would not have to take him all the way home, but only one mile along the way. Then after a mile he could go into another home and get another escort for the next mile.

The Lord Jesus said, "If you have the real righteousness which comes from God, you won't go only one mile because you have to, you will go two miles, because you want to."

Another law was this: If one Israelite came to another and asked for help, the one who was asked would have to give it to the one who asked him. If he asked for a loan, the other Israelite was expected to give it to him. It was expected, of course, that the loan would be repaid. However, according to the Old Testament law, every seven years all debts were cancelled. Consequently, some people did not want to lend anything in the sixth year, because they were taking a big risk that they wouldn't be repaid. But Jesus said that if the man were in need and came to you for help, even if it was the sixth year, you would give generously to him, if the righteousness of God were in you.

This is not human nature. But it is the way you would deal with each other if you were doing right in the sight of God. Doing only what the law requires is not enough, if the love of God is in your heart.

Perhaps in all of the Sermon on the Mount, one of the hardest sayings is: "Love your enemy."

In the first place you might well ask the question, "Why should I?"

The answer is this: "In order that you may be known as the children of your Father which is in heaven – in order that your actions may resemble those of your heavenly Father."

"For he maketh his sun to rise on the evil and on the good, and sendeth rain on the just and on the unjust." Since God does so many things so graciously to all people, whether they acknowledge Him or not, you – if the Spirit of God dwells in you – will also do good to all mankind.

This does not mean to love your enemies more than you love your friends, nor to love them in place of your friends. It means to love them in spite of the fact that they treat you as an enemy.

If you really belong to God, this is the way you will live. "Be ye perfect, even as your Father which is in heaven is perfect." If God is your Father, others should be able to see the family resemblance in you.

Chapter 4

RIGHTEOUSNESS EXCEEDING THE LAW

What You Should Do First

What is the Sermon on the Mount all about? Three verses, each containing the word "first," will give you a pretty good idea.

1. "First be reconciled to thy brother, and then come and offer thy gift" (Matthew 5:24).

2. "Seek ye first the kingdom of God, and his righteousness; and all these things shall be added unto you" (Matthew 6:33).

3. "Thou hypocrite, first cast out the beam out of thine own eye; and then shalt thou see clearly to cast out the mote out of thy brother's eye" (Matthew 7:5).

"First be reconciled to thy brother" indicates that our personal relationship to others shows our relationship to God. In his first epistle, John wrote that if any man love not his brother, and says that he loves God, he is a liar. Loving one's brother and loving God is the same piece of cloth.

If I do not seek the welfare of others, I am sinning. Why? Because sin is "any want of conformity to the law of God." And God's law is grounded in God's basic nature. Anything that is like God is acceptable. Anything not like Him is not acceptable. And God seeks the welfare of all men.

"Seek ye first the kingdom of God" concerns our relationship to things. How common it is for Christians to struggle to get the things of this world, to strive to get enough money for all the things they want. None of these things may be wrong in themselves, but any one of them can become so important to you that your whole attention may be given over to it.

The righteousness of God mentioned in this verse refers to the conduct which comes from being right with God by faith. If you place your trust in Jesus Christ, His righteousness is shared with you and you are counted righteous in the presence of God. If your first concern is to be right with God, "all other things shall be added unto you."

Will this turn out to be very impractical? After all, if you are going to pay your rent and feed your family, you will have to work for a living.

One thing you can be sure about: When God rules your life, He won't allow you to be lazy. When God directs you, you won't neglect your work. The very fact that you are a Christian means that you work as if you owned the place. So if you let the Lord have His way in your heart, you won't need to worry about your job or about anything else. "All these things will be added unto you."

What God is first of all interested in is that you count most important your personal relationship to Him. If you are yielded to God, you won't need to worry about things. As a matter of fact, the worrying soul is a sinning soul.

When I was younger, I thought worrying was a virtue. I felt that if I worried a lot I was doing well; if I didn't worry, I was worried about myself. But now I realize this was wrong.

If I say that my life belongs to God, my worrying is actually an advertisement to the world that I don't really trust God. You see, the person who worries is actually forgetting the promises of God.

"First cast out the beam out of thine own eye" deals with judging other people. If you have an idea that another Christian ought to be different than he is, remember this: If you judge him, you will be judged. If you can see faults in someone else, you should first look inward to search out those same faults within yourself.

Of course, you can't help but recognize when another person does something that looks wrong. But first, make sure you judge yourself. If you match yourself against the truth of God, you will have a better understanding of how God's truth applies to someone else.

The Sermon on the Mount brings out the inner nature of true righteousness. As we examine ourselves according to the standards of the righteousness of God as taught by Jesus, we will see how inadequate we really are. And so we learn to judge ourselves.

This self-judgment is preliminary to the entire gospel message. For as we see our inadequacy, we turn to Jesus Christ, who is adequate for everything. He it is who can transform us and make us into a likeness of Himself. You see, it is a great thing that a sinner can come to the Saviour, but it is a still greater thing that when he comes to the Saviour, he will not stay in his sin. He will be set free. He will be changed by God Himself.

Playing to the Grandstand

Take heed that ye do not your alms before men, to be seen of them: otherwise ye have no reward of your Father which is in heaven. Therefore when thou doest thine alms, do not sound a trumpet before thee, as the hypocrites do in the synagogues and in the streets, that they may have glory of men. Verily I say unto you, They have their reward. But when thou doest alms, let not thy left hand know what thy right hand doeth: That thine alms may be in secret: and thy Father which seeth in secret himself shall reward thee openly (Matthew 6:1-4).

The Lord Jesus continually stressed that the truth of God's will is something more than the rules and regulations that the religious leaders of His day had established. In chapter 5 He discussed this in reference to the Old Testament law. In chapter 6 He discussed it in reference to various religious practices.

Almsgiving means giving to the poor. This is a practice that all godly men are expected to observe. Jesus taught, "Do not your alms before men, to be seen of them." This does not mean that you have to hide yourself when you are helping others, however. It is speaking about your motivation in doing it.

There is a great contrast between the social significance and the spiritual significance of your conduct. The two are not the same. Something may be pleasing in the sight of man but be an abomination in the sight of the Lord.

When you are doing a good deed, do it for the Lord's sake. Don't keep a record of your personal goodness. If you do it for the Lord, He will reward you. If you do good to be praised by men, their praise will be your reward. It is possible to fool even your own relatives about your goodness, so that they may exclaim, "My, what a good person he is!" But God knows the motivation of your heart in doing good.

What you do to be seen of men fosters pride in your heart. What you do for the glory of God fosters humility. When you think of how much God has done for you and how little you actually do for others, your little contribution of goodness does not seem to count for anything. And this produces humility. God loves the humble but resists the proud.

However, when the Bible says that you should give in secret, it does not mean that you should hide when you are doing it. If you give five dollars to the poor, you do not need to send it anonymously in an unmarked envelope. If you give five dollars to the poor and you are doing it to make an impression on a business partner or on the church ushers, that is exactly the value of the act. God is not impressed by it, because you are not doing it for Him.

But suppose, when the offering is being taken for the poor, you give five dollars and the reason you give it is because you think God would be pleased. Since no one could know why you are doing it, it is really being done in secret, as far as man is concerned. All of this is known to God, and God will give you His reward.

Whether you realize it or not, you always have a gallery, like a ballplayer with a grandstand full of spectators. Some players are known to perform better when the grandstand is full, because they want to be applauded by men. You have your grandstand, too. But it makes a big difference who is in your grandstand.

When a young person goes to a strange city, he may conduct himself honorably. In his heart he cherishes the folks back home. In his grandstand, you might say, are his parents and his friends. And because he lives his life as though they were looking at him, his life is honorable and decent.

Jesus Christ taught that you should live your life knowing that God is in the grandstand. If you live your life always conscious that God is watching, there is a reward for you in heaven.

THE SECRET OF TRUE PRAYER

And when thou prayest, thou shalt not be as the hypocrites are: for they love to pray standing in the synagogues and in the corners of the streets, that they may be seen of men. Verily I say unto you, They have their reward. But thou, when thou prayest, enter into thy closet, and when thou hast shut the door, pray to thy Father which is in secret; and thy Father which seeth in secret shall reward thee openly. But when ye pray, use not vain repetitions, as the heathen do: for they think that they shall be heard for their much. speaking. Be not ye therefore like unto them: for your Father knoweth what things ye have need of, before ye ask him. After this manner therefore pray ye: Our Father which art in heaven, Hallowed be thy name. Thy kingdom come. Thy will be done in earth, as it is in heaven. Give us this day our daily bread. And forgive us our debts, as we forgive our debtors. And lead us not into temptation, but deliver us from evil: For thine is the kingdom, and the power, and the glory, for ever, Amen. For if ye forgive men their trespasses, your heavenly Father will also forgive you: But if ye forgive not men their trespasses, neither will your Father forgive your trespasses (Matthew 6:5-15).

In prayer, as in many other phases of your life, you can choose whether you wish to please men or God. Once again, what really matters is the intention of your heart. Why are you praying? Whom are you trying to please?

Some people take the phrase, "When thou prayest, enter into thy closet," very literally. So they go to their bedrooms to pray; they refuse to pray anywhere else. If this verse really meant that, there would never be any such thing as public prayer.

When the Lord Jesus said, "Enter into thy closet," I think He meant that since nobody but God knows how you feel, turn your heart over to Him alone. "Shutting the door of the closet" would mean shutting out any consideration of this world's affairs. Some people can hardly talk to God because they are thinking so much about their business. Others are thinking about their pleasure. That is not being separated unto God. Jesus said to shut out every other consideration but your relationship with God. You may have dealings with God all by yourself, but God will openly benefit you in front of others.

Some people have the mistaken notion that prayer forces God into action. They seem to think that if you pray a certain amount, God will bless you, and if you pray twice as much He will bless you twice as much. But that is not the way it goes.

They think that by repeating and repeating they are persuading God or they are building up their requests in front of God. All of this Jesus called "vain." "Your Father knoweth what things ye have need of, before ye ask him." You don't have to repeat it over and over because He already knows.

In what is commonly called the Lord's Prayer, there are a number of lessons you can learn.

The prayer begins with the word *Our*. This suggests united prayer. You see, if you were alone, you would say *my*, but when you say *our*, it means that you are joining with other people.

"Which art in heaven" tells us something about God. It is a good thing in praying to bring to mind something true about God as you begin to pray.

"Hallowed be thy name" begins the prayer in honor and worship of God.

"Thy kingdom come" is a quick way of saying, "May thy will be done."

In praying "Give us this day our daily bread" you are asking God for virtually everything that pertains to your life in this world· your food, your shelter, your clothing. It means that you recognize that these things come from God.

"Forgive us our debts" is discussed later by Christ: "For if you forgive men their trespasses, your heavenly Father will also forgive you."

Though this prayer itself is relatively short, it points directly to certain things that you want to keep in mind. This does not mean that you are limited to use only these words. He said, "After this manner, pray ye," or "Pray in this fashion."

A study of "The Lord's Prayer" will indicate there are certain elements in prayer: (1) you honor God; (2) you ask for God's will to be done; (3) you ask God to help you in your personal affairs.

Perhaps you may think, "If a person really trusts Christ, he shouldn't have to ask for anything, since God already knows what he needs."

But no, this isn't the way God wants it. As your heart is responsive to God, He wants you to seek certain things from Him. Your request is like opening your hand to receive the benefits that God desires to give you. It is as though the Lord God had offered you some delicious food and you are extending your hands palms-up to receive it. This is the nature of true prayer.

WHAT IS FASTING?

Moreover when ye fast, be not, as the hypocrites, of a sad countenance: for they disfigure their faces, that they may appear unto men to fast. Verily I say unto you, They have their reward. But thou, when thou fastest, anoint thine head, and wash thy face; That thou appear not unto men to fast, but unto thy Father which is in secret: and thy Father, which seeth in secret, shall reward thee openly (Matthew 6:16-18).

In His discussion of religious activity, the Lord Jesus mentions the much misunderstood practice of fasting. Fasting as we commonly understand it, refers to doing without a normal amount of food or drink. But it can include much more than your diet.

Think of it this way: Any time you refrain from doing something that would be normal under those circumstances, because you do not want to be distracted from your personal fellowship with God, you could call it "fasting." Fasting means to abstain from natural practices in order to be more sensitive to spiritual things.

A human being has physical interests and spiritual interests. As a child of Adam you have relationships in this world, but as a child of God you have relationships with Him. One is in the flesh; the other is in the spirit. If you want to give your time to spiritual things, you won't have as much time for fleshly things. Throughout history, spiritually-minded people have often abstained from material things in order to be more sensitive to spiritual things.

Andrew Bonar, a Scottish minister, kept a diary in which he recorded experiments he made in fasting. He told, for example, that on occasion when he was going to partake of the Lord's Supper, he would not eat any food for a certain length of time before. He varied his procedure: one time he did not eat for an entire day prior to the Lord's Supper; then prior to the next observance of Communion, he ate. Each time he carefully noted the effect on himself. Then he compared his spiritual experiences on these two occasions. He found that the time he fasted, he was quite unusually spiritually sensitive.

When I was in school, a fellow student from Minnesota experimented with fasting. For a week he ate nothing. He reported to the rest of us concerning the effect that he felt the fasting had on him spiritually.

Generally speaking, he concluded that doing without food was not the point. However, when he was abstaining from food in order to draw nigh to God, there was spiritual benefit in it. In this way he felt that fasting could be wholesome for Christians.

Too often we limit the idea of fasting to food. But actually, I believe that more people fast for spiritual reasons than we ordinarily recognize. For example, a man might refrain from going to a Major League baseball game in order to take time to pray. I think that would be fasting. A family may make a rule never to stay out late on Saturday night in order that they might be prepared for worship on Sunday. I think that would be fasting, too. Some young people refrain from certain practices because they think that it is better for them spiritually if they refrain. I think that would be fasting as well. Anything that you abstain from for spiritual reasons would be a matter of fasting.

Make it a practice of denying yourself any pleasure likely to distract you from God, and when you do this, do it as unto the Lord, and not unto men. Then you would be following the Lord's teaching in this passage.

What Is Your Treasure?

Lay not up for yourselves treasures upon earth, where moth and rust doth corrupt, and where thieves break through and steal: But lay up for yourselves treasures in heaven, where neither moth nor rust doth corrupt, and where thieves do not break through nor steal: For where your treasure is, there will your heart be also. The light of the body is the eye: if therefore thine eye be single, thy whole body shall be full of light. But if thine eye be evil, thy whole body shall be full of darkness. If therefore the light that is in thee be darkness, how great is that darkness! (Matthew 6:19-23).

Anything can be your treasure if you value it as such. It is not the thing in itself; it is the way you cherish it. Some things may be of little worth in themselves, but because you value them highly, they become your treasures.

Jesus warned against allowing things of the world to become too precious. When He said, "Lay not up for yourselves treasures upon earth," He meant, "Do not let your values be centered down here." Naturally, you have material possessions: food, shelter, clothing, friends. All of these things you will value to a certain extent. Thus they could become treasures to you.

Anything you have of this world's goods can be lost. That includes even your health, strength and life. But the Lord Jesus said that you should not let any of these things become your greatest treasures. Instead, "Lay up for yourselves treasure in heaven."

How can you "lay up treasures in heaven"?

It is hard to think about heaven at all, because we can't picture it very clearly. Usually when we try to think about heaven, we make another earth out of it. The best way to think of heaven is to remember that God is there. Certainly, we will have fellowship with friends and loved ones. But most important is the fact that in heaven we will have eternal fellowship with the Lord Himself.

While you may find it difficult to gain an intellectual picture of heaven, you can put your heart there. It is interesting and somewhat strange that Jesus said, "Where your treasure is, there will your heart be also." He didn't say, "Where your heart is, there will your treasure be."

Suppose you are given a ring. The moment it is yours, you admire it. You begin to cherish it. Even when you aren't wearing it, you think about it. In fact, you can't forget it. Your heart may become attached to the ring, so wherever that ring is there your heart is also. When we do things here on earth that are pleasing to God, we can look forward to joy with the Lord in heaven: this expectation of joy can become a treasure to our hearts.

It is not easy to understand the passage which begins, "The light of the body is the eye." If I am in a beautiful room with magnificent chandeliers, ornate windows and exquisite furniture, how do I know it? I can only know it because my eyes tell me. Light shows up things to my consciousness by coming to my eye. When the Bible says, "If your eye be single, the whole body shall be full of light," the word *single* means "clear." Let me put it this way: "If your eye is not blurred." If your eye is focused clearly and you understand it fully, the whole body is full of light.

"If thine eye be evil" does not necessarily mean morally evil, but rather functioning poorly. If you have a cataract over your eyes, when you open them and light falls on them you can't see and the whole body is in darkness.

You have just one heart. If you give your affection to the things of this world, you cannot give it to the things of God. If you are interested in your car or your house and those things are completely engaging your attention, you will not be able to see anything else. You will be blind to spiritual things. But if you have your eye "single," so that your mind is not cluttered up with things of this world and you can see spiritual things, the whole body will be full of light: you will see things as they really are.

Don't Worry

No man can serve two masters: for either he will hate the one, and love the other; or else he will hold to the one, and despise the other. Ye cannot serve God and mammon. Therefore I say unto you, Take no thought for your life, what ye shall eat, or what ye shall drink; nor yet for your body, what ye shall put on. Is not the life more than meat, and the body than raiment? Behold the fowls of the air: for they sow not, neither do they reap, nor gather into barns; yet your heavenly Father feedeth them. Are ye not much better than they? Which of you by taking thought can add one cubit unto his stature? And why take ye thought for raiment? Consider the lilies of the field, how they grow; they toil not, neither do they spin: And yet I say unto you, That even Solomon in all his glory was not arrayed like one of these. Wherefore, if God so clothe the grass of the field, which to day is, and to morrow is cast into the oven, shall he not much more clothe you, O ye of little faith? Therefore take no thought, saying, What shall we eat? or, What shall we drink? or, Wherewithal shall we be clothed? (For after all these things do the Gentiles seek:) for your heavenly Father knoweth that ye have need of all these things. But seek ye first the kingdom of God, and his righteousness; and all these things shall be added unto you. Take therefore no thought for the morrow: for the morrow shall take thought for the things of itself. Sufficient unto the day is the evil thereof (Matthew 6:24-34).

No one can go north and south at the same time and no one can go up and down at the same time. Jesus said it this way: "No man can serve two masters."

If you have one pail and it is full of honey, you can't fill it full of milk. If it is full of milk, you can't fill it with honey. Life is like that. You can't have both. Jesus said, "You cannot serve God and mammon."

The Lord Jesus went on to say when your heart and mind are trusting God you can live a life free from anxiety. The phrase, "Take no thought," really means, "Do not be anxious." In other words, do not be preoccupied with concern about your physical needs, because you, in the sight of God, are much more important than what you eat, drink or wear.

Jesus illustrated His point by referring to the "fowls of the air." When I was younger, this illustration always bothered me. I was almost ashamed that anything in the Bible could be as impractical as this. I expect the truth was that I had an idea that this passage was saying that a bird would just sit on a fence post and that God would come and drop a worm in its mouth. But I should have known better.

I knew that birds don't sow, reap or gather into barns, but they certainly are not inactive. In the morning they wake up before you do. You no doubt have heard the phrase "getting up with the chickens." Certainly birds aren't lazy.

When a woodpecker bangs his bill against the side of a tree, he is trying to scare the bugs out from under the bark. But do you know what? He is actually expecting that bugs are there.

This, I believe, is what the Lord wants to teach us. When you go out in the morning, look for what God has prepared for you. God will provide for you, just as He provides for the birds.

Next, Jesus referred to "the lilies of the field." This too seems to be a difficult illustration to understand. How could a little lily be more glorious than the mighty monarch Solomon? Is a little flower more wonderful than a royal coronation with all its gold, silver, purple, silks, satins and furs? But stop and think a bit.

If you stripped Solomon of all his gold, jewelry and adornments, what would you have? You would see a scrawny individual who would look like any other man. Now go out and look at that flower again. It hasn't any paint on it, nor any clothing, nor is it laden with silver and gold. What the flower is, it is from the inside out as God made it. It is exactly as you see it. But when you look at Solomon in all his glory, you see the trappings hung on him.

This is what the Lord Jesus had in mind. If you yield yourself to God, something will happen to you from the inside out. You won't have to pretend. You won't have to put on an act. You will really be something that is acceptable to God and helpful to mankind, because God made you that way.

As God feeds the birds and clothes the flowers, so He will provide for you. Worry will not provide your material needs, but trust in God will not only provide material food and clothing but spiritual food and clothing as well. "Seek ye first the kingdom of God and his righteousness, and all these things shall be added unto you."

Chapter 5

MEASURING UP TO GOD'S YARDSTICK

WHAT GOD WANTS OF YOU

You may be tall or short, strong or weak, smart or dull, but the Bible isn't concerned about such things. The Bible focuses upon your relationship with God.

If you plan to live in an obedient relationship with the living God, your actions must be under His control. No longer will you do what you want, but now you will want to do what God wants. Instead of trying to live your life yourself, you yield yourself to God so that God might work His will in you.

The Sermon on the Mount points out the results of yielding yourself to the will of God. Several of these results are mentioned in Matthew 7.

First, when you are controlled by the will of God, you will be much more concerned about judging yourself than about judging anyone else. In case of a conflict between you and someone else, the tendency will be to reflect on your own conduct, appraising and correcting what is at fault in your own life, rather than judging the other person.

David is a good example of this. When his son Absalom usurped the throne, King David had to flee to save his life. As he traveled through a rather narrow place between cliffs an enemy rolled stones down on him and cursed him.

One of David's lieutenants said, "Let me go and get that man. I will cut off his head."

But David replied, "Let him curse me. Maybe God told him to curse."

David was not disposed to judge the other man's conduct. Let the judging of others be left to God. If you want to do any judging, judge yourself.

Although you are not to judge others, this does not mean that you are not to exercise spiritual discernment. It does not mean that you will enjoy the fellowship of everyone, nor that you should share your spiritual experiences with everyone. Some people have no appreciation of spiritual things. Talking to them spiritually is like talking with someone who can't understand English. Some people are sensitive only to those things which they can see, hear, smell, taste or touch. To such people spiritual things have no value.

You are not to judge these people, as if you were a judge on a bench. They are in God's hands; God is their judge. But if you are inwardly being guided by the Spirit of God, you will exercise discernment in dealing with such people.

Although there are some people with whom you will not be able to communicate regarding the matters that mean most to you, you can always communicate with God. In fact, God wants you to talk with Him. No matter what problems you face, He wants you to ask Him for help.

In any situation you will do your part, expecting God to do His part. You'll work to the best of your ability, expecting divine assistance. This is part of what is meant when Jesus said, "Ask . . . knock . . . seek."

In any frustration of life, you will study the situation carefully and then act in the light of what you know to be God's will, looking constantly for divine guidance. You may wonder, "How will I know what I should do?"

One good rule to follow is this: Put yourself in the place of other people who are involved. Sympathize with them and consider what you would do if you were in their place.

Someone has wisely said, "Pray as if it all depended on God; work as if it all depended on you." Remember at all times that God is more eager to bless you than you are to receive His blessing.

SHOULD CHRISTIANS JUDGE?

Judge not, that ye be not judged. For with what judgment ye judge, ye shall be judged: and with what measure ye mete, it shall be measured to you again. And why beholdest thou the mote that is in thy brother's eye, but considerest not the beam that is in thine own eye? Or how wilt thou say to thy brother, Let me pull out the mote out of thine eye; and, behold, a beam is in thine own eye? Thou hypocrite, first cast out the beam out of thine own eye; and then shalt thou see clearly to cast out the mote out of thy brother's eye. Give not that which is holy unto the dogs, neither cast ye your pearls before swine, lest they trample them under their feet, and turn again and rend you (Matthew 7:1-6).

You do not treat a baby as you would treat a ten-year-old. Instead, you ask yourself, "How much does the baby understand?" Your answer to that question determines how you handle the baby.

Perhaps you have had the experience of disciplining a child rather severely before you suddenly realized that the child didn't even understand what the problem was. Immediately you would try to approach the problem from a different aspect.

In His dealings with you, God does not have to wait to find out how much you understand. He knows. God deals with you according to your understanding. If you are critical of another person's work, God will be especially critical of yours. If you judge a person for his unkindness, God will carefully examine you to see how kind you are.

However, if you see faults in another person, but do not judge them, nor penalize them in your mind, God will take note of your attitude and treat you accordingly. "Blessed are the merciful, for they shall obtain mercy" is exactly what Jesus is teaching here.

"And why beholdest thou the mote that is in thy brother's eye, but considereth not the beam that is in thine own eye?" The mote is a little splinter, and the beam is a large plank. Jesus is asking "Why are you paying more attention to the little splinter in your brother's eye, than you are to the large plank in your own?" Of course you are eager to straighten the other fellow out. But how ridiculous it is to try to straighten him out when "behold a beam is in thine own eye!"

The word hypocrite in verse 5 means a two-faced person. A hypocrite is a man who looks one way at a neighbor, condemning him, and another way at himself, excusing himself. The Lord takes notice when you are harsh in your condemnation of others but indulgent in your estimation of yourself. He will not accept such a double standard in judging.

In the first five verses of this passage, you are told, "Don't judge." In the next verse, however, you must judge. You have to judge in order to know who the "dogs" are and who the "swine" are. The fact of the matter is that you can't help noticing what is going on around you, if you keep your eyes open. It is quite easy to tell when a man is obedient to God and when he is not. This is not judging others; it is merely being aware of the facts of life. Judging others involves your appraisal of their motivation. Although Jesus warns you not to judge another man's heart, you can certainly note his conduct. You can observe how he acts, but why he acts that way must be left to God. God knows if the man does not know any better. God knows if the man is acting in ignorance. If you did what he is doing, you might be very wrong, since you might know better what should be done.

While you must not judge motivation, you must notice conduct in order to recognize the dogs and the swine. Left alone, a
dog is not too fussy about what he eats. He seems to have little
sense of taste. Jesus is talking about someone who does not have
any spiritual taste when He says, "Give not that which is holy
unto dogs." Don't spread out the holy things of God before people
who do not care about them.

Only a person who has lived on a farm can understand the
reference to swine. Pigs get very hungry; rapacious is the word for
it. When they want to be fed, they let you know. They squeal
and push and shove and squeal some more. When you throw in
the food, they care nothing about Emily Post manners.

If the pigs were to come to you and you spread pearls before
them, they would think that these gems were gravel and would
trample them underfoot. They would get their feet in the trough
and squeal for more food. Pearls wouldn't mean anything to them
as pearls. "They would turn again and rend you," means they
would still be hungry and bite at you. They would come after you
for more food.

In discussing spiritual things with others, you must exercise
judgment. The Lord may have done some things for you that others
might not understand. If you start talking about some wonderful
things the Lord has done for you and there is someone present
who laughs at you, that would be a good time to keep quiet. That
person may be like the dog, without a sense of taste. Or he may
be like the pig, looking for something else altogether.

When you have told some people what the Lord is doing for
you, and you learn they have not even listened, it is truly tragic.
They had no appreciation of the blessing you were telling about:
they really wanted to hear something interesting to them and quite
different from what you were telling.

KNOCKING AT GOD'S DOOR

Ask, and it shall be given you; seek, and ye shall find; knock,
and it shall be opened unto you: For every one that asketh receiveth; and he that seeketh findeth; and to him that knocketh
it shall be opened. Or what man is there of you, whom if his
son ask bread, will he give him a stone? Or if he ask a fish,
will he give him a serpent? If ye then, being evil, know how to
give good gifts unto your children, how much more shall your
Father which is in heaven give good things to them that ask
him? Therefore all things whatsoever ye would that men should
do to you, do ye even so to them: for this is the law and the
prophets (Matthew 7:7-12).

Here is one of the most remarkable promises about prayer you will ever find. The challenge is just as broad, deep and long as you can possibly imagine it. There are no qualifications. There are no conditions, except to ask.

You may say, "I don't think that can be true." I would ask you, "Why?" If you reply, "Well, I just haven't seen it," my answer would be, "How many times have you seen anyone ask?"

Now, to bring this down closer to home, "How many times have you asked God?" You know that James says: "You have not, because you ask not."

The person who goes into life looking for the blessing of God, receives it. It reminds you of the birds who go out in the morning looking for the worm they think is there. They seem always to expect to find.

"Seek and ye shall find." You can't seek sitting down or standing still. Go out and look around and you shall find. Seeking involves your judgment, your examination, your appraisal, but while you are seeking you are expecting that God has prepared for you. It will be your joy to find He has.

Knocking is also an activity. Knocking on a door is usually a hard thing for me to do. Maybe it is hard for you, too. But unless you knock, the door won't be opened. The promise is that when you knock, it will be opened.

If I told you that God has promised that if you will prepare the soil properly and sow wheat in the ground, you would get wheat, you would say, "Of course. If you don't put the seed in the ground, you won't get wheat." In just the same way, if you pray you will have, and if you don't pray you won't have. It is as simple as that. God wants to help you, but His help is extended to those who ask Him for it. He will be found of the people who seek Him, and He will open the door for the people who knock.

Immediately after these verses on prayer, Jesus sets forth the Golden Rule in verse 12. For a long time I used to wonder, "Why bring that in here?" I think now that I see the reason. Asking is not a matter of words, seeking is not a matter of a flashlight and knocking is not just with your knuckles. Putting the Golden Rule next to these instructions on prayer suggests that you can act in such a way that you are really asking God for blessing. "Whatsoever ye would that men should do to you, do ye even so to them," does not mean that you will get others to do things for you. It means that you should think of what you would like the other person to do for you, and then you do that for him, because in that way you will be acting on "love thy neighbor as thyself."

If you do that, you will find that you will be asking God for blessing, seeking His way and knocking for entrance into eternal treasures. It will be His faithful benevolence to bless you according to your asking.

STRAIT AND STRAIGHT

Enter ye in at the strait gate: for wide is the gate, and broad is the way, that leadeth to destruction, and many there be which go in thereat: Because strait is the gate, and narrow is the way, which leadeth unto life, and few there be that find it (Matthew 7:13,14).

Of all that the Lord Jesus said, this is probably His most ignored saying. From the sound of many sermons I've heard, everyone in the world is going to end up all right. Many church members, who should know better, talk as if no one will ever be lost. But this isn't what Jesus said.

When Jesus said, "Enter ye in at the strait gate," He did not mean "straight." It does not mean "straight" as a ruler, nor not twisted, nor in a direct line, nor the shortest distance between two points. The word *strait* means narrow or tight. It implies a narrow corridor, a tight place. You have heard of the Straits of Dover and the Straits of Gibraltar. A strait, you see, is a narrow body of water that connects two larger bodies of water.

"Enter ye in at the strait gate, for wide is the gate" (it is easy to get in) "and broad is the way" (it is easy to travel) "which leadeth to destruction."

Now what does this mean? It means that man does not naturally travel God's road. He does not want to go through a tight spot to take the road that leadeth to life.

Jesus told Nicodemus, "Except a man be born again, he cannot see the kingdom of God" (John 3:3).

You might say, "Well, that doesn't seem very broadminded." You are right, it doesn't. There is nothing wide nor loose when it means coming to God. There is only one way to approach God. You come to God through the Lord Jesus Christ on Calvary's cross.

Some years ago in California, I was talking to a college student. Suddenly he interrupted me. "It seems to me," he said, "you put all your hopes on one person."

"Is that the way it seems?"

"Yes," he said, "it looks as if you are trusting everything to Jesus Christ. It is just as if you were hanging yourself up on a hook on the wall and everything depends upon that hook. But what if that hook gives way?"

"You mean," I said, "if it turns out that Jesus Christ is not true, then where will I be?"

"Yes, where will you be?"

"I'll be lost, that's all. It's as simple as that." Then I looked up at him and asked, "Tell me this; if that hook does not give way and if it holds and if Jesus Christ is true, then what?"

"I guess you'd call yourself saved."

"That's right," I said. "By the way, what hook are you hanging on?"

The only way to God is through the Lord Jesus Christ. Anyone can come to God, but you cannot come to God any way you choose. Jesus said, "*I* am the way, the truth, and the life: no man cometh to the Father but by me" (John 14:6). He is the only way.

You see, God in heaven had one Son, the Lord Jesus Christ. He sent Him into the world one time. We are to understand He is the way of salvation.

Perhaps you will say, "Not many people believe that." I expect that is true. The Lord Jesus said, "Few there be that find it." I wish it were not so, but it is.

I can well understand the Apostle Paul, who, when he spoke about Israel said, "My heart's desire and prayer to God for Israel is that they might be saved." In another place he said, "I could wish myself accursed from God for my kinsmen after the flesh." But this was not necessary. There was one accursed from God on their behalf, and that was the Lord Jesus Christ on the cross.

. This is the one strait gate through which we must come in. It leads to life, and anyone can find it.

WATCH OUT FOR WOLVES

Beware of false prophets, which come to you in sheep's clothing, but inwardly they are ravening wolves. Ye shall know them by their fruits. Do men gather grapes of thorns, or figs of thistles? Even so every good tree bringeth forth good fruit; but a corrupt tree bringeth forth evil fruit. A good tree cannot bring forth evil fruit, neither can a corrupt tree bring forth good fruit. Every tree that bringeth not forth good fruit is hewn down, and cast into the fire. Wherefore by their fruits ye shall know them (Matthew 7:15-20).

All through the Bible the people of God were troubled with false prophets, men who claimed to speak for God but did not. The Apostle Paul had to deal with them, even as Jeremiah did. And there are false prophets among us today, too.

Some people seem to have the idea that you should never question anything that is said in the pulpit. When a man gets up to preach, everything he says is supposed to be the gospel truth. Now it is true anyone may speak for God, but it also sadly is true there are those who claim to do so, who do not.

The Lord Jesus said that false prophets "come to you in sheep's clothing, but inwardly they are ravening wolves." A sheep is mild and innocent. Of all the farm animals, it is the most harmless. On the other hand, a wolf is about as vicious a creature as you will find. Jesus said that although the outward manner of false prophets may be mild, gentle, sweet and harmless, they are hungry for your life's blood.

You can tell a false prophet, Jesus said, "by their fruits." You won't know them by their arguments. You won't know them because they look ungodly. But "ye shall know them by their fruits": by the consequences of their work.

Suppose a new doctor came into your community. How would you know if he were any good? You certainly couldn't tell by looking at him. You could not tell by glancing around his office. He might have all the latest medical equipment and still be an inefficient doctor. How could you tell? Find out if he has ever done anything for anyone. Hear the testimony of his patients.

Suppose you needed a lawyer. How would you select one? It would be by his reputation. You'd select the man who has shown in his past performance that he can do what you want to have done.

Recently some friends were asking me about some of the well-known leaders in the church today. I was being asked if I had confidence in them. With reference to one man they mentioned, I had to say, "No, I don't have confidence in him."

My friends seemed upset, "Aren't you terribly harsh?"

"Oh," I said, "I haven't said anything against him. I just told you I did not have confidence in him."

Now they seemed puzzled: "What do you mean?"

I replied, "You asked me if I had confidence in that man. You did not ask me if he was any good. You just asked me if I had confidence in him, and I said, 'No.'"

"Well, why not?"

"For one simple reason, I do not know him. I have not seen any of his work."

Then they asked one further question: "How would you know if he were trustworthy?"

I replied, "I am in the world to preach the Gospel. The thing that concerns me is that individuals shall be brought to God. So I want to know this: Does this man bring anyone to God? When he talks, does a man's faith grow? Or does the hearer get more confused all the time? If a man talks about the Gospel in such a way that his listeners believe less when he is through than they did when he started, he is not trustworthy." And I am sorry to say there are such preachers and teachers.

If a man preaches in such a way that you become conscious of sin, righteousness and judgment to come, God the Holy Spirit is working through that man. Any man's preaching that causes his listeners to feel that they are sinners, that makes them wish that they were holy, that makes them understand that they will come face to face with God–that man has the evidence of the Holy Spirit. You could trust him to preach the truth of the Gospel.

DON'T BE FOOLED

Not every one that saith unto me, Lord, Lord, shall enter into the kingdom of heaven; but he that doeth the will of my Father which is in heaven. Many will say to me in that day, Lord, Lord, have we not prophesied in thy name? and in thy name have cast out devils? and in thy name done many wonderful works? And then will I profess unto them, I never knew you: depart from me, ye that work iniquity. Therefore whosoever heareth these sayings of mine, and doeth them, I will liken him unto a wise man, which built his house upon a rock: And the rain descended, and the floods came, and the winds blew, and beat upon that house; and it fell not: for it was founded upon a rock. And every one that heareth these sayings of mine, and doeth them not, shall be likened unto a foolish man, which built his house upon the sand: And the rain descended, and the floods came, and the winds blew, and beat upon that house; and it fell: and great was the fall of it. And it came to pass, when Jesus had ended these sayings, the people were astonished at his doctrine: For he taught them as one having authority, and not as the scribes (Matthew 7:21-29).

In this final chapter of the Sermon on the Mount, Jesus gave one warning after another. He realized that people can be fooled about religion very easily, and so these warnings were given to help people not to be deceived.

He warned them that not everyone who thinks he is in the kingdom of heaven really is. Some are merely fooling themselves. He was not talking about murderers or thieves. He was talking about people who claimed to be good, people who had preached in His name, who had cast out demons, who had done many wonderful works for Jesus.

Why would the Lord say, "I never knew you"?

When do you know someone? It isn't when you know his name, where he was born, what he does for a living, etc. It is when you have talked with him face to face and have had dealings with him.

Once in a while I hear a Sunday school teacher or even a

minister who makes me wonder if he really knows the Lord. Of course, I am not his judge, but I cannot help but wonder. He may have a great amount of education and may have amassed many facts regarding the Bible, but somehow there is no indication that he has ever had fellowship with Jesus Christ. And, sad to say, if that man does not know the Lord, the Lord will not know him. The Lord said that no one would come into the kingdom of heaven whom He did not know personally.

Though the parable of the wise man and foolish man is a simple story, it contains a great deal of truth. Each man built a house and apparently both houses were equally well-built. There is no indication that there was any difference in the design or the structure of the two houses. Yet one of these houses was destroyed in the storm while the other house stood firm.

In your church there may be two people doing equal work. Perhaps both of them sing in the choir; maybe both of them give regularly; maybe both have families to whom they are faithful; maybe both have good reputations in the community. One of them, however, is helped day in and day out because he personally knows the Lord Jesus Christ. The very faithfulness that he has is not his own: it is the faithfulness of the Lord Jesus Christ in him.

The other person does not know the Lord Jesus. He does everything by imitating other Christians. Since his father went to church, he goes to church. Since his wife wants to give to the church, he gives to the church. Since his children go to Sunday school, he goes to Sunday school. If you were to ask him, "Do you know the Lord Jesus Christ?" he would have to say, "I know about Him. I have read about Him." But he does not really know Jesus. His house may be an excellent looking structure, but it is not on a sound foundation.

Paul wrote, "Other foundation can no man lay than that is laid, which is Jesus Christ." The person who is trusting Christ will stand the test. He has committed himself to God. Such a person will do the sayings of Christ because he wants to do them. He wants to do them because Christ is in him, "the hope of glory."

Everything that the Lord Jesus Christ said in the Sermon on the Mount about righteous living He personally performs. When you receive Him as your Saviour and Lord, He brings into your soul His own personal performance. He Himself in you does the things that are pleasing in the sight of God.

Chapter 6

THE GREAT PHYSICIAN BEGINS HIS PRACTICE

How Jesus Proved His Power

When Jesus came into this world, He not only came preaching and teaching about the kingdom of God, but He also came healing all kinds of sicknesses. You see, when sin entered the world, it ruined man. It made his eyes blind and his ears deaf and his feet paralyzed. When Jesus came, He removed the effects of sin. This was demonstrated in His healing works.

In the Sermon on the Mount, Jesus taught that true righteousness came from an inner desire to do the will of God sincerely.

Suppose you read the Sermon on the Mount and decide that you want to do what it says. As you try to live up to it, you fail over and over again. Soon you realize that you can't do the will of God by yourself. And when you come to that realization, you have actually taken the first step toward God.

How then is it possible for anyone to please God, you may ask?

Only Jesus Christ Himself can do the will of God. He is the only one who ever, from the bottom of His heart, really wanted to do only His Father's will. If you let Christ come into your heart and live in you, He will give you inner impulses and urges that will move you to do the will of God. You will now be a citizen of the kingdom of God. You will be eager to obey God's will.

This creates a problem. In your heart you might want to do the will of God, but in your flesh, with its habits of self-indulgence, you would rather do something else. No matter how many times you have heard the things of Jesus Christ, your own ego is not willing to surrender all to God. The self is naturally opposed to God because the self is dead in trespasses and sin.

But God can raise the dead. The power of God can overcome human nature. God can overrule natural processes. To illustrate this, you can read Matthew 8 and 9 which graphically show Christ's power over nature.

You will read about the leper who fell down before the Lord Jesus and said, "Lord, if thou wilt, thou canst make me clean." And He did, because Jesus of Nazareth had power to overcome disease. You will read of the centurion who said, "My servant is sick nigh unto death. Speak the word and he will get well." When Jesus spoke the word, immediately the servant began to recover. You will read how the Lord Jesus found that Peter's mother-in-law was sick and He healed her. You will read of a palsied man whose friends brought him to Jesus for healing. You will read of a storm at sea which became suddenly calm when Jesus said, "Be still." You will read of two demon-possessed men who were freed by the power of Jesus Christ.

These works of power illustrate the truth that Christ Jesus can set you free from natural limitations of any kind. Christ has power over spiritual disease as well as physical disease.

Do you remember when Jesus was criticized because He ate with publicans and sinners? Jesus told the Pharisees that doctors didn't spend their time with people who were well but with those who were sick. Jesus was a doctor of men's souls. And He still is. People who think they are spiritually well will not be helped by the Lord. Only those who recognize their illness will come for healing.

WHAT FAITH CAN DO

When he was come down from the mountain, great multitudes followed him. And, behold, there came a leper and worshipped him, saying, Lord, if thou wilt, thou canst make me clean. And Jesus put forth his hand, and touched him, saying, I will; be thou clean. And immediately his leprosy was cleansed. And Jesus saith unto him, See thou tell no man; but go thy way, shew thyself to the priest, and offer the gift that Moses commanded, for a testimony unto them. And when Jesus was entered into Capernaum, there came unto him a centurion, beseeching him, And saying, Lord, my servant lieth at home sick of the palsy grievously tormented. And Jesus saith unto him, I will come and heal him. The centurion answered and said, Lord, I am not worthy that thou shouldest come under my roof: but speak the word only, and my servant shall be healed. For I am a man under authority, having soldiers under me: and I say to this man, Go, and he goeth; and to another, Come, and he cometh; and to my servant, Do this, and he doeth it. When Jesus heard it, he marvelled, and said to them that followed, Verily I say unto you, I have not found so great faith, no, not in Israel. And I say unto you, That many shall come from the east and west, and shall sit down with Abraham, and Isaac, and Jacob, in the kingdom of heaven. But the children of the kingdom shall be cast out into outer darkness: there shall be weeping and gnashing of teeth. And Jesus

— understanding, also!

said unto the centurion, Go thy way; and as thou hast believed, so be it done unto thee. And his servant was healed in the self-same hour. And when Jesus was come into Peter's house, he saw his wife's mother laid, and sick of a fever. And he touched her hand, and the fever left her: and she arose, and ministered unto them. When the even was come, they brought unto him many that were possessed with devils: and he cast out the spirits with his word, and healed all that were sick: That it might be fulfilled which was spoken by Esaias the prophet, saying, Himself took our infirmities, and bare our sicknesses (Matthew 8:1-17).

Jesus' ministry was first described in these words: "Jesus went about all Galilee, teaching in their synagogues, and preaching the gospel of the kingdom, and healing all manner of sickness and all manner of disease among the people" (Matthew 4:23). In Matthew 5-7 you find the Sermon on the Mount, which is devoted to teaching and preaching. Now in Matthew 8 and 9 you find works of power, the healing ministry of Jesus. Having set forth in His teaching what God offers to do for anyone who will yield himself to God, Jesus now demonstrates the power of God to encourage men to believe that God can do what He says.

Whenever God reveals His will to you, He calls on you to respond in a certain way. The trouble is, humanly speaking, you will not respond that way. In fact, you may not even be able to respond that way. Your own human limitations will keep you from obeying the will of God.

The Lord Jesus reveals that He can overcome natural limitations and He demonstrates this by His works of healing.

First, He healed an incurable disease, leprosy. There were cases in Biblical times where the disease had been arrested, but it was commonly known as an incurable disease. So when a leper came believing that Jesus could heal him, it showed great faith. And this is the first step in coming to God—believing that God is able. Later on you will believe more. But at first all you need to believe is that God can.

After Jesus touched him, immediately his leprosy was cleansed. The word "immediately" takes it away from natural processes. But how did Jesus do it? This work shows the operation of a power greater than nature.

Even so when you come, believing that God can, you can expect the experience of being made able to respond immediately to Him by a power that is greater than the power of nature.

After this Jesus told the healed leper to show himself to the priests, the people in that day who were representing the Word of God, and tell them that what the Bible had promised was actually coming to pass. The leper's words to the priests were a testimony to them, a way of helping them understand, of giving them insight. Even though the priests had not been able to help the leper, Jesus sent the man back to them to let them know what God can do.

Next, Jesus healed the servant of a centurion. Once again there was great faith placed in Jesus. The centurion believed that Jesus didn't even need to see the servant. The Lord needed only to say the word and it would be done. For this faith Jesus commended him. This, Jesus said, is the kind of faith that those who are gathered together in the kingdom of heaven will have. We may be sure this is the kind of faith that will build the church today.

After this, Jesus healed Peter's mother-in-law. In this case, Peter apparently did not ask for help. Here we see that the Lord will help you even before you ask for it. This is one of the fringe benefits that come to any Christian family. Because Peter believed in the Lord Jesus Christ and invited Him into his home, his mother-in-law was healed. There is no evidence that she exhibited the faith of the leper or of the centurion. God blesses not only those who call on Him, but the promise embraces "you, and your household."

This section of Scripture closes with a quotation from Isaiah, "Himself took our infirmities and bare our sicknesses." Does He actually take sickness on Himself? This is what it says. And what ever is true physically, is true spiritually. If you are sick with unbelief, if you are sick with envy, if you are sick with resentment against God, God is able to heal by taking your infirmity on Himself.

DISCIPLESHIP CAN BE DANGEROUS

Now when Jesus saw great multitudes about him, he gave commandment to depart unto the other side. And a certain scribe came, and said unto him, Master, I will follow thee whithersoever thou goest. And Jesus saith unto him, The foxes have holes, and the birds of the air have nests; but the Son of man hath not where to lay his head. And another of his disciples said unto him, Lord, suffer me first to go and bury my father. But Jesus said unto him, Follow me; and let the dead bury their dead. And when he was entered into a ship, his disciples followed him. And, behold, there arose a great tempest in the sea, insomuch that the ship was covered with the waves: but he was asleep. And his disciples came to him, and awoke him, saying, Lord, save us: we perish. And he saith unto them, Why are ye fearful, O ye of little faith? Then he arose, and rebuked the winds and the sea; and there was a great calm. But the men marvelled, saying, What manner of man is this, that even the winds and the sea obey him! (Matthew 8:18-27).

This is the important question of the whole account.

Two men wanted to follow Jesus Christ. The first was a scribe, a student of the Scriptures, an educated man. Jesus said to him, "The foxes have holes, and the birds of the air have nests, but the Son of man hath not where to lay his head." In other words, "Think it over. It is going to cost you something. I have nothing to give you, not even a place to stay."

If you plan to follow Jesus Christ, consider the cost. You can be sure of this: It will cost you something.

Another prospective follower of Jesus wanted to take care of his father before following Him. Jesus told him, "Follow me, and let the dead bury their dead." The young man was willing to follow, but he felt he had certain social obligations which should come first.

This matter of burying his father apparently was an oriental custom which meant that the son would stay home until the father died. It did not mean that the father was already dead. In other words, the young man was saying, "Wait until my father dies, and then I'll be free to follow you."

The answer which Christ gave indicated that spiritual relationships were more important than human relationships. There is no social obligation that should stand between you and God's will for you. Nothing is as important as obeying the inward call of God.

Right after that, Jesus and His disciples were in a storm at sea. It was a time of obvious danger. Here we may note at once that just because you become a follower of the Lord, you need not expect everything to be sweet and lovely. Actually, deciding to follow the Lord may mean real danger.

The only reason those disciples were in the boat was that they were following the Lord's instructions. By obeying Him they got into a very dangerous situation. Though the storm was raging, Jesus was asleep. Feeling the desperate need of any help He could give, His disciples woke Him up. Remember that many of these disciples were veteran fishermen on this Sea of Galilee. This little sea had a bad reputation for sudden storms. This particular storm frightened them greatly.

It may seem strange for Jesus to say, "Why are ye fearful?" or "Why are ye upset?" For no matter how bad the storm was, these disciples could have been trusting God. This may be why Jesus called them men "of little faith."

Faith is not always the same size. You can have little faith, you can have more faith, and you can have much faith. These disciples had little faith. But let us not despise "little faith." After all, their faith got them on the boat; it had them following the Lord Jesus Christ. What then is "little faith"? Perhaps you

what is wrong with "a little faith"?

could say it is beginning faith. These disciples had enough faith to commit themselves to God. And so they were following the Lord. They had that much faith. They even followed Him on the boat. They had that much faith. And they even called on Him in trouble. They had that much faith. Any faith is good. Even a little faith is good. You may learn more, but that little faith will get you started.

"Then he arose, rebuked the winds and the sea, and there was a great calm. But the men marvelled, saying, What manner of man is this, that even the winds and the sea obey him." That is what they learned in the time of crisis. You do not ask for trouble, but when trouble comes, you can learn about the Lord, if you look to Him for help.

They Cared About Their Pigs

And when he was come to the other side into the country of the Gergesenes, there met him two possessed with devils, coming out of the tombs, exceeding fierce, so that no man might pass by that way. And, behold, they cried out, saying, What have we to do with thee, Jesus, thou Son of God? art thou come hither to torment us before the time? And there was a good way off from them an herd of many swine feeding. So the devils besought him, saying, If thou cast us out, suffer us to go away into the herd of swine. And he said unto them, Go. And when they were come out, they went into the herd of swine: and, behold, the whole herd of swine ran violently down a steep place into the sea, and perished in the waters. And they that kept them fled, and went their ways into the city, and told every thing, and what was befallen to the possessed of the devils. And, behold, the whole city came out to meet Jesus: and when they saw him, they besought him that he would depart out of their coasts (Matthew 8:28-34).

As He journeyed in the country, the Lord met two men "exceeding fierce." These men were "possessed with devils" and apparently could not think freely. Their minds were not their own. They were compelled from within to do violent things. The only place they were allowed to live was the graveyard.

Some people today don't believe in devils. They say that such a story as this is unscientific. But we cannot accept such a view. If devils do not exist, then the prince of devils does not exist either. And if Satan does not exist, then the story of Christ's temptation in the wilderness is only a story. If men do not believe in evil spirits, how can they believe in the Holy Spirit? How can they believe in angels? It is to be feared they do not.

But there are demons. They existed in the time of Jesus and

they still exist today. Don't let anyone fool you. It is just as possible to be possessed with demons as it is possible to be filled with the Holy Spirit. If a man is possessed with an evil spirit, he will be compelled to do evil. He won't know why; he will just do it, because he is compelled to do it. If a man is filled with the Holy Spirit, he will do those things which are pleasing to God.

These "demon possessed" men did not have control of themselves, yet they recognized Jesus Christ. Obviously, the man himself wasn't speaking, but rather the demons inside him. They may have known a time is coming when all evil will be destroyed. So when they heard of the coming of Jesus, they wondered, "Is this the time of our destruction already"?

When they asked Christ, "Let us go into this herd of swine," and Jesus permitted it, the swine themselves became demon possessed. The swine then did something that they felt compelled to do.

After the swineherds told the townsfolk what had happened, the people became panicky. They "came out to meet Jesus" and told Him to go away. Because Jesus had come two men had been healed, but the city did not care about that. Because Jesus had come their swine had been destroyed. And they did care about that!

How Can You Help Others

And he entered into a ship, and passed over, and came into his own city. And, behold, they brought to him a man sick of the palsy, lying on a bed: and Jesus seeing their faith said unto the sick of the palsy; Son, be of good cheer; thy sins be forgiven thee. And, behold, certain of the scribes said within themselves, This man blasphemeth. And Jesus knowing their thoughts said, Wherefore think ye evil in your hearts? For whether is easier, to say, Thy sins be forgiven thee; or to say, Arise and walk? But that ye may know that the Son of man hath power on earth to forgive sins, (then saith he to the sick of the palsy,) Arise, take up thy bed, and go unto thine house. And he arose, and departed to his house. But when the multitude saw it, they marvelled, and glorified God, which had given such power unto men (Matthew 9:1-8).

Some of the other gospels tell us that four friends carried this man to Jesus. When they arrived there was such a crowd that they could not get in the front door, so they climbed up on the roof, opened up the tile, and let the man down on a stretcher in front of the Lord Jesus. In response to the faith of these friends, Jesus blessed the man they brought.

Sometimes you might get discouraged in witnessing to others

or in inviting others to church. You get the feeling that it doesn't do any good. Here is a lesson for you. It was the faith of the friends that brought about the healing of this man who was sick of the palsy. It may well be your faith that will bring blessing to those about whom you are concerned. Faithfulness in bringing someone to church or in encouraging someone to pray will be honored by God. If you as a parent are faithful to God and come before God with your children and pray for them, God will look at your faith and will bless and keep those whom you cherish and hold dear.

Jesus said, "Son, be of good cheer. Thy sins be forgiven thee." Yet that is not what the friends came to ask for. They wanted to see the man walking again. At the moment, they did not seem to get what they wanted, but they got something far more important. When they came to God and established a relationship with Him, they received something far more important than physical healing.

When Jesus said, "Thy sins be forgiven thee," the scribes immediately said, "That's not right. No man can forgive sins. He is blaspheming."

Isn't this a strange thing? The scribes may have accepted the healing as a wonderful happening, but when Jesus forgave sins, they objected. In other words, they doubted that a man could be forgiven. They had no idea of the atoning work of Christ.

Then the Lord Jesus said, "That you may know that the Son of man hath power on earth to forgive sins, [in other words, that you may know that Jesus Christ can work a reconciliation with God] (then saith he to the sick of the palsy,) Arise, take up thy bed, and go unto thine house." The lesson here seems to be that the significance of New Testament miracles is to show that the Lord Jesus Christ can do all things, even the most difficult, the forgiveness of your sins.

ONLY SICK PEOPLE NEED A DOCTOR

And as Jesus passed forth from thence, he saw a man, named Matthew, sitting at the receipt of custom: and he saith unto him, Follow me. And he arose, and followed him. And it came to pass, as Jesus sat at meat in the house, behold, many publicans and sinners came and sat down with him and his disciples. And when the Pharisees saw it, they said unto his disciples, Why eateth your Master with publicans and sinners? But when Jesus heard that, he said unto them, They that be whole need not a physician, but they that are sick. But go ye and learn what that meaneth, I will have mercy, and not sacrifice: for I am not come to call the righteous, but sinners to repentance (Matthew 9:9-13).

Matthew had probably heard Jesus speak before. Probably he was well aware of the preaching, the teaching and the miracle working of Jesus of Nazareth. But at this specific time there was a specific call to this specific man named Matthew.

Shortly after responding to Christ's call, Matthew prepared a banquet for Jesus. To this banquet he invited his old friends. Since Matthew himself had been a man of the world, his old friends were also men of the world.

No doubt this change in Matthew would affect his old friends. The same thing happens today. Quite often when a businessman becomes an earnest Christian, his friends become interested in accepting Christ, too. If such a man, they reason, thinks there is something in the Gospel, maybe there is.

When the Pharisees saw the motley crowd at the banquet, they said to Christ's disciples, "Why eateth your master with publicans and sinners?" The implication, of course, was that if He were really a spiritually-minded man, He would associate only with religious people, and not with such worldly people.

Jesus' answer is proverbial: "You don't need a doctor if you are well. You need one only when you realize you are sick." The implication is, "I am in the world to be a spiritual doctor. I came to help sick people, so they are the ones with whom I must associate." The Gospel must be preached to those who need it and those who are really willing to recognize that need.

Then Jesus said, "But go ye and learn what that meaneth, I will have mercy and not sacrifice." Mercy is from God to man. Sacrifice is from man to God. Jesus is far more interested in what God will do for me and in me than in what I will do for Him. You cannot bribe your way into God's presence by sacrifice; your salvation results from God's great mercy. The Lord Jesus Christ did not call righteous people to reward them; He called sinners to save them. The righteous are not called to be approved. Sinners are called that they might repent.

In this you might say, "Isn't the Lord Jesus discriminating against a certain class of people?" Let me remind you that there is not a man who does not sin. "All have sinned and come short of the glory of God." Since all are sinners, what did Jesus mean when He spoke as He did to the Pharisees? Put it this way: Some people think they are righteous. As long as a man feels he is righteous, he won't feel that he needs a Saviour. A man must realize he is lost, before he starts crying for a Saviour. But when a man knows he is a sinner, he will look for help.

As long as you think you are all right, all you are seeking is approval. The Lord Jesus Christ will then be unable to do anything for you. But the humble, the contrite, the brokenhearted, the poor in spirit are the ones who will receive help, because they are desperate enough to want it and to ask God for it.

Chapter 7

WHAT GOD CAN AND WILL DO

Meeting Your Need

Man needs help. As a moral being he knows what is right and wrong and is responsible for his choices. But sad to say, while many men are wise enough to know they are wrong in themselves, they may not know what is right nor are they good enough to be able to do it. Because of this we say men are sinners.

Man not only does wrong, but actually, while he may want to escape the consequences of wrongdoing, he does not have in his heart a desire to do really what is acceptable in God's sight. This makes him feel guilty, and soon he despairs of hope. He despairs because he cannot see any relief from his predicament. If he knows anything, he knows that "whatsoever a man soweth, that shall he also reap." He also knows that he has not done what his Creator wanted him to do. So he expects to pay the consequences.

Such a man is ignorant of God. He may admit there is a God, but he has no idea what God is like. He can look at the heavens and think of God as the Creator, but this is about all he can know concerning God. He may have an idea that God is something like himself, but in this he is wrong, because man is a sinner and God is holy. Therefore God would not act as sinful man acts.

For instance, if someone pushes you, your first natural idea is to push him in retaliation. This is human, but it is not like God. Similarly, since man has rejected God, man assumes that God has rejected him. Wouldn't this be the natural thing for God to do? And so man lives his life, not asking for help, because he does not think that there is any help available. Consequently the average man is stuck in his own helplessness. And he has lost all hope of ever getting out of that hole. If you do not have the understanding of a Christian, you probably feel that living is all up to you, and you are not getting it done.

But there is hope. In loving-kindness God sent Jesus Christ

78

into the world "to seek and to save that which was lost." You may know that, like a sheep, you are lost; you don't know the way home. And you are afraid that any moment a wolf may come. But instead of a wolf it is the shepherd, looking for his sheep. This is the way that the Lord Jesus Christ comes to you.

Paul said, "God commendeth his love toward us, in that while we were yet sinners, Christ died for us (the ungodly)" (Romans 5:8). Such is God's kindness that He sends Jesus to give a new and better life to the man who is a failure. Jesus gives you not another chance, so that you can fail again, but a different life. As the first life was the life of Adam, the second life is the life of God. In the first life you are a child of Adam, but in the second life you are a child of God.

Jesus came to this world not to repair what is broken, but to replace it with something new and different, and infinitely better.

Suppose you are trying to row a boat across a lake and a storm comes up. The wind is blowing so hard that you cannot go ahead. The more you try, the farther off course you are swept. You are in danger of being swamped by the waves. Then someone comes in a motorboat. He pulls you out of your leaky boat and puts you in his motorboat. You don't have to row any more. You ride, because he has the power to take you. Being saved by Jesus Christ is like that. What you have in Jesus Christ is better than anything you ever had before. When He comes to save you He does not come to put you back where you were; He comes to put you on a higher level from which you will not fall.

Jesus often used illustrations to show that this was so. One of the things that He taught was that patching up what is broken and torn is useless. If you have an old garment with a hole in it, you don't patch it with a new piece of cloth. You get a new garment.

Of course, people raise questions when Jesus Christ offers to give them something brand new in place of their old and broken-down model. One person might say, "It is too late. My soul is dead. There is no use in talking to me."

Here you might remember how a ruler came to Jesus and said, "My daughter has died." Then he added, "But if you will come, you can put your hand on her and she will live." And this is the answer to those who say, "My soul is dead": God can raise the dead.

Someone else might say, "It just can't be done. It's a good idea, but it's impossible."

Do you remember the story of the woman with an issue of blood? She had been ill for twelve years. She had tried everything. Doctors had tried to help her and they had pronounced the disease incurable. Yet she came to Jesus saying, "If I but touch the hem of his garment, I shall be whole." She did, and she was. Here is the answer for any of us. If you come to Him and touch Him, you too can be healed of your soul's affliction, no matter how incurable it may seem.

Someone else might say, "He won't have time for me. I need help, but I'm not that important to Him."

Do you remember those two blind men walking along the street and crying, "Thou Son of David, have mercy on us"? Even the disciples told them to keep quiet. But they kept on calling out. Jesus took notice of them and restored their sight. "According to your faith be it unto you," He said.

Someone else might say, "I have gone too far. I am in bondage. I cannot do my own thinking. I am controlled by ideas and thoughts I don't even understand."

Do you remember the dumb man, possessed with the devil? That demon had such control over the man's spirit that he could not even speak. But when they brought him to Jesus, He delivered him.

Why are all these miracles recorded in Matthew 9? To show you what Jesus Christ can and will do for you. The Lord Jesus, after all, did not come to set forth a philosophy or an ideology. He did not come to explain the secrets of the universe, nor even to argue the benefits of virtue. He came to save you. And He can do it!

Creating Something New

> Then came to him the disciples of John, saying, Why do we and the Pharisees fast oft, but thy disciples fast not? And Jesus said unto them, Can the children of the bridechamber mourn, as long as the bridegroom is with them? but the days will come, when the bridegroom shall be taken from them, and then shall they fast. No man putteth a piece of new cloth unto an old garment, for that which is put in to fill it up taketh from the garment, and the rent is made worse. Neither do men put new wine into old bottles: else the bottles break, and the wine runneth out, and the bottles perish: but they put new wine into new bottles, and both are preserved (Matthew 9:14-17).

The disciples of John, and the Pharisees as well, often went without food and drink in order to heighten their spiritual sensitivity to the truth that they were trying to grasp. We call this "fasting." Naturally they were surprised that Christ's disciples didn't fast.

Christ's disciples seemed joyful and carefree; they acted as if they were fortunate and rich. John's disciples couldn't understand it. When they tried to approach God, they restricted themselves. To them, religion was largely a matter of "you don't do this" and "you don't do that." But the disciples of Christ didn't seem to worry about what they shouldn't do. John's disciples couldn't help but ask Jesus of Nazareth why this was so.

In the answer the Lord Jesus gave, He indicated that as long as you have the Almighty God in you by His Holy Spirit, showing you the things of the Lord Jesus Christ, you will not be conscious of being deprived of anything. You will actually feel that you have everything. For this reason His disciples seemed so happy and glad.

Other people might very well wonder when they see your Christian joy: "Why do you look so happy? You act as if you had just won a great fortune." This is true. You have won a great fortune, because you have found out that God has received you and that you now belong to Him.

In the gospel of John is the well-known passage about the necessity of being born again (John 3). The gospel of Matthew says much the same thing in verses 16 and 17 of this chapter. Here Jesus says that when God works in you, He does not improve your own human nature and make it good enough; He creates something entirely new.

The first illustration Jesus used is about putting a patch on an old garment; the second is about putting new wine into an old bottle.

Some years ago the freezing unit in our refrigerator broke down. I called the merchant from whom I had bought it, and he sent a repairman. However, the repairman did not come to repair the unit; he came to replace it. I had thought that he would take it apart, see what the trouble was, and fix it. Instead, he took the unit out. When I questioned him about it, he said, "That is the way we do it. We don't repair this unit here. We send it back to the factory, and they will rebuild it. What we do is give you a totally new unit."

This is what Jesus was saying, "I am not coming to repair the unit in your spiritual life; I am coming to give you a new engine."

In understanding the second illustration, you need to understand that the bottles were not made of glass. These bottles, or more properly wineskins, were made from leather. After wine was put in one of these wineskins, it fermented. When it fermented, it gave off gas, and the skins were stretched. Now if you emptied that stretched leather and filled it with new wine and the new wine fermented, there would not be any stretch left in that leather, and it would burst. So new wine had to be put in new wineskins. Once again, Jesus is saying, "I have not come to improve you.

I've come to give you an entirely new and different life."

When you receive the Lord Jesus Christ as your Saviour, something new begins in you. It is not an improvement of the old nature; it is not a finding in yourself something good which can be properly developed; it is not a changing of your old way of doing things. Every man who receives Jesus Christ becomes a new creature. When you receive Jesus Christ, you become a new creation. God begins something new in you. From now on, you have a new disposition, a disposition that desires to do the will of God, because you now have in you a new life: the life of God – eternal life.

Raising the Dead

> While he spake these things unto them, behold, there came a certain ruler, and worshipped him, saying, My daughter is even now dead: but come and lay thy hand upon her, and she shall live. And Jesus arose, and followed him, and so did his disciples. And when Jesus came into the ruler's house, and saw the minstrels and the people making a noise, He said unto them, Give place: for the maid is not dead, but sleepeth. And they laughed him to scorn. But when the people were put forth, he went in, and took her by the hand, and the maid arose. And the fame hereof went abroad into all that land (Matthew 9:18-19,23-26).

Notice the faith of this ruler. He did not come to Christ as a matter of routine. He came because he really believed. This is the same kind of faith that the leper had, who said, "Lord, if thou wilt, thou canst make me clean." It is the same kind of faith that the centurion had, who said, "Speak the word only, and my servant shall be healed."

Although the girl was dead, the ruler had confidence in Jesus Christ. And he held to his faith in spite of the mourners who scoffed. These mourners were professional wailers who came to sing woeful songs of lament after a person had died. They were a part of every funeral in that country. These mourners had seen many, many dead people, and they had never seen any of them come back to life. Naturally, they thought that both Jesus as well as the ruler who had faith in Him had gone crazy.

Before working the miracle, Jesus put these mourners out of the house. You see, there are some things that unbelievers will never be allowed to witness. Unbelievers will never see the full reward of the righteous.

Of course, there are some who have sincere doubts and questions. God knows the heart. He understands the sincere people who have difficulty in believing. But often, when He wants to perform a great deed, the unbelievers are put out, and the believers are gathered together to be eye-witnesses.

But God doesn't always raise the dead. He raised this girl, and He raised Lazarus, but there were people who were dying all over Judea and Galilee that He didn't raise up. He certainly didn't go up and down the countryside stopping funerals just to show off. He raised the dead in this case to illustrate the truth that God can raise men from spiritual death. Just as this maid was actually dead, you might feel that you are spiritually dead. But just as Jesus could raise the maid in response to faith, so you can be encouraged that if you believe in Him, He can raise you from spiritual death.

HEALING THE HOPELESS

And, behold, a woman, which was diseased with an issue of blood twelve years, came behind him, and touched the hem of his garment: For she said within herself, If I may but touch his garment, I shall be whole. But Jesus turned him about, and when he saw her, he said, Daughter, be of good comfort: thy faith hath made thee whole. And the woman was made whole from that hour (Matthew 9:20-22).

This poor woman had long suffered from her affliction. What a discouraging thing it must have been! And how expensive it surely was! She had spent all the money she had and yet, according to Mark, she grew worse, instead of better. Luke, who was himself a physician, said that she "had spent all her living upon physicians, neither could be healed of any."

Obviously, this woman was in dire need. But in addition to this desperate need, she also had faith. It was this faith that brought her to Jesus. She did not say, "If I could only find a new brand of medicine"; or "If I could only go to the hospital in Jerusalem"; or "If I could only get into a better climate." No, she said, "If I may but touch his garment." Her faith was in Jesus Christ, and she was gloriously healed.

Today many people are in desperate need. Some have trouble because of inner weaknesses and limitations, and in distress they seek to have the condition changed. Doctors may help them physically, and friends may help them socially. But the kind of help that comes from God through the Lord Jesus Christ is a change of the inner nature, a change of the actual person himself.

The Lord Jesus Christ did not change this woman's environment. He changed her, and she was immediately different. Immediately the issue of blood was dried up. An actual change took place in her. And when you exercise your faith in Jesus Christ, there will be an immediate consequence of the Lord's working in your heart.

Her part in this whole matter was that she touched Him; she came to Him. She did not come out of curiosity or to pass away a few idle hours. She did not come to experiment. She came expectantly. She expected Him to help her. And He did!

Maybe a friend of yours is suffering from some inner affliction. Maybe that friend is in bondage to a habit. Maybe he is enmeshed in some evil. Whatever the situation may be, whenever you have a friend who feels hopelessly trapped, you can tell him, "With God nothing is impossible." If he but reaches out and touches the hem of His garment, he too can find salvation. Encourage one another to turn to Him, for He can do for you more than you ask or think.

Opening Blind Eyes

And when Jesus departed thence, two blind men followed him, crying, and saying, Thou son of David, have mercy on us. And when he was come into the house, the blind men came to him: and Jesus saith unto them, Believe ye that I am able to do this? They said unto him, Yea, Lord. Then touched he their eyes, saying, According to your faith be it unto you. And their eyes were opened; and Jesus straitly charged them, saying, See that no man know it. But they, when they were departed, spread abroad his fame in all that country. As they went out, behold, they brought to him a dumb man possessed with a devil. And when the devil was cast out, the dumb spake: and the multitudes marvelled, saying, It was never so seen in Israel. But the Pharisees said, He casteth out devils through the prince of the devils. And Jesus went about all the cities and villages, teaching in their synagogues, and preaching the gospel of the kingdom, and healing every sickness and every disease among the people (Matthew 9:27-35).

Perhaps you get a little confused when you read of the great miracles of healing which Jesus performed. You may wonder whether you should expect those things today. I will not say that such miracles could not take place today, but remember this: when Jesus was on earth, He was demonstrating these things in human form. He was healing men's bodies then to show that He can heal men's souls any time.

Do you remember when they brought the palsied man to Him, and the Lord Jesus said, "Thy sins be forgiven thee"? Those friends were seeking physical healing. Why then did the Lord say, "Thy sins be forgiven thee"? The reason is this: the purpose of His coming into the world was to deliver men from sin rather than to heal their physical diseases. "Thou shalt call his name Jesus, for he shall save his people from their sins" (Matthew 1:21).

So when Jesus healed physical blindness, He was illustrating that He could also open the eyes of the soul. Now two blind men had come to Him in faith. In the very way they addressed Him, "Thou Son of David," you could know they had spiritual perception, even though they were physically blind. They recognized that He was the heir to David's throne. Jesus touched their eyes and said, "According to your faith, be it unto you." Thus they received the blessing of Christ.

Perhaps you are living a life in which, day in and day out, you are not blessed. Maybe you are distressed. Maybe your family is not turning out the way you want them to turn out. Maybe your business is troubling you. Maybe your health is a problem. Whatever it is, you realize that you do not have the help and favor of God. Is it possible that the reason that you are not being blessed is that you are not exercising your faith? Since the Lord works "according to your faith," perhaps that is why you receive nothing at all. You are not trusting Him.

Afterward Jesus told these two blind men, "See that no man know it." Why did the Lord Jesus say this? Perhaps it was because the Lord Jesus knew that, as He became more and more prominent, public opposition to Him would increase to the point of His crucifixion. In one place He said, "My hour is not yet come." He knew that the time had not come for Him to end His ministry, so He told them, "Don't tell anyone. Keep it quiet." But despite what He said, they "spread abroad his fame in all that country."

Following this miracle, Jesus cast a devil out of a dumb man. The people marveled, but the Pharisees criticized. Here is a strange thing. Jesus set a man free from the domination of an evil spirit so that he could talk, and the religious leaders criticized Him for it. They said He was actually working with the devil himself.

Even in our day some religious leaders will criticize the preaching and the teaching of the Gospel even when souls are saved and lives are changed.

ANSWERING YOUR PRAYER

But when he saw the multitudes, he was moved with compassion on them, because they fainted, and were scattered abroad, as sheep having no shepherd. Then saith he unto his disciples, The harvest truly is plenteous, but the labourers are few; Pray ye therefore the Lord of the harvest, that he will send forth labourers into his harvest (Matthew 9:36-38).

There is a multitude like this living in your town. They are in the neighborhood school, in the university, in the shops, in the banks, in the crowds on the city sidewalks, in the throngs that choke the highways.

As Jesus described the people He saw, they seemed to have no strength; they seemed overcome by their situation; they were scattered abroad as sheep having no shepherd. He was moved with compassion on them.

Jesus said these people were ripe for a spiritual harvest. They were ready to be gathered in. Even as He told His disciples then, He tells you today that there is a great opportunity to win souls for the kingdom of God. But sad to say, few people really care about the spiritual condition of their fellow man.

Isn't it interesting that He did not say, "Make sure that you go"? Instead, He said, "Pray ye therefore the Lord of the harvest that he will send forth labourers into his harvest." This should be your first concern. Pray that God may send out men and women who will show others the Gospel of Jesus Christ. In the Great Commission which concludes the gospel of Matthew, we are told to go into all the world and preach the Gospel, but this is a call to prayer. Here you are to pray that God will move in the hearts of those who can serve Him. As you pray, some young man may decide to devote his life to take the Gospel to Africa, Brazil, Japan or Korea. In answer to your prayer, he will feel he must go.

But there is a harvest field in this country, too. How many people on your street have been without Christian visitation? A neighbor's personal witness, reinforced by his consistent Christian life, is one of the greatest missionary activities. Being a witness in your neighborhood is work that needs to be done. But it depends on people who are inwardly urged to do it and upon individuals who feel that they want to do it. What will keep you doing it? What will cause you to keep visiting? What will make you keep bringing children to Sunday school? Here is the answer: Inwardly you will be strengthened to do it. And the source of this inner strength may be found where someone else is praying for you.

Certainly you should pray for yourself and for your own needs. But here God has asked that you pray to Him to send out workers both at home and abroad. The ministry of prayer is equally as important as the ministry of preaching and teaching the Gospel. As you pray, someone else may be led to go.

Chapter 8

HOW TO BE A SERVANT

The Value of a Servant

Humanly speaking, the Gospel of the Lord Jesus Christ would long since have been forgotten if it had not been for faithful servants. These servants include apostles and martyrs, missionaries and ministers, Sunday school teachers and church officers, as well as witnesses for Christ in the home and in the community. Some of these servants were translators. You can read the Bible in English today because faithful men of God risked their lives to bring you the Gospel. Many of these servants were Christian parents who brought up their children to believe in God, teaching them Bible stories, hymns and prayers and living before them with sweetness and light. In many different ways, many different people have served to spread the Gospel of Christ.

In Matthew 9:36 we read, "When he saw the multitudes, he was moved with compassion." Here we can see what moves the servant of God. As the Apostle Paul said: "The love of Christ constraineth us" (II Corinthians 5:14). This motivation is an inner concern for others.

As we look out upon the multitudes of whom Christ spoke, we too may sense their suffering and overwhelming frustration. We know that they are fainting before the impossibility of the life they are obliged to live. As Jesus said, they are like sheep scattered without a shepherd. And what concerns us is that we know the Shepherd and we know how He wants to help them.

In Matthew 10:1-4, which records the selection of the twelve apostles, you can see the call of the servants. If you wish to become a servant, you must first get to know the Master. In these verses Jesus called His servants out from among His disciples that they should be His apostles. These apostles were then empowered by the Lord to do His work.

In Matthew 8 and 9 you saw how the Lord Jesus delivered men from the consequences of sin by overcoming disease, demons and death. Now He called some of His disciples to be His apostles, and gave them power to do similar work.

Matthew 10:5-15 records the commissioning of His apostles. Jesus was specific as to where He wanted them to go. He said, "Go not into the way of the Gentiles, nor into the cities of the Samaritans, but go rather to the lost sheep of the house of Israel, and preach to them." Later, we know, the Lord Jesus gave the Great Commission in which He told all His servants to go into all the world. But at this time these apostles were sent only to "the house of Israel."

These servants were specifically guided not only as to where they were to go, but as to when they were to go and what they were to say. They were told also how they were to serve. They were told to be dependent upon the Lord and upon the Lord's people. This can be a very humbling experience for the servant, but it is also very much worthwhile. He will learn as never before that he is not his own, and also in the last analysis that he is dependent altogether on the Lord.

In Matthew 10:16-31 Jesus warns His servants to beware of men, because they will be facing great opposition. And strangely, this opposition will come from among their own people, even from their own household. They can expect this opposition, because "the servant is not greater than his master." "He came unto his own and his own received him not."

Yet the servant is comforted to know that he will be safe in the care of God. The very hairs of your head are numbered, Jesus said, and God who watches every sparrow will certainly watch over you. Whenever you begin to testify in the name of the Lord, the Lord Himself will come and will help you. He also promised His disciples that He would personally be faithful to them. If they would confess Him, He would confess them. Even though their own families would oppose them, the Lord would be with them and comfort them.

Everything the Master has, the servant will share. When you identify yourself with the Gospel of Jesus Christ, some people will treat you as if they did not want to have anything to do with you. But others will give you special help, because you are a servant of Christ. You will receive benefits you do not even deserve. When you belong to Him, every defeat you have, He shares; every victory He has, you share. You are His partner as well as His servant.

Matthew 11:1-19 is a record of John the Baptist, a true servant of the Lord, and how John expressed his concern about the Lord's program. Thus in Matthew 11:7-15, the servant, John the Baptist, shared the reproach of his Master, Jesus Christ. The people who turned against Christ, turned against him. Finally in Matthew 11:16-19, Jesus commended John as a great man, "greater than any man born of woman," even though he was yet not appreciated by those who saw him.

Chapters 9 and 10 have been dealing with servants. By their faithfulness, servants of Christ have brought the Gospel to you, that you might believe and have eternal life. Such servants are very important to us, but they are precious to the Lord. Whatever anyone does to a servant of the Gospel is considered by the Lord as having been done to Him personally, whether bad or good.

The Call of the Servants

And when he had called unto him his twelve disciples, he gave them power against unclean spirits, to cast them out, and to heal all manner of sickness and all manner of disease. Now the names of the twelve apostles are these: The first, Simon, who is called Peter, and Andrew his brother; James the son of Zebedee, and John his brother; Philip, and Bartholomew; Thomas, and Matthew the publican; James the son of Alphaeus, and Lebbaeus, whose surname was Thaddaeus; Simon the Canaanite, and Judas Iscariot, who also betrayed him. These twelve Jesus sent forth, and commanded them, saying, Go not into the way of the Gentiles, and into any city of the Samaritans enter ye not: But go rather to the lost sheep of the house of Israel. And as ye go, preach, saying, The kingdom of heaven is at hand. Heal the sick, cleanse the lepers, raise the dead, cast out devils: freely ye have received, freely give. Provide neither gold, nor silver, nor brass in your purses. Nor scrip for your journey, neither two coats, neither shoes, nor yet staves: for the workman is worthy of his meat. And into whatsoever city or town ye shall enter, enquire who in it is worthy; and there abide till ye go thence. And when ye come into an house, salute it. And if the house be worthy, let your peace come upon it: but if it be not worthy, let your peace return to you. And whosoever shall not receive you, nor hear your words, when ye depart out of that house or city, shake off the dust of your feet. Verily I say unto you, It shall be more tolerable for the land of Sodom and Gomorrha in the day of judgment, than for that city (Matthew 10:1-15).

Out of the total number of His disciples, the Lord Jesus called a few to be apostles to serve Him in a special way. A disciple is a learner, anyone who enrolls to study and learn. An apostle is a servant, sent out with a message. A disciple is an inquirer who comes to learn; an apostle is a missionary who goes to tell.

If anyone is going to be a servant of Christ, he must first be in fellowship with Jesus. Personal relationship is primary. Note the word "his" in verse one; they belonged to Him.

At this time He gave these apostles power to perform the promises of God. He did not tell them to teach, nor to approach those who had never heard. He told them to go to those who had some knowledge of the Gospel and to bring the significance of it into their understanding.

Each apostle is listed by name. Anyone who goes out to serve the Lord, whether he be a minister, deacon, elder, Sunday school teacher, friend, brother, sister or parent, is known individually by the Lord. "He calleth his own sheep by name." Serving the Lord is personal and individual.

The list included Judas Iscariot, "who also betrayed him." The servants of the Lord are not automatically always obedient. For instance, if you should be called to be a minister of the Gospel, this would not mean that everything you do will be right. Just because you are called to serve is no guarantee that you will be faithful. Remember Judas.

These apostles were told not to go into the way of the Gentiles nor the Samaritans, "but go rather to the lost sheep of the house of Israel." Israel had the Scriptures. They had God's promises. The Gentiles did not have any knowledge of the Scriptures nor the promises of God. What the Israelites lacked was the effectual working of these promises. The Word of God had lost its power in their lives.

Jesus said to these apostles, "Heal the sick, cleanse the lepers, raise the dead, cast out devils; freely ye have received, freely give."

In this way they were to put power into their religion, and life into what had become a sort of dead orthodoxy. The operation of the will and the power of God in the lives of people is promoted by men who act as the servants of the Lord and preach as apostles with power, bringing the promises of God into a state of operation in the hearers.

Opposition to the Servants

Behold, I send you forth as sheep in the midst of wolves: be ye therefore wise as serpents, and harmless as doves. But beware of men: for they will deliver you up to the councils, and they will scourge you in their synagogues; And ye shall be brought before governors and kings for my sake, for a testimony against them and the Gentiles. But when they deliver you up, take no thought how or what ye shall speak: for it shall be given you in that same hour what ye shall speak. For it is not ye that speak, but the Spirit of your Father which speaketh in you. And the brother shall deliver up the brother to death, and the father the child: and the children shall rise up against their parents, and cause them to be put to death. And ye shall be hated of all men for my name's sake: but he that endureth to the end shall be saved. But when they persecute you in this city, flee ye into another: for verily I say unto you, Ye shall not have gone over the cities of Israel, till the Son of man be come. The disciple is not above his master, nor the servant above his lord. It is enough for the disciple that he be as his master, and the servant as his lord. If they have called the master of the house Beelzebub, how much more shall they call them of his household? Fear them not therefore: for there is nothing covered, that shall not be revealed; and hid, that shall not be known. What I tell you in darkness, that speak ye in light: and what ye hear in the ear, that preach ye upon the house tops. And fear not them which kill the body, but are not able to kill the soul: but rather fear him which is able to destroy both soul and body in hell. Are not two sparrows sold for a farthing? and one of them shall not fall on the ground without your Father. But the very hairs of your head are all numbered. Fear ye not therefore, ye are of more value than many sparrows (Matthew 10:16-31).

If you want to talk, you can always find someone who will let you talk. Of course, he may not always listen, but you can talk as much as you want. However, when you ask him to respond, you may run into stiff opposition.

People will fight to stay in their present condition. If they are in ignorance, they want to stay that way. If they are in blindness, they want to stay that way.

Jesus sent His apostles forth as sheep among wolves. They were to be harmless, not doing anyone any injury; helpless, not even defending themselves. But they were to be wise as serpents in their ways.

Is this true today? Does Christ send forth His witnesses in the same way today? Yes, this is true of anyone who wants to serve the Lord. If you want to be useful in bringing the promises of God into operation in other people's lives, you will soon discover that they will resent the insinuation that you think what they are doing is not all right. As a servant of Christ, you will not stir up any unnecessary contention. You will be as wise as you can and as harmless as you can as you proceed in your witnessing.

But what did Jesus mean when He said, "Beware of men"? Does that mean to avoid men? No, you can't avoid them. You have to deal with men. But it means to be prepared for opposition. In other words, don't be surprised when "they deliver you up to the councils." Men will mistreat you. And many times they will do it for religious reasons. Religious people themselves may give you the fiercest opposition.

To each of His servants Jesus gave this comforting assurance: "You are not to worry about what to say when they put you on the spot. You will not be left alone. The Lord will be with you. The Holy Spirit will give you the words to say at the right time."

Also the Lord said, "But when they persecute you in this city, flee ye into another." Do not make a last ditch fight in every situation as it arises. If you are bearing witness for the Lord, and people oppose you, let them be. Offer your testimony wherever you can, but when it is no longer acceptable, leave them with the Lord. Other people need your witness, and before you are finished with your ministry the Lord Himself will take over for you. In other words, He'll be there. It is for you to sow the seed. He won't let it lie there long. He will work with that seed and make it bring forth fruit.

THE CHALLENGE OF THE SERVANTS

Whosoever therefore shall confess me before men, him will I confess also before my Father which is in heaven. But whosoever shall deny me before men, him will I also deny before my Father which is in heaven. Think not that I am come to send peace on earth: I came not to send peace, but a sword. For I am come to set a man at variance against his father, and the daughter against her mother, and the daughter in law against her mother in law. And a man's foes shall be they of his own household. He that loveth father or mother more than me is not worthy of me: and he that loveth son or daughter more than me is not worthy of me. And he that taketh not his cross, and followeth after me, is not worthy of me. He that findeth his life shall lose it: and he that loseth his life for my sake shall find it. He that receiveth you receiveth me, and he that receiveth me receiveth him that sent me. He that receiveth a prophet in the name of a prophet shall receive a prophet's reward; and he that receiveth a righteous man in the name of a righteous man shall receive a righteous man's reward. And whosoever shall give to drink unto one of these little ones a cup of cold water only in the name of a disciple, verily I say unto you, he shall in no wise lose his reward (Matthew 10:32-42).

When you confess Christ before men, you openly identify yourself with the name of the Lord Jesus Christ. You admit to all people that you are trusting in Him. When you do that here on earth, the Lord Jesus in heaven openly admits to His Father that you belong to Him. But if you are not willing to line up with the Lord Jesus Christ down here, He will not Himself line up with you up there. What you do with Him now is what He will do with you then.

However, it is not always easy to confess Christ. Such confession may turn your family or your community against you. At home there are people who will misunderstand. They will think that whenever you put the Lord first, you are neglecting them. As a Christian you will be considerate of your family, but you will also remember that *first* you belong to the Lord, and *then* you belong to your own family.

Your biggest opposition in the Christian life will come from among your closest friends. Some people have misunderstood the verse, "He that loveth father and mother more than me is not worthy of me." Jesus is not saying that you should not love your parents. He is saying that you should not love them more than you love Christ. Loving is not just sentiment. It is not a matter of how you feel; it is the way you do. Your love will govern your actions. All human social relationships, past, present and future, must be kept in second place when you are serving Him.

When anyone so commits himself to Christ as to seek really to do His will and get others to do His will, he shares in all that belongs to Christ. You will share His rejection and you will share His acceptance. You will get blamed for more than you are responsible for, and you will get credit for more than you are responsible for. But above all else, you will be closely, intimately associated with your Lord and Master. You will be an heir of God, and joint-heir with Jesus Christ.

THE EXAMPLE OF A SERVANT

And it came to pass, when Jesus had made an end of commanding his twelve disciples, he departed thence to teach and to preach in their cities. Now when John had heard in the prison the works of Christ, he sent two of his disciples, And said unto him, Art thou he that should come, or do we look for another? Jesus answered and said unto them, Go and shew John again those things which ye do hear and see: The blind receive their sight, and the lame walk, the lepers are cleansed, and the deaf hear, the dead are raised up, and the poor have the gospel preached to them. And blessed is he, whosoever shall not be offended in me (Matthew 11:1-6).

The popular interpretation of this passage is that John the Baptist who was now in prison began to doubt the Lord Jesus and so sent his two disciples to find out whether or not he had made a mistake in baptizing Him. I really do not think such an understanding of this passage is true.

Look closely at the story. What prompted John's inquiry? According to verse 2 he asked because he heard of the works of Christ while he was imprisoned. This does not say that when he was suffering and when he was downhearted he sent these men. It wasn't that he heard of any failures in Christ's ministry. It wasn't when John heard that some people were rejecting Christ. No, it was "when he heard the works," and we know the works were glorious. It was the wonderful works of Christ that prompted the question.

John's faith never weakened. Did he not say that Christ would come? When he saw the Lord Jesus Christ, he said, "Behold the Lamb of God." That means, "Behold the One who is going to die for sinners." So when John the Baptist himself was put in prison, he wasn't surprised. Such treatment was to be expected, for the servant is not greater than the master. He had preached about the coming of One who would die. Why should he then be discouraged in the face of his own possible death?

John also knew the Old Testament promises. The Old Testament said that God would send the Messiah, His chosen One. It also said (1) that Messiah would suffer and die, and (2) that Messiah would rule as king. Many of the Jewish scholars in those days thought that there would be two Messiahs. One would come like a *Lamb* and One would come like a *Lion*. It was difficult for them to see how the same person could both die and rule. The one truth that these scholars did not see clearly was the fact of the Resurrection. In Revelation the writer saw into heaven; he saw the throne; on the throne was "the Lamb as it had been slain." This is what the Old Testament scholars did not see in their time. The slain one was raised from the dead! "He was dead, and is alive, and liveth forevermore." This was manifested in Revelation after Calvary, the Resurrection and the Ascension. So John asked, "Art thou he that should come, or look we for another?" Are you Jesus of Nazareth the coming King which was promised, or is there another one who is coming?

As far as John the Baptist was concerned, he had no question of Jesus of Nazareth being the Lamb of God. But you see, when he heard the works of Christ, it made him wonder as to whether He was also the King. Would the Lamb be setting the lame man free of his lameness? Would the Lamb be opening the eyes of the blind? Would the Lamb be setting the men free from the power of Satan? Would the Lamb be raising the dead? In the Old Testament those things were associated with the King. Now here is this one whom John the Baptist had identified as the Lamb of God and He was doing these things! "Are you the king," he asked, "or is there another one coming to rule?"

Notice carefully how the Lord Jesus Christ answered. He did not say, "Now you tell John to be of good courage; everything that he believed is all right." No, Jesus did not make any inference that John's faith was weak. Instead He said, "Go and show John again those things which you do hear and see." And then He demonstrated more of the wonderful works! In verse 5 Jesus outlines these things: "The blind receive their sight, and the lame walk, the lepers are cleansed, and the deaf hear, the dead are raised up, and the poor have the gospel preached unto them." That was the Old Testament prediction of the coming of the King. So He actually said, "You go back to John and say, 'This is what is happening, and blessed is he whosoever shall not be offended in me.'" I believe that when John the Baptist received this message, he was triumphantly assured, "He is the King, too!"

John was not the kind of man who would be much upset at the prospect of death. When men get close to the Lord Jesus Christ, they don't fear death that much. You pass through death. It is a dark corridor, but it is not a hole in the ground. It is more like a tunnel. The other end is open, and you pass through it into the very presence of God. It is not the end of anything but this life, and it is the beginning of another. It is passing from darkness into light.

As far as John the Baptist was concerned, I think he was able to die in blessed assurance knowing that the One whom he heralded was not only the Lamb of God, but also the Lion of the tribe of Judah. He was not only our Passover Lamb; He was also our King of kings and Lord of all.

The Reward of a Servant

And as they departed, Jesus began to say unto the multitudes concerning John, What went ye out into the wilderness to see? A reed shaken with the wind? But what went ye out for to see? A man clothed in soft raiment? behold, they that wear soft clothing are in kings' houses. But what went ye out for to see? A prophet? yea, I say unto you, and more than a prophet. For this is he, of whom it is written, Behold, I send my messenger before thy face, which shall prepare thy way before thee. Verily I say unto you, Among them that are born of women there hath not risen a greater than John the Baptist: notwithstanding he that is least in the kingdom of heaven is greater than he. And from the days of John the Baptist until now the kingdom of heaven suffereth violence, and the violent take it by force. For all the prophets and the law prophesied until John. And if ye will receive it, this is Elias, which was for to come. He that hath ears to hear, let him hear. But whereunto shall I liken this generation? It is like unto children sitting in the markets, and calling unto their fellows, And saying, We have piped unto you, and ye have not danced; we have mourned unto you, and ye have not lamented. For John came neither eating nor drinking, and they say, He hath a devil. The Son of man came eating and drinking, and they say, Behold a man gluttonous, and a winebibber, a friend of publicans and sinners. But wisdom is justified of her children (Matthew 11:7-19).

John the Baptist was a living, walking representation of the Old Testament message. In his life he manifested the law of God.

He was not only a prophet, but also a preparer of the way for the Lord Jesus Christ. He was the herald of the coming King. The Old Testament said, "Behold I send my messenger before thy face which shall prepare thy way before thee" (Malachi 3:1). The Lord Jesus said that John was the fulfillment of this Old Testament prediction. Jesus identified John the Baptist with the Elijah whom the Old Testament said must come before Messiah came.

Paul said that the law is your schoolmaster to bring you to Christ. Thus John the Baptist also was a schoolmaster to bring people to Christ. He did not spend time in setting forth the Ten Commandments. That had been done by Moses. John stressed the importance of a sincere response to the law. He did not tell the people to bring sacrifices. He told them that when they brought the sacrifices, they should bring them in the proper frame of mind. He did not even tell them to turn to God; he told them that when they did turn to God, they should do it with their hearts and not merely with their lips. He preached that every man is responsible before God. The worst sinner as well as the most pious church member is under obligation to come to God and confess his sins.

And when you come before God to confess your sin, make sure that you mean it. This is the message that John preached.

Jesus had the highest regard for John the Baptist, for He said, "No one born of woman is greater than he." Yet He also said, "He that is least in the kingdom of heaven is greater than he."

What did He mean by this seeming contradiction? Man to man John was second to no man, yet those privileged to live after the day of Pentecost, after the Holy Spirit was given to the Christian church, can avail themselves of even greater blessing than John the Baptist had.

John suffered violence. He was taken and thrown into prison. Under the most ridiculous circumstances, he was beheaded. This is the way men always try to deal with the law of God. They treated John the Baptist violently, and even so they seek to handle God's revelation violently. To this day, men are trying desperately to destroy both the work of God and the Word of God.

There is an old saying "the voice of the people is the voice of God." But this is not true. The way the public responds to the true servant of God is utterly unreliable. You cannot go by public opinion. The fickle public criticized John for being too narrow and Jesus for being too broad-minded. No Christian servant can please everyone all the time. It is good to remember you are not asked to please men; you are asked to please God. After all, you are not a servant of men, but a servant of God.

Chapter 9

IN THE FACE OF GROWING OPPOSITION

How Jesus Reacted

Nothing indicates the sinful nature of man as clearly as his opposition to the Gospel. Isaiah said, "The ox knoweth his owner, and the ass his master's crib: but Israel doth not know, my people doth not consider" (1:3). This was the sad experience of Christ's ministry: "He came unto his own, and his own received him not" (John 1:11). It continues to be so even today.

You can call to mind many great men in history who were associated with various great ideas. Who takes any offense at these men now?

On the other hand, when you mention Jesus Christ, some people refuse to listen. Why is this?

I believe it is because the Lord Jesus demands a response on the part of every man. His hand is always outstretched, and as soon as any man sees the outstretched hand, he must do something. If he refuses to take it, he must turn away from it. Sometimes men hammer nails into that outstretched hand today, even as they did at Calvary. Sad to say, sometimes those most implacably opposed to Jesus Christ, are religious people. Even today church people may oppose the evangelistic preaching of the Word of God and the men of God who proclaim it.

In Matthew 11, the Lord Jesus appraises such response. He points out that although miracles were done in certain cities, the citizens in those cities did not repent. When warned, they did not respond. Judgment is coming, Jesus said, and these cities will be judged according to their opportunity.

Will you be judged by your opportunity? Many millions of people do not have the Bible. You do. Millions of people do not know that God answers prayer. You do. You feel sorry for the millions because they do not turn to God, but if *you* don't turn to God, where does that leave you? What will Christ say to those who believe the Bible is the Word of God, but do not read it?

In this atmosphere of neglect and rejection, Jesus Christ gave a remarkable invitation: "Come unto me, all ye that labor and are heavy laden, and I will give you rest." In the midst of people who refused to pay attention, He spoke these words. Yes, even when there is a sophisticated rejection of the Gospel on the part of some, the gracious offer of salvation is still set forth to others, so that whosoever will may come.

As usual some of the strongest opposition to Jesus Christ came from the Pharisees. Though they were known for their zeal in promoting the law of God, they bitterly turned against Jesus Christ. They fasted, they prayed, they gave tithes. Yet they resented the call to repent. They claimed to be great because of their keeping the law, but Jesus was not impressed with their claims. They set themselves up as being the children of Abraham and He told them, "If you were the children of Abraham, you would have followed me, because Abraham spoke of me." This infuriated them. They wanted to be the leaders of the people, but the people were following Jesus of Nazareth instead. Out of envy they became His deadly enemies.

Openly, they criticized Him and tried to trap Him. First, they criticized His disciples for breaking the regulations about the Sabbath. When the Pharisees saw the disciples walking through a harvest field eating wheat, they accused them of harvesting. But Jesus answered their charges from Scripture. He could have used other arguments, but He turned to the Scriptures which they professed to follow. David, Jesus said, had even eaten bread from the holy place of the tabernacle when he was hungry. Thus he illustrated from Scripture that hunger can ignore certain regulations.

Next, the Pharisees put Him on the spot with a test case. In the synagogue on the Sabbath, they brought to Him a man with a withered hand. They wanted to see what He would do.

His response began by going back to the writings of Moses. Moses had told them how to keep the Sabbath. Although they were not supposed to work on that day, if a man found an ox in the ditch, he could help the ox out. And that was work. If he found a sheep in a pit, he could rescue the sheep. That was work, too. Yet such work of mercy was allowable on the Sabbath day in the Old Testament Scriptures.

After He had reminded them of the writings of Moses, Jesus reasoned with them. There is nothing wrong with reason. When interpreting Scripture you should use your head. Get the Scripture before you, compare Scripture with Scripture and then reason it out.

Jesus' reasoning was this: A man is more important than a sheep. If a concession were made to set aside the ritual law about the Sabbath on account of a suffering sheep, how much more should it be set aside on account of a suffering man? After He had set up this principle, He turned to the man with the withered hand and healed him. Everyone saw that Jesus would heal whenever there was need. The Son of man is Lord even of the Sabbath day.

The Pharisees then made plans to do away with Jesus, but Jesus "withdrew himself." He avoided open conflict. He was firm in presenting the truth, but He was not contentious. He was peaceable and not provocative. He was fulfilling a prophecy from Isaiah which stated that He shall not strive, nor cry, neither shall any man hear His voice in the streets (42:2). In spite of this, however, the Pharisees remained His persistent enemies to the end.

CONDEMNATION FOR THE COMPLACENT

Then began he to upbraid the cities wherein most of his mighty works were done, because they repented not: Woe unto thee, Chorazin! woe unto thee, Bethsaida! for if the mighty works, which were done in you, had been done in Tyre and Sidon, they would have repented long ago in sackcloth and ashes. But I say unto you, It shall be more tolerable for Tyre and Sidon at the day of judgment, than for you. And thou, Capernaum, which art exalted unto heaven, shalt be brought down to hell: for if the mighty works, which have been done in thee, had been done in Sodom, it would have remained until this day. But I say unto you, That it shall be more tolerable for the land of Sodom in the day of judgment, than for thee. At that time Jesus answered and said, I thank thee, O Father, Lord of heaven and earth, because thou hast hid these things from the wise and prudent, and hast revealed them unto babes. Even so, Father: for so it seemed good in thy sight. All things are delivered unto me of my Father: and no man knoweth the Son, but the Father; neither knoweth any man the Father, save the Son, and he to whomsoever the Son will reveal him (Matthew 11:20-27).

The public may think Christians are supposed to be spineless and weak. Some may even believe this is what is meant by the meekness of Christ. But let's get this straight. Christ's attitude toward the sinner is gracious and merciful, but His judgment of sin is always stern and severe.

Jesus was certainly not mild regarding Chorazin and Bethsaida. The Bible says that He upbraided them. "Upbraid" is an old English word; your dictionary might tell you that this means to scold. But a slang word comes closer to its meaning: "He bawled them out."

This "bawling out" may apply just as much to you as it did to these old-time cities. After all, haven't you seen people turned to God by the Gospel of Jesus Christ? Haven't you heard of the mighty works that have been done through evangelism? And what has your response been? If you have been surrounded by the goodness and grace of God and yet have not turned to Christ, what He said to these cities is applicable to you as well.

Notice, however, that these cities were not necessarily evil cities. He did not scold them because they were sinful in their conduct. He scolded them because, when they saw the evidence of the power of God, they did not turn to God. He said some of the harshest words of His whole ministry to good people who were smugly complacent. Jesus said that those with greater knowledge of the things of God deserve the greater blame when they disobey God. If you have heard the Gospel all your life and yet fail to respond to it, you will receive greater condemnation than a vile murderer who had never heard the Gospel.

There is a great change of mood in Matthew 11. In quiet prayer, Jesus thanked God for revealing Himself to "babes" rather than to the wise and the prudent. "Wise" includes the sophisticated, the philosopher, the intellectual. The "prudent" is the one who is thoughtful and cautious, the unemotional, the scientific, the analytical. God has hidden Himself from such people and has revealed Himself unto babes. Is that because the Gospel is so simple? Or is it because the Gospel is so personal that God Himself actually wants to deal with people genuinely? "Except ye be as little children, ye shall not enter the kingdom of heaven."

But Jesus Christ can reveal God the Father to you. He reveals Him by the Holy Spirit within your heart. Only those who are inwardly empowered by the Holy Spirit can really know the Fatherhood of God.

COMFORT FOR THE WEARY

> Come unto me, all ye that labour and are heavy laden, and I will give you rest. Take my yoke upon you, and learn of me; for I am meek and lowly in heart: and ye shall find rest unto your souls. For my yoke is easy, and my burden is light (Matthew 11:28-30).

"Come unto Me" is the personal call of the Lord Jesus Christ to your soul. There is no substitute for personal fellowship with Him. If you want His help, come; if you want His guidance, come; if you want His salvation, come.

You can be glad He does not say, "Come unto Me, all ye that have kept the rules," nor "Come unto Me, all ye that have never sinned." The only condition is that you labor and are heavy-laden. This brings hope to those who really care about their spiritual burdens. You will find no comfort anywhere in the Bible for the person who doesn't care, nor for the nonchalant. In the Book of Revelation, Jesus said, "Because thou art lukewarm, and neither cold nor hot, I will spue thee out of my mouth" (3:16). The Lord looks upon the heart.

What does it really mean to be "heavy-laden"? Does it refer to someone who has to do two day's work in one day? No, let's put it this way: the heavy-laden are those who mourn because of the sins they have committed.

To the heavy-laden, Jesus promised "rest." This word "rest" is wonderful. It does not mean that you are in a semi-lifeless state. It does not mean that Jesus will never call on you to do anything. In the cemetery, on the headstones of many graves, are the initials *R.I.P.* It means "Rest in Peace." ·But that is not the kind of rest that Jesus gives.

Jesus was talking of the kind of rest you have when things work harmoniously, when you have no friction, no contention, no conflict.

Also, Jesus spoke of a yoke. If you have ever driven oxen, you know that the harness which is placed on an ox consists mostly of a heavy wooden yoke laid across the neck. An ox usually holds his head low. His shoulders are higher than his head. When he pulls his load, he puts his shoulders into the yoke and pushes. "Take my yoke upon you" means "be willing to be like an ox that is hitched to work." Yield yourself to the will of God as an ox yields itself to its yoke. The ox that is well-broken to work will let you put the yoke upon him; he will drop his head down and let the yoke settle on his neck. But some oxen are rebellious or what the Bible calls "stiff-necked." They will hold their heads up; when they do that, the yoke slides back and galls their shoulders and they are unable to put any power into their pulling. There are many stiff-necked people too who refuse to cooperate with the will of God.

"My yoke is easy" means that it is made so that it will fit naturally to your shoulders. If you are not stiff-necked, you'll find that it is not hard to obey God. "My burden is light" means that while there will be some consequences in the way of responsibility when you accept Christ as Lord and Master, you will not find such to be irksome. You will find it is an easy thing to serve the Lord, when you yield to Him and accept His control.

TROUBLE IN THE CORNFIELD

At that time Jesus went on the sabbath day through the corn; and his disciples were an hungred, and began to pluck the ears

of corn, and to eat. But when the Pharisees saw it, they said
unto him, Behold, thy disciples do that which is not lawful to do
upon the sabbath day. But he said unto them, Have ye not read
what David did, when he was an hungred, and they that were
with him; How he entered into the house of God, and did eat
the shewbread, which was not lawful for him to eat, neither for
them which were with him, but only for the priests? Or have
ye not read in the law, how that on the sabbath days the priests
in the temple profane the sabbath, and are blameless? But I
say unto you, That in this place is one greater than the temple.
But if ye had known what this meaneth, I will have mercy, and
not sacrifice, ye would not have condemned the guiltless. For
the Son of man is Lord even of the sabbath day. And when
he was departed thence, he went into their synagogue (Matthew
12:1-9).

The Pharisees criticized the disciples for "plucking ears of corn."
"Corn" as used in the Bible does not mean our Indian Corn. This
is an old English word for "grain." Even today in Britain, people
use the word "corn" to mean any kind of grain, either wheat,
oats, barley or rye.

The "corn field" through which the disciples were passing was
probably a wheat field. The Pharisees saw them picking ears of
wheat and rubbing the kernels in their hands. So they were accused of threshing on the Sabbath day. The Pharisees, of course,
were always very critical and sensitive about outward conduct,
but they probably would never have noticed what the disciples
were doing if they had not been looking to find fault.

When you have a disposition to find fault, you are like the
Pharisees were then. What's wrong with finding fault? The truth
is that when you are looking for faults in people, you don't love
them. Do you like to have others tell you about your children's
faults? Do you spend your time looking for flaws in members of
your own family? No, because you love them. Now what about
others, especially those people with whom you have trouble getting
along? When you watch them, what are you looking for? Are you
looking to find mistakes?

In your own community, you may find that one man doesn't
keep his yard clean, another does not park his car right, another
has a dog that barks too much, another has vines that grow over
on your property and another plays his radio too loud. No doubt
all around you is fault, fault, fault. Now if you let your mind feed
on these faults, you will never grow in love. The Pharisees went
to Jesus with their criticism, not to His disciples. They didn't really
care about the disciples and what they did. They were concerned
about Jesus. They wanted to "get something on Him."

The Lord did not answer as He could have. He could have

pointed out that the disciples had not eaten much, or that they were ignorant of that regulation. But instead He accepted their accusation and He answered it by the Word of God which the Pharisees claimed to follow. He referred back to what King David had done one time. It is not only that King David had done this, but the big thing is that it was not even called a sin, nor held in any way against David. You will remember the Bible said that David "did all things after God's own heart, save in the matter of Uriah the Hittite."

Still using the Scriptures, Jesus said that even the priests do some work on the Sabbath. Every Sabbath they killed animals and brought them in for sacrifice. Even today Christian workers often labor harder on Sunday than on any other day. Yet they are doing an act which is necessary for the glory of God and the worship of God.

Then a third time Jesus referred to Scripture, quoting, "I will have mercy and not sacrifice." God is more interested in mercy being shown than in sacrifice being given. He is more interested in deeds motivated by love, than in deeds motivated by legalistic and grudging obedience.

ACCUSATION ON THE SABBATH

And, behold, there was a man which had his hand withered, And they asked him, saying, Is it lawful to heal on the sabbath days? that they might accuse him. And he said unto them, What man shall there be among you, that shall have one sheep, and if it fall into a pit on the sabbath day, will he not lay hold on it, and lift it out? How much then is a man better than a sheep? Wherefore it is lawful to do well on the sabbath day. Then saith he to the man, Stretch forth thine hand. And he stretched it forth: and it was restored whole, like as the other. Then the Pharisees went out, and held a council against him, how they might destroy him. But when Jesus knew it, he withdrew himself from thence: and great multitudes followed him, and he healed them all; And charged them that they should not make him known: That it might be fulfilled which was spoken by Esaias the prophet, saying, Behold my servant, whom I have chosen; my beloved, in whom my soul is well pleased: I will put my spirit upon him, and he shall shew judgment to the Gentiles. He shall not strive, nor cry; neither shall any man hear his voice in the streets. A bruised reed shall he not break, and smoking flax shall he not quench, till he send forth judgment unto victory. And in his name shall the Gentiles trust (Matthew 12:10-21).

Jesus was in the synagogue on the Sabbath day when a man with a crippled hand was brought to Him. The Old Testament Scriptures said that no work should be done on the Sabbath day, but there were exceptions, especially regarding works of necessity or mercy. The prohibition of work on the Sabbath referred mostly to those things one did for profit or pleasure. Such things were to be suspended, but acts of charity and mercy could be performed any time. However, in this case, the man was brought to test the Lord Jesus as to what He would do.

Jesus referred to an example found in the Old Testament of a sheep falling in a pit. If this happened on the Sabbath, the owner was allowed to do what was necessary so that he could get his sheep out. Necessity would overrule regulations. Ritual conditions would be set aside for actual physical need even in the case of a sheep or an ox.

So Jesus asked, "How much then is a man better than a sheep? If you would do this for a sheep on the Sabbath day, should you not do it for a man?" Then he healed the crippled hand in plain view of everyone.

After this, the Pharisees decided that the only way they could stop Jesus was to kill Him. So they held a meeting to discuss how to do it most righteously.

"But when Jesus knew it, he withdrew himself from thence."

Was He frightened? No, He was not. He did not fear death even when He stood in Pilate's judgment hall. Then why did He flee from the Pharisees? Needless controversy is not good. In any fight innocent people often get hurt. In this case the innocent people who might have gotten hurt could have been the disciples. They certainly weren't prepared as yet to stand on their own.

Jesus avoided open conflict at this time in fulfillment of a prophecy in Isaiah which said, "He shall not strive." The prophecy continues by saying, "A bruised reed shall he not break, and smoking flax shall he not quench" (Isaiah 42:3). "A bruised reed" refers to a man who has been broken down and isn't what he ought to be. Flax was used for fire. If the flax was wet, it would not burn easily, but would smoke. According to this prophecy, Jesus wouldn't put water on smoking flax to extinguish the little fire that was still left. He is not going to break men who are imperfect.

So He would not stir up strife; if it came, He would try to avoid it. He did not plan a defense party, nor organize His disciples into an army, nor make plans for a great debate.

Although He would do everything He could to avoid conflict, He would not refuse to do good. Even though doing good aroused the hostility of the Pharisees, He still healed the man with the crippled hand on the Sabbath. He did what was in His heart.

Since they could not intimidate Him, the Pharisees decided that they would have to kill Him.

WHO IS ON SATAN'S SIDE?

Then was brought unto him one possessed with a devil, blind, and dumb: and he healed him, insomuch that the blind and dumb both spake and saw. And all the people were amazed, and said, Is not this the son of David? But when the Pharisees heard it, they said, This fellow doth not cast out devils, but by Beelzebub the prince of the devils. And Jesus knew their thoughts, and said unto them, Every kingdom divided against itself is brought to desolation; and every city or house divided against itself shall not stand: And if Satan cast out Satan, he is divided against himself; how shall then his kingdom stand? And if I by Beelzebub cast out devils, by whom do your children cast them out? therefore they shall be your judges. But if I cast out devils by the Spirit of God, then the kingdom of God is come unto you. Or else how can one enter into a strong man's house, and spoil his goods, except he first bind the strong man? and then he will spoil his house. He that is not with me is against me; and he that gathereth not with me scattereth abroad (Matthew 12:22-30).

When the people asked, "Is not this the Son of David?" they meant, "Is not this the King that the Bible promised?" In the Old Testament when the prophets spoke of the Messiah who would sit on the throne of David, a distinguishing characteristic of the Messiah would be the miracles which He would perform. Since Jesus did such miracles, the people naturally asked, "Is not this the Son of David?"

Today when a great evangelist preaches and many are turned to God, immediately the word spreads throughout the area. Some people will say, "What a great man of God this evangelist must be!" But others will criticize the evangelist because of his methods or his message. They will call him unwise or superficial.

The ministry of Jesus provoked a similar reaction. When the Pharisees heard of Christ's miracles, they said that Satan was helping Him perform miracles.

On the former occasion when Jesus answered the Pharisees, He quoted Scripture. This time He did not. This time He argued from common sense. You don't need to use the Bible to prove that two and two are four. Similarly, it just doesn't make sense to say that Satan would cast out Satan. Using common sense, Jesus asked, "How could you walk into a man's house and take out his property, unless you first restrained the owner?" The only way a man could be freed from the clutches of the devil would be by restraining the devil first. And anyone who can do this must be stronger than the devil. In this way He claimed both that He was against the devil, and that He was more powerful.

Then He said soberly, "He that is not with me is against me, and he that gathereth not with me, scattereth abroad." He knew what the Pharisees were doing. Their criticism was actually opposition to God.

The conversation began as the Pharisees questioned whether Jesus was on Satan's side. But the Lord Jesus soon made them see how ridiculous that question was. The real question was, "Who is on the Lord's side?"

Chapter 10

HOW THE MASTER TEACHER TAUGHT

The Technique of the Teacher

We call Him a teacher. He came to teach us about God, His Father. But God is infinite and we are finite. God is eternal and we are temporal. God is holy and we are sinful. In fact, there is hardly anything about God that you could express in the language of man, because we know only those things we can see, hear, taste, smell and touch.

And so, you see, it was an extremely difficult task to take the eternal truth of God and show these things in the language and thought forms of sinful man. Yet that is exactly what the Gospel is. It is a message from the eternal God in heaven to sinful man on earth.

God is invisible and we can know only what we see. The Bible says, "Eye hath not seen, nor ear heard, neither have entered into the heart of man, the things which God hath prepared for them that love him. But God hath revealed them unto us by his Spirit" (I Corinthians 2:9,10).

So here is your first clue: God has revealed Himself in the Scriptures. Even though this revelation of God is brought to man in the words of man and in the thought forms of man, it is not the word of man. It is the Word of God, but it is the Word of God in human language.

The whole idea of such a revelation is set forth in the coming of the Lord Jesus Christ, in that He came into the world in the form of man. We call Him the incarnate Word. In Him the eternal became temporal, and the infinite became finite.

Every criticism leveled against Jesus of Nazareth can be leveled against the Bible. In each case, you have the fact that when God became incarnate in human form, He made Himself subject to the approach of man. Man would handle Him to see what he could see.

One of the major ministries of Jesus Christ on earth was to

open up to men's understanding the Word of God. In teaching, He followed a very common procedure: proceed from the known and go to the unknown.

You bring an object lesson to children and get across to their minds some intellectual idea. You can do this because there is a similarity of design between that which is seen and that which is unseen.

Paul wrote, "For the invisible things of him from the creation of the world are clearly seen, being understood by the things that are made, even his eternal power and Godhead." In other words, nature can teach us about God. In His teaching, Jesus demonstrated how this could be done.

Actually, Jesus had three main teaching devices: (1) He used nature. He spoke about trees, fruit, sheep, grass and flowers. (2) He used Scripture. When the Pharisees accused Him of breaking the Sabbath day, He referred to Scripture showing how David had eaten shewbread on the Sabbath. (3) He also used reason. When the Pharisees accused Him of being in league with Satan, He used reason to show them that this did not make any sense. Satan would not cast himself out.

Probably Jesus' favorite method of teaching was the parable or illustration. "Without a parable spake he not unto them." The Chinese have a saying that "a picture is worth a thousand words." A parable is a verbal picture.

Take, for example, the story of the Good Samaritan. That could be translated into a thousand different languages and dialects and still mean only one thing. Or consider the parable of the Lost Sheep. What person could ever understand the Gospel as well, if we did not have that story about the ninety-nine sheep that were safe in the fold, and the one that was out astray, and how the shepherd went out to look for it?

In the 12th and 13th chapters of Matthew you can see Jesus as the Master Teacher in action. When His family came and appealed to Him to get away from the conflict with the Pharisees, He replied, "He that doeth the will of my Father which is in heaven is my mother, sister and brother." He picked up a human relationship and made it mean something spiritually.

The 13th chapter has seven parables explaining the nature of the kingdom of God. Jesus told about the sower who went forth to sow. There were four different kinds of soil and the condition of the soil determined the kind of crop. This is the clearest explanation of people's response to the Gospel that you could find. Some will hear the Scriptures and some will refuse to listen. Some will listen superficially but will not really understand. Some will respond honestly but will be involved in so much of life in this world that they cannot really obey. Some will respond fully and be blessed.

Other parables such as the parable of the wheat and the tares and the parable of the net indicate the problem caused by those who look like Christians, but really aren't. The parables of the mustard seed and the leaven describe the spread of the Gospel. The parables of the treasure in the field and the goodly pearl tell of the worth of the Gospel.

In all these parables you can witness the Master Teacher at work, teaching eternal truths by telling simple stories from nature. To this day this would be recognized as teaching at its best. It is important to notice that the Lord followed principles of procedure that are valid even to this day.

The Sin Against the Spirit

Wherefore I say unto you, All manner of sin and blasphemy shall be forgiven unto men: but the blasphemy against the Holy Ghost shall not be forgiven unto men. And whosoever speaketh a word against the Son of man, it shall be forgiven him: but whosoever speaketh against the Holy Ghost, it shall not be forgiven him, neither in this world, neither in the world to come. Either make the tree good, and his fruit good; or else make the tree corrupt, and his fruit corrupt: for the tree is known by his fruit. O generation of vipers, how can ye, being evil, speak good things? for out of the abundance of the heart the mouth speaketh. A good man out of the good treasure of his heart bringeth forth good things: and an evil man out of the evil treasure bringeth forth evil things. But I say unto you, That every idle word that men shall speak, they shall give account thereof in the day of judgment. For by thy words thou shalt be justified, and by thy words thou shalt be condemned (Matthew 12:31-37).

Blasphemy against the Holy Spirit is not a matter of taking the name of the Holy Spirit in profanity. Blasphemy against the Holy Spirit is more sober, more serious than that. It means a belittling of the work of the Holy Spirit, a slandering of the results of the Spirit and an attributing the works of the Spirit unto Satan.

The work of the Holy Spirit is to present Jesus Christ. He convinces the world of sin, righteousness and judgment to come. When people become conscious of sin, and when they begin to hunger and thirst after righteousness and desire to escape the coming judgment, this is the work of the Spirit. When this work is depreciated as being only human, those who make such insinuations are speaking against the Holy Spirit of God.

When a man listens to the preaching of the Gospel and his heart is changed, this is the result of the Spirit. But when a man hears that sin is just a human weakness and that the gospel miracles did not really happen and that it is doubtful if there will be a future resurrection and judgment, no matter what the result may seem to be, you can be sure that type of preaching is not from the Holy Spirit of God. An evil tree, Jesus said, brings forth evil fruit and a good tree brings forth good fruit. You can tell the quality of the preaching by the quality of its fruit. If the preaching turns men to God, it has been honored by the Holy Spirit. Men who criticize that kind of preaching are only displaying the perversity of their evil hearts. Those who truly love God will give Him the praise and the glory for such preaching and will honor the Holy Spirit who worked to produce such results.

THE SIGN OF JONAH

Then certain of the scribes and of the Pharisees answered, saying, Master, we would see a sign from thee. But he answered and said unto them, An evil and adulterous generation seeketh after a sign; and there shall no sign be given to it, but the sign of the prophet Jonas: For as Jonas was three days and three nights in the whale's belly; so shall the Son of man be three days and three nights in the heart of the earth. The men of Nineveh shall rise in judgment with this generation, and shall condemn it: because they repented at the preaching of Jonas; and, behold, a greater than Jonas is here. The queen of the south shall rise up in judgment with this generation, and shall condemn it: for she came from the uttermost parts of the earth to hear the wisdom of Solomon; and, behold, a greater than Solomon is here. When the unclean spirit is gone out of a man, he walketh through dry places, seeking rest, and findeth none. Then he saith, I will return into my house from whence I came out; and when he is come, he findeth it empty, swept, and garnished. Then goeth he, and taketh with himself seven other spirits more wicked than himself, and they enter in and dwell there: and the last state of that man is worse than the first. Even so shall it be also unto this wicked generation (Matthew 12:38-45).

In Old Testament days, the prophet who claimed to speak for God was expected to show a sign. For instance, Moses was given two signs by God–a rod that turned into a serpent and his hand that became leprous. Similarly in the early church, any man who claimed to be a minister of the Gospel was examined very carefully. Paul said, "Truly the signs of an apostle were shown before you." In the Book of Revelation the Lord Jesus Christ commends the church that checked on its preachers to see if they showed the signs of authenticity.

So when certain scribes and Pharisees asked Jesus for a sign, they were not asking for anything unusual. Although they had just heard His warning about belittling the work of the Holy Spirit, they were interested in trapping Him in some way. So now they sought a sign.

In His answer, Jesus referred to "an evil and adulterous generation." Whenever you read the word "adulterous," remember how the Old Testament prophets used it. Certainly the Bible uses this word to refer to physical, sexual adultery, but it also uses it to refer to spiritual adultery. As a husband is to be committed to his wife, so man's heart is to be committed to God. When man's heart wanders from God, it becomes adulterous. When Jesus called the people an adulterous generation, He meant that while with their lips they served God, with their hearts they really were interested in and allured by something else.

Jesus told the scribes and Pharisees that the only sign they would see would be the sign of Jonah. The sign of Jonah was that as Jonah "was three days and three nights in the whale's belly; so shall the Son of man be three days and three nights in the heart of the earth." Thus the sign was the Resurrection of Jesus Christ. By this He meant to say that the Resurrection was the supreme sign that Jesus Christ was the authentic Messiah. He went on to point out that Nineveh repented when Jonah preached, whereas He was far greater than Jonah and yet Jerusalem did not repent. He also said that the Queen of Sheba came a long way to see the riches of King Solomon, yet though He was far greater than Solomon no one had been impressed by Him.

Jesus then gave another stern warning about neglecting the work of the Holy Spirit. He spoke of a man who had been possessed by an evil spirit. This man swept the evil spirit out of the house, but he brought nothing in to take the place of the evil spirit. So when the evil spirit saw the empty house in such perfect order he invited seven other spirits to return with him to take possession, so that the man's last state was worse than his first.

This is a story that Jesus told to religious people. It is a story that would apply just as much today as it did to the Pharisees then. This could happen in a Christian home. Today it could happen to any church member. With godly training a man might be free from a great many unclean things, but unless he were born again he would revert to his own human nature. Even though his heart was empty of evil habits, swept and garnished, yet such a person could soon find himself completely obsessed with evil. The work of the Holy Spirit is necessary to produce true godly living.

HUMAN AND SPIRITUAL RELATIONS

While he yet talked to the people, behold, his mother and his brethren stood without, desiring to speak with him. Then one said unto him, Behold, thy mother and thy brethren stand without, desiring to speak with thee. But he answered and said unto him that told him, Who is my mother? and who are my brethren? And he stretched forth his hand toward his disciples, and said, Behold my mother and my brethren! For whosoever shall do the will of my Father which is in heaven, the same is my brother, and sister, and mother (Matthew 12:46-50).

One of the most subtle methods of attacking the Lord Jesus Christ is to emphasize His humanity to such an extent that you ignore His deity. It is possible to think of Him as a man to such an extent that you forget He was God. He was not a man who became the Son of God; He was the Son of God who became a man. And when He became a man He never stopped being the Son of God. This needs to be remembered.

In Matthew 12 Jesus faced all kinds of opposition, but the climax came when His own human family came to appeal to Him. In His reply Jesus did not disparage human relationships, but rather He exalted the spiritual relationships.

At times you may have to distinguish between the spiritual — that which is pleasing to God — and the human — that which is pleasing to man. Sometimes you may please man and God at the same time. Sometimes human relationships and spiritual relationships are both served. But at other times this is not true.

You are born once of the flesh as a human creature. By the grace of God you may be born again of the Spirit as a spiritual creation. Then you are a child of Adam in the flesh but a child of God in the Spirit. It is important to remember that your relationship with God always comes first.

Although the relationship with God comes first, your human relationship will not suffer. When the Lord Jesus was hanging on the cross, one of the last things He did was arrange a permanent home for His mother. He called John to Him and, pointing to His mother, said, "Behold your mother"; and then said to Mary, pointing to John, "Behold your son." So we see that even in His last hour Jesus had not ignored the importance of human relationships. But when His mother and brothers stood outside as recorded in Matthew 12 seeking to influence His work, He emphasized that spiritual relationships come first.

Apparently His family had come to get Him out of trouble. They probably feared the consequences of the open opposition by the scribes and the Pharisees.

Some people will say that Mary held influence over Jesus Christ and that she still does. This passage is a clear answer to that. No matter where you search in Scripture you will never find one instance where Mary persuaded Jesus to do anything other than He wanted to do. In this case when she came with the brothers, He did not even go out to speak to her. He simply sent word that the things of the Lord were more important than earthly family ties.

THE SOWER AND THE SEED

The same day went Jesus out of the house, and sat by the sea side. And great multitudes were gathered together unto him, so that he went into a ship, and sat; and the whole multitude stood on the shore. And he spake many things unto them in parables, saying, Behold, a sower went forth to sow; And when he sowed, some seeds fell by the way side, and the fowls came and devoured them up: Some fell upon stony places, where they had not much earth: and forthwith they sprung up, because they had no deepness of earth: And when the sun was up, they were scorched: and because they had no root, they withered away. And some fell among thorns; and the thorns sprung up, and choked them: But other fell into good ground, and brought forth fruit, some an hundredfold, some sixtyfold, some thirtyfold. Who hath ears to hear, let him hear. And the disciples, came, and said unto him, Why speakest thou unto them in parables? He answered and said unto them, Because it is given unto you to know the mysteries of the kingdom of heaven, but to them it is not given. For whosoever hath, to him shall be given, and he shall have more abundance: but whosoever hath not, from him shall be taken away even that he hath. Therefore speak I to them in parables: because they seeing see not; and hearing they hear not, neither do they understand. And in them is fulfilled the prophecy of Esaias, which saith, By hearing ye shall hear, and shall not understand; and seeing ye shall see, and shall not perceive: For this people's heart is waxed gross, and their ears are dull of hearing, and their eyes they have closed; lest at any time they should see with their eyes and hear with their ears, and they should understand with their heart, and should be converted, and I should heal them. But blessed are your eyes, for they see: and your ears, for they hear. For verily I say unto you, That many prophets and righteous men have desired to see those things which ye see, and have not seen them: and to hear those things which ye hear, and have not heard them. Hear ye therefore the parable of the sower. When any one heareth the word of the kingdom, and understandeth it not, then cometh the wicked one, and catcheth away that which was sown in his heart. This is he which received seed by the way side. But he that received the seed into stony places, the same is he that heareth the word, and anon with joy receiveth it. Yet hath he not root in himself, but dureth for a while: for when tribulation or persecution ariseth because of the word, by and by he is offended. He also that received seed among the thorns is he that heareth the word; and the care of this world, and the deceitfulness of riches, choke the word, and he becometh unfruitful. But he that received seed into the good ground is he that heareth the word, and understandeth it; which also beareth fruit, and bringeth forth, some an hundredfold, some sixty, some thirty (Matthew 13:1-23).

This chapter contains seven stories or parables about the kingdom. Only three are explained, but these three explanations give a clue as to the interpretation of the other four.

When the Lord Jesus told a parable, the hearer could grasp its natural meaning easily. Some would hear it only as an interesting story and go away thinking what a good story-teller Jesus was. But willing hearts would grasp a spiritual meaning.

The first parable is called the "Sower and the Seed" or "The Parable of the Soil." In this story the sower sows the seed everywhere. According to the old manner of sowing seed, the sower carried a sack of seed on his shoulder and took a handful of seed at a time and threw it over the area where he was walking. Some seed fell on pathways where people had walked through the field. Since the path was hard, the seed would not be covered up, so the birds soon came and picked it up.

Jesus explained that there are some people like that, who hear the Word but do not understand it. The Gospel lies on their hearts like a kernel of wheat on the open road. What a person does not understand is soon forgotten.

The second soil He described was stony ground. The seed sprang up quickly, but the heat of the day caused these plants to wither and die. This symbolizes those who listen superficially to the Gospel, but they never let it grip their lives. They believe it intellectually, but it doesn't affect their hearts. They may grasp the Gospel, but they are unwilling to let the Gospel grasp them. At the first sign of trouble those hearers let go of what they had heard.

The third soil was thorny ground. This represents a person who listens and understands, but whose mind is preoccupied with other things. Before he responds fully to what he heard, he remembers that he has his business, his family, his community and his personal activities. He has his own plans for his life. "Business is business," he says, and so he gives earthly matters first place. Luke says about such people, "These are they which are choked with cares and with riches and with the pleasure of this life, that bring no fruit to perfection." This is their tragedy. They probably have many good things. A man's business is a good thing; his home is a good thing; his family is a good thing. But when any good thing comes ahead of God, that good thing becomes an enemy of the best.

The fourth soil is good ground. This indicates those who hear the Word, understand it, and more than that, participate in it.

It is not that they are so good nor so pious, nor so spiritually-minded. But they are wise because they put first things first. These are the people who bring forth fruit to the glory of God. What was thus set out in this parable is what happens every time the Gospel is preached. The same message may produce many different results in different people, because their hearts are in different conditions. Everyone who heard the parable would understand what happens in the sowing of seed in the field. But such as would be willing to obey God would see the spiritual truth being implied and demonstrated in the parable.

THE WHEAT AND THE TARES

Another parable put he forth unto them, saying, The kingdom of heaven is likened unto a man which sowed good seed in his field: But while men slept, his enemy came and sowed tares among the wheat, and went his way. But when the blade was sprung up, and brought forth fruit, then appeared the tares also. So the servants of the householder came and said unto him, Sir, didst not thou sow good seed in thy field? from whence then hath it tares? He said unto them, An enemy hath done this. The servants said unto him, Wilt thou then that we go and gather them up? But he said, Nay; lest while ye gather up the tares, ye root up also the wheat with them. Let both grow together until the harvest: and in the time of harvest I will say to the reapers, Gather ye together first the tares, and bind them in bundles to burn them: but gather the wheat into my barn. Then Jesus sent the multitude away, and went into the house: and his disciples came unto him, saying, Declare unto us the parable of the tares of the field. He answered and said unto them, He that soweth the good seed is the Son of man; The field is the world; the good seed are the children of the kingdom; but the tares are the children of the wicked one; The enemy that sowed them is the devil; the harvest is the end of the world; and the reapers are the angels. As therefore the tares are gathered and burned in the fire; so shall it be in the end of this world. The Son of man shall send forth his angels, and they shall gather out of his kingdom all things that offend, and them which do iniquity; And shall cast them into a furnace of fire: there shall be wailing and gnashing of teeth. Then shall the righteous shine forth as the sun in the kingdom of their Father. Who hath ears to hear, let him hear (Matthew 13: 24-30; 36-43).

In the Lord's interpretation of this parable, He explains that He is the One who sowed the good seed. His enemy, who sowed the tares, is the devil. Both the Lord Jesus and the enemy are real persons. Satan is just as real as the Lord Jesus.

According to Jesus the tares are the children of the wicked one! Some people say that all men are the children of God. Certainly all men are the creatures of God, for God made all men and

He gave His Son to die for all men. But the Bible clearly states that some men are the children of the evil one. They get their ideas from him, just as we who are the children of God are to get our ideas from the Holy Spirit.

But who is a child of the kingdom and who is a child of the enemy? God knows, but you and I don't know. How easily you might be deceived because God lets them both grow in the same field day after day! You might even imagine that He does not know the difference. You could not make a bigger mistake. He knows who is who.

You might say, "Here is a person who is preaching some strange thing, but if he were not a child of the kingdom, God would surely stop him." That is not true. For one reason or another, God may not stop that person immediately. Actually He may seem to hinder His own, because "whom the Lord loveth he chasteneth, and scourgeth every son whom he receiveth" (Hebrews 12:6). Often Christians may have more trouble than non-Christians. But that doesn't prove anything. This is not the day of judgment. God is not dealing with people the way they deserve. For this reason you should be very careful how you judge. If you see what seems to be evidence that one person is being blessed you must be careful in your judgment. If you think that someone must be doing wrong because things seem to be going against him, you must be careful. Remember the wheat and the tares grow together; they look alike.

But the harvest is coming. At that time there will be a separation. God has set a time for the end of this world. Then the angels will collect all the wicked, and will cast them into a furnace of fire. There "shall be wailing and gnashing of teeth."

This is what is so shocking about this story. It is a parable of the kingdom of God, and it shows us that whenever there are children of the kingdom there are also counterfeits. Both will make the same profession and join the same church, but God knows the difference, and He alone will be the Judge. These imitation believers can live all their lives in fellowship with true believers, but the Lord Himself knows His own and in the harvest time He will call them out for Himself.

Chapter 11

UNBELIEF AND ITS RESULTS

OBEYING DESPITE DOUBT

When the Lord told Peter to launch out into the deep and let down his net for fish, he replied that he had been fishing all night and had not caught any but went on to say "Nevertheless at thy word I will let down the net." I wouldn't be surprised if Peter the fisherman had grave doubts about the wisdom of doing it. I am inclined to think he didn't really expect to catch any fish. But Peter did what the Lord commanded anyway. He obeyed. He had such an attitude toward the Lord that if Jesus told him to do something, he would do it, even if he had real doubts. It seems clear that doubts did not determine his actions.

A major element in believing is obedience. Because you feel a certain act is what God wants you to do, you obey Him. You may still have some doubts: you may not feel sure as to how it will all work out, but because you believe in God, your faith takes the form of obedience to His will. Even when doubt may be present, obedience is the result of an exercise of faith. Faith does not mean you are sure about the outcome; it means you are sure about the Lord.

Unbelief is different from doubt. You don't need any reason for unbelief. Unbelief is the condition in which you simply do not act. Sometimes it is because you won't, but it is *always* because you don't. Unbelief is when you do not take the medicine. You may forget it. You may have misplaced it. You may have no confidence in it. You may be more interested in other things. But the point is this: You don't take the medicine. Unbelief is like darkness, which is best defined as the absence of light. Unbelief is like death, which is best defined as the absence of life. Unbelief is the absence of faith.

Unbelief may arise from ignorance or indifference, but it is never really innocence. Man is always responsible for his separation from God. Unbelief is a form of vagrancy, a spiritual vagrancy.

The bum on a park bench is like an unbeliever in the Gospel. A soldier asleep when he is on guard duty, a baby sitter oblivious to the needs of the baby is like unbelief. Unbelief is paying no attention to God. Unbelief is man's "No" to God's promises.

In Matthew 13 you find that Jesus marveled at the unbelief of His neighbors. Why did He marvel? They had heard His wisdom, they had heard His preaching, they had seen His works, and they had witnessed His power. But they would not believe. To Him this was amazing.

Unbelief does not change God, but it does have a terrific power. It can actually hinder the operation of God's grace in this world. "And he did not many mighty works there because of their unbelief."

The sovereignty of God is not exercised in forcing men to believe. The Lord Jesus sat outside Jerusalem and wept, "O Jerusalem, Jerusalem . . . how often would I have gathered thy children together, even as a hen gathereth her chickens under her wings and ye would not!" (Matthew 23:37). It is obvious He had no intention of forcing them to obey.

In the Old Testament God granted the children of Israel the desire of their hearts and sent a leanness to their souls. Over and over again God complained to His people, "I wanted to bless you, but you would not."

Four Little Parables

Another parable put he forth unto them, saying, The kingdom of heaven is like to a grain of mustard seed, which a man took, and sowed in his field: Which indeed is the least of all seeds: but when it is grown, it is the greatest among herbs, and becometh a tree, so that the birds of the air come and lodge in the branches thereof. Another parable spake he unto them; The kingdom of heaven is like unto leaven, which a woman took, and hid in three measures of meal, till the whole was leavened. All these things spake Jesus unto the multitude in parables; and without a parable spake he not unto them: That it might be fulfilled which was spoken by the prophet, saying, I will open my mouth in parables; I will utter things which have been kept secret from the foundation of the world. Again, the kingdom of heaven is like unto treasure hid in a field; the which when a man hath found, he hideth, and for joy thereof goeth and selleth all that he hath, and buyeth that field. Again, the kingdom of heaven is like unto a merchant man, seeking goodly pearls: Who, when he had found one pearl of great price, went and sold all that he had, and bought it (Matthew 13:31-35; 44-46).

The reading of this passage may seem to imply that some people could not understand the Gospel even if they wanted to. The prophet Isaiah clears up this problem plainly: "Their eyes they have closed lest at any time they should see with their eyes and hear with their ears, and should understand with their hearts and should be converted, and I should heal them" (Isaiah 6:10; Acts 28:27).

Apparently they did not want to understand the spiritual meaning. The Lord, who knows the heart of man, reveals His truth in such a way that the willing person will see it and the unwilling will not.

Years ago, my wife presented me with a picture which I have cherished ever since. It depicted a monk on his knees before an open Bible. Light streamed through a window. This godly man wanted light from heaven to shine on the Word that he might see its meaning, and God gave him that light.

Christ spoke in parables so that as you considered them you could grasp enough of the truth to want more, if you were really interested. Any time you are willing to accept the truth, the Holy Spirit will show you more in the very Scripture you have been reading.

The parable of the mustard seed stresses the fact that only a little Scripture is necessary to enable a great faith to grow. The tiny seed has an amazing capacity for growth.

The parable of the leaven is similar. You put a little bit of leaven of yeast in the dough and it spreads throughout the entire batter. Even a little truth introduced into the heart will grow and spread. Bible students give other interpretations of these parables, but the obvious meaning seems to be along the line noted above.

Parables were given to convey ideas. Such ideas should not be difficult to grasp. We may expect their meaning to be plain.

Another pair of parallel parables deals with the treasure in the field and the pearl of great price. Here the meaning is plain: Having found out what is available in the Gospel, nothing on earth will take the place of it. You will get rid of anything and everything in order to receive the promises of God.

Two men were once in a train together. Years earlier they had been pals in school, but had been separated shortly after graduation and hadn't seen each other since. One of the men had become wealthy and prominent, but he had no faith in God. The other was an obscure person, but one who had a deep faith in God. Suddenly the train crashed; some of the passengers were killed, including the son of the Christian man. Searching the wreckage the Christian found the body of his boy. Despite the tragic shock he seemed to have such an inner peace that his rich friend later said to him, "Bill, I tell you I would give everything that I have if I could have faith like yours."

The Christian looked at him and replied, "Tom, that is just what it would take."

To enter into the blessing of God, one must be willing to forsake all else for the privilege of knowing Him and trusting Him.

THE SEPARATION OF THE WICKED

Again, the kingdom of heaven is like unto a net, that was cast into the sea, and gathered of every kind: Which, when it was full, they drew to shore, and sat down, and gathered the good into vessels, but cast the bad away. So shall it be at the end of the world: the angels shall come forth, and sever the wicked from among the just, And shall cast them into the furnace of fire: there shall be wailing and gnashing of teeth. Jesus said unto them, Have ye understood all these things? They say unto him, Yea, Lord. Then said he unto them, Therefore every scribe which is instructed unto the kingdom of heaven is like unto a man that is an householder, which bringeth forth out of his treasure things new and old (Matthew 13:47-52).

As a net is cast into the sea, so the Gospel is preached in all the earth. All types of people respond to the Gospel and for various reasons. Some of these reasons are legitimate and some aren't. This would seem naturally to be true in mass evangelism, but just because all of the responses are not genuine does not mean that mass evangelism is a wrong approach. This way of preaching the Gospel has been greatly blessed by God.

As soon as the net is full, the fishermen draw it to shore and gather the good into vessels, while they throw the bad away. This is the same truth which was brought out in the parable of the wheat and the tares.

This parable also points to the end of the world, which in this case does not refer to this earth, but rather to our present age. When the Bible speaks of the end of the world, it means the end of things as they are now.

The nets are brought in, as if all the fish were good. But the time of separation is coming. This is a clear indication of a future judgment.

When Jesus asked His followers if they understood His seven parables, they replied, "Yea, Lord." Then He said, "If you do, you are like a householder, which bringeth forth out of his treasure things new and old." God's truth opens for you new opportunities. As you learn more you will find new dimensions for living. When you know the truth of the kingdom of God, many promises in Scripture will have a deeper meaning to you, because you will understand more fully how they can be carried out.

For instance, if you consider, "The Lord is my shepherd, I

shall not want," you know quite well that you are not an actual sheep, yet you know from the truth of the kingdom of God that Jesus Christ will be in you to guide you as a shepherd guides his sheep into green pastures. He will lead you into understanding the truth in a way that will feed your soul. Likewise these ideas will come into your heart as you read the Old Testament promises. When you recieve any new truth of the kingdom of God in your heart you will find new dimensions in all the Scripture that you ever knew.

LIMITED BY UNBELIEF

And it came to pass, that when Jesus had finished these parables, he departed thence. And when he was come into his own country, he taught them in their synagogue, insomuch that they were astonished, and said, Whence hath this man this wisdom, and these mighty works? Is not this the carpenter's son? is not his mother called Mary? and his brethren, James, and Joses, and Simon, and Judas? And his sisters, are they not all with us? Whence then hath this man all these things? And they were offended in him. But Jesus said unto them, A prophet is not without honour, save in his own country, and in his own house. And he did not many mighty works there because of their unbelief (Matthew 13:53-58).

As you read this portion of Matthew, did you notice the question His neighbors asked? "Is not this the carpenter's son?"

This is one of the two passages in Scripture where the word carpenter is mentioned in connection with Jesus. In one place He is called "the carpenter," and in another He is called "the carpenter's son." But in both places the people who referred to Him in this way were those who did not believe in Him. Isn't it strange then that in the Christian church today so many people speak of Jesus as "the carpenter of Nazareth"?

Actually we have no *real* evidence that He was ever a carpenter as far as His own activity went. When He was twelve, He went down from Jerusalem with His mother and stepfather and "was subject in all things to Mary and Joseph." Since Joseph was a carpenter, Jesus may have worked with him, but this is only an inference. It is quite true that the general custom in those days was that the trade of the head of the house was usually the trade of the children particularly in the case of the oldest boy, but this wasn't always the case.

In our day so much interest is directed to the humanity of Christ and so much is said about His manhood. There is real danger that we will consider Him as only a human being. If we keep talking about Him as only a man, we shouldn't be surprised if some do not believe in Him as God.

It was the Son of God who gave His life for us. We must put our faith in the fact that it was the Son of God who went to Calvary's cross. The Son of God laid down His life. The Son of God was raised from the dead. The Son of God is in the presence of God right now. And it is the Son of God in whom we put our trust.

The neighbors who emphasized His humanity doubted Him. Their doubt was followed by a state of unwillingness to believe. This unbelief actually limited His working in their midst: "And he did not many mighty works there because of their unbelief."

I wonder if our modern emphasis on the humanity of Christ is the reason why so many of our churches today are so powerless. I wonder if the reason why some people are so powerless in prayer is because they think of Him only as a man. The church that talks about Him only as a man has only human strength and power; the church that regards Him as God has divine strength.

ADMISSION WITHOUT SUBMISSION

At that time Herod the tetrarch heard of the fame of Jesus, And said unto his servants, This is John the Baptist; he is risen from the dead; and therefore mighty works do shew forth themselves in him. For Herod had laid hold on John, and bound him, and put him in prison for Herodias' sake, his brother Philip's wife. For John said unto him, It is not lawful for thee to have her. And when he would have put him to death, he feared the multitude, because they counted him as a prophet. But when Herod's birthday was kept, the daughter of Herodias danced before them, and pleased Herod. Whereupon he promised with an oath to give her whatsoever she would ask. And she, being before instructed of her mother, said, Give me here John Baptist's head in a charger. And the king was sorry: nevertheless for the oath's sake, and them which sat with him at meat, he commanded it to be given her. And he sent, and beheaded John in the prison. And his head was brought in a charger, and given to the damsel: and she brought it to her mother. And his disciples came, and took up the body, and buried it, and went and told Jesus (Matthew 14:1-12).

Amazing, isn't it, how a man can find it difficult to believe in Jesus and yet very easy to believe in the most fantastic ideas otherwise. Here is such a case. Herod heard of the preaching and power of Jesus and commented, "This is John the Baptist raised from the dead."

Some folks refuse to believe the creation story of the Bible, and yet they are willing to stretch their imagination to believe in some weird and amazing theories about the origin of the world.

Others refuse to believe in what the Bible has to say about life after death, but dream up fanciful notions to give themselves a degree of hope for the future. Herod was a man like that.

Although the death of John had taken place earlier, it is recounted here. John had apparently condemned Herod for marrying his own sister-in-law. But at a birthday party, Herod's stepdaughter danced before him and Herod promised her whatever she wanted. It was the kind of promise a man might make in the time of hilarity, perhaps by impulse. Having consulted with her mother, the young girl responded by asking for John the Baptist's head.

Herod apparently was sorry he had to behead John, but he did it "for the oath's sake." Isn't that strange? Here is a man with very little morality on any level keeping a drunken promise. How often you find that to be true! People who ordinarily do not have any integrity say, "Well, I gave my word, I've got to stand by it."

I know of a young woman who broke her marriage vow and went away with another man. When the time came that she wondered whether or not she should seek to repair the damage she had done, she said, "Well, I gave my promise to this other man; I can't break it." She had broken her promise to her true husband, but she could not break her promise which she had made in sin.

There is no virtue in this kind of consistency. The fact that Herod was sorry does not really help in any way. Certainly, we would be sorry. How many wicked men are sorry! But it is no great virtue to be sorry when you have made a fool of yourself. "Nevertheless for the oath's sake, and them which sat with him at meat, . . ." There you have it. You see, he wanted to look as if he were a man of his word.

Don't feel sorry for John. The whole event was much more terrible for Herod than it was for the beheaded saint. It is not as important that you live down here for a few years longer as it is that you live in eternity with God. Herod is the one for whom you should be sorry. The real tragedy is that when John first told him the truth about himself, he neglected to respond to it. He had a chance to repent; he had a chance to choose what was right; he had a chance to forsake sin. But the sad fact is that he failed to respond to the message of truth when it was plainly put before him.

There is a great snare in *admission* which does not lead to *submission*. You may admit the truth, but this is futile if you do not submit to God. Herod will forever serve as an illustration of the danger of "the half-way mark."

Five Loaves and Two Fishes

When Jesus heard of it, he departed thence by ship into a desert place apart: and when the people had heard thereof, they followed him on foot out of the cities. And Jesus went forth, and saw a great multitude, and was moved with compassion toward them, and he healed their sick. And when it was evening, his disciples came to him, saying, This is a desert place, and the time is now past; send the multitude away, that they may go into the villages, and buy themselves victuals. But Jesus said unto them, They need not depart; give ye them to eat. And they say unto him, We have here but five loaves, and two fishes. He said, Bring them hither to me. And he commanded the multitude to sit down on the grass, and took the five loaves, and the two fishes, and looking up to heaven, he blessed, and brake, and gave the loaves to his disciples, and the disciples to the multitude. And they did all eat, and were filled: and they took up of the fragments that remained twelve baskets full. And they that had eaten were about five thousand men, beside women and children (Matthew 14:13-21).

In Scripture when you read of "a desert place," it does not mean a place of only sand and gravel. It means an uninhabited place, a deserted place, one where you could be alone.

In this passage, Jesus probably withdrew into the wilderness to get away from the crowds. He had heard of the death of John the Baptist and was deeply moved. He wanted to be alone, so He left the cities of Galilee and the crowds of people. Although He left the people, the people did not leave Him. They wanted to be with Him so much that they followed Him into "a desert place."

When Jesus saw this crowd, He sensed their great need. So in spite of the fact that He had come away to rest, He responded to this need. He healed their sick. In the evening, His disciples advised Him to send the people home. It was as if they said, "It is late in the afternoon. It is time they were getting their supper, so end what you are doing and send them away." This proposal would seem to be the practical sensible thing to do.

Jesus responded with the words, "Give ye them to eat."

In another gospel we are told how the disciples reacted: "How can we do it? We don't have enough to feed them. If we spent all the money we have, we would not have enough to feed them." All they had was five loaves and two fishes. The loaves were small and so were the fish, but that didn't seem to make any difference. With more than 5,000 people, it certainly wouldn't matter much how big the five loaves were or how big the two fish were.

Then the well-known miracle took place. Perhaps you have read of naturalistic explanations of this miracle. Some will sug-

gest that when Jesus took the lunch of one person and gave it
to others, everyone in the crowd shared their lunches with each
other. Such an explanation ruins the whole point of this incident. We do well to remember that when a man explains something by explaining it away, he has not explained anything at
all. The feeding of the five thousand was a supernatural miracle.
There is no other true explanation.

Once when I was pastor, I was concerned because I did not
see evidence of the spiritual growth in my congregation that I
wanted to see. One day as I was praying, the Lord reminded me
of the incident in which the Israelites were confronted by the Red
Sea. At that point Moses called upon God, and God said, "What
is that in thine hand?"

Moses replied, "A rod."

God said, "Go and use it."

Moses was told to go down to the sea, raise up his rod and
command the sea.

And then I realized that inasmuch as I was the pastor, God
wanted me to speak the word He gave to me. If I faithfully did
my part, God would be faithful to do His part.

I did not feel at all that I had enough faith to do anything.
I felt like these disciples who said, "We have but a few loaves
and a few small fishes."

Then God spoke further to me: "Bring it hither to me." He
wanted me to bring to Him what I had, surrender it to Him and
let Him bless it. It turned out to be enough. When I did what
He wanted me to do, God kept His promise in a wonderful way,
and our whole congregation was truly blessed. Maybe some of
you who read this are face to face with some needy situation and
the Lord has told you, "Go and do."

Perhaps you have already replied, "I can't. I am not equipped
to do it." Do not be surprised when He will ask, "How much
do you have?" If you find you are obliged to say: "Just a pitiful
little bit," you may expect to hear Him say, "Bring it to me."
When you turn over to Him the little you have, He will bless it
and you will see that it will be enough. As in the story of the
feeding of the five thousand, you will find that there will be more
remaining afterward than there was in the beginning.

Chapter 12

DEMONSTRATING THE POWER OF GOD

BELIEVING IN BIBLE MIRACLES

The Bible reports the mighty works of God from time to time throughout its pages. Again and again the revelation of God to His people was punctuated by some event wherein the usual processes of nature were overruled by the will of God. At certain periods of history these miracles occurred more commonly than at other times.

Such a period occurred during the Exodus when there were many amazing events. The crossing of the Red Sea was a major miracle, but the cloud by day and the pillar of fire by night were miracles that continued for forty years. Manna fell from heaven, water sprang from a rock, quail were brought miraculously. The Israelites entered the Promised Land by crossing the Jordan River in a miraculous manner, and again in the battle of Jericho the walls fell down miraculously.

Just such a period of miracles occurred again in the time of Elijah and Elisha. In the Biblical account of these prophets one miracle after another is recorded.

But at no time in history were there ever so many miracles as occurred in the life of the Lord Jesus Christ.

As a young man, I did not believe in God and I did not believe in the Bible. Later, however, when I became sufficiently interested in the Gospel to start reading the New Testament, all these miracles challenged me. I thought no one could be expected to believe these things. At times I felt it was really too bad that you could not get to the Gospel of Jesus Christ without facing all these impossible stories. I even tried to forgive the writers for putting them in the Bible. I tried to believe the Bible leaving out the miracles. I was willing to accept as a fact that Jesus of Nazareth was a wonderful man who set a great example, but I felt that I couldn't believe any more than that.

But as I read on in the New Testament, I found that Paul

made it plain in Romans 10:9: "If thou shalt confess with thy mouth the Lord Jesus, and shalt believe in thine heart that God hath raised him from the dead, thou shalt be saved." By that time I wanted to be saved, but this verse made it clear that for me to be saved, I had to believe in the Resurrection. As I read further I found that Paul did not change this demand at all in I Corinthians 15. Either Jesus Christ was raised from the dead or everything in the Gospel was just foolishness, Paul said. I remember that it occurred to me to go through the New Testament and cut out everything about miracles. To my astonishment I realized that if I would do that I would have very little left but conjunctions and connecting phrases.

Why would all these miracles be recorded in Scripture? Why are there so many things so hard to believe? Gradually I began to understand that these miracles are in the gospels to demonstrate that Jesus of Nazareth was the Son of God. The power Jesus showed over nature was the power of God over nature.

As a young agnostic I was faced especially with the problem of the Resurrection. I tried to believe it, even as Paul said I must. One day I asked myself, "Why do I find it so difficult to believe in the Resurrection?"

I answered myself, "It couldn't have happened, because I have never seen it happen and I have never heard of it happening since."

Then I recalled that the Bible itself claimed that the Resurrection was absolutely unique. So I felt I must find another explanation.

My second answer was, "Miracles like the Resurrection are contrary to everything I know."

Then I asked myself, "Do I claim to know everything?"

No, I had to admit that there were many things I did not know. Then could it be possible that the Resurrection was one of those things outside my own range of knowledge?

I had always understood that the Bible claimed that God was the Creator of the world, that He was outside it like a man is outside a machine He builds, and that He actually manages it. But could God bring a person back to life? Quickly I answered my own questions: If I could believe that God made me in the first place, it would not be such a difficult thing to believe that God could bring me back to life. If I could accept the idea that God was big enough to create, couldn't I believe in a God big enough to resurrect? In creation, God made me out of nothing. In resurrection, He certainly could bring me back into existence again. The more I thought about that, the more I realized that if

I could believe in the creation of the world, I should not have any trouble believing in the Resurrection.

At that time God gave me grace to believe. For me it was a terrific experience. It was as though my whole intellectual sky had been covered until then with a great big circus tent. The limit of what I could hear, see, taste, smell and touch was the limit of everything I knew. It was then as though some great giant had reached down to the horizon and had begun to rip it wide open, tearing the whole sky apart. There was more to this universe than I had ever dreamed. I had been thinking only in physical terms, but now I saw there were spiritual realities also.

From that time on it was never hard for me to see that the miracles were merely a demonstration that the Almighty God is at work. In Matthew 14 is the record of the miracle of the feeding of the five thousand. This is Almighty God at work. When you read how Jesus walked on the water, here was God in human form. When you read of that woman of Canaan whose daughter was "grievously vexed with a devil," and how Jesus healed her, you are reading of God at work. And when you read of how 4,000 were fed, once again you see Jesus demonstrating the almighty power of God. Apparently these events are recorded here for the same purpose as when they occurred in the first place. Miracles are evidences of the almighty power of God, and are some indication of the nature of the salvation work of God. They prepare our hearts to be able to believe that God can and will raise the dead.

PETER'S "LITTLE" FAITH

And straightway Jesus constrained his disciples to get into a ship, and to go before him unto the other side, while he sent the multitudes away. And when he had sent the multitudes away, he went up into a mountain apart to pray: and when the evening was come, he was there alone. But the ship was now in the midst of the sea, tossed with waves: for the wind was contrary. And in the fourth watch of the night Jesus went unto them, walking on the sea. And when the disciples saw him walking on the sea, they were troubled, saying, It is a spirit; and they cried out for fear. But straightway Jesus spake unto them, saying, Be of good cheer; it is I; be not afraid. And Peter answered him and said, Lord, if it be thou, bid me come unto thee on the water. And he said, Come. And when Peter was come down out of the ship, he walked on the water, to go to Jesus. But when he saw the wind boisterous, he was afraid; and beginning to sink, he cried, saying, Lord, save me. And immediately Jesus stretched forth his hand, and caught him, and said unto him, O thou of little faith, wherefore didst thou doubt? And when they were come into the ship, the wind ceased. Then they that were in the ship came and worshipped him, saying, Of a truth thou art the Son of God. And when they were gone over, they came into the land of Gennesaret. And when the men of that place had knowledge of him, they sent out into all that country round about, and brought unto him all that were diseased; And besought him that they might only touch the hem of his garment: and as many as touched were made perfectly whole (Matthew 14:22-36).

Many of the miracles of Jesus were done in public for the multitudes to see, but this miracle was done in semi-private for the disciples. The purpose of this miracle was to confirm their faith in Him. These apostles had responded to His call and were following Him. But, after all, they were still human beings. He worked to build their confidence and strengthen their faith, by demonstrating His power before them.

In this incident the ship was in the middle of the Sea of Galilee. It was "tossed with waves: for the wind was contrary." Mark reports that the disciples were "toiling in rowing." They were "digging furiously" for all they were worth, because of the storm. As these disciples knew well, a squall on the Sea of Galilee could be very dangerous. So the disciples were in danger. It will help our understanding to remember they were where they were because Jesus had told them to go. They could naturally expect Him to help them.

Then Jesus came walking on the water. The disciples couldn't believe their eyes. They were greatly disturbed. Thinking that He was a ghost, they cried out in fear. When Jesus told them that it was He, Peter responded with: "Bid me come unto thee on the water."

Jesus said, "Come." To his credit Peter was willing to go through with it. He stepped out of the boat and walked on the water, "but when he saw the wind boisterous, he was afraid." I can't say for certain which way he was looking when he started out. But I can think he was looking at Jesus. However, suddenly he realized where he was. He looked around and saw the waves were mounting up; the wind was howling; danger was surrounding him; "he was afraid." It was then that he began to sink.

Often our spiritual experience depends on which way we are looking. If we look at trouble, we will become downhearted and discouraged. In the time of distress we should look to Jesus. That is what Peter did even as he began to sink. Immediately Jesus stretched out His hand, caught him and said, "O thou of little faith, wherefore didst thou doubt?"

Jesus did not rebuke Peter for "little faith." I realize it was *little* faith, but at least it was faith. It was enough faith to get Peter started, even though it was only a little. A little faith can get you started, too. And if you start walking with the Lord, you'll learn more and more. If you have just a little faith and exercise it, God will begin to work. Then you can believe more and more.

When they came into the ship, the wind ceased, and all the disciples acknowledged, "Of a truth thou art the Son of God." That was the very truth Jesus was trying to demonstrate. These disciples needed to be convinced that Jesus of Nazareth was really the Son of God. This conviction would be important for their own spiritual experience, and for the power of the message they would carry to the world.

When you are confronted by some sudden storm of events, that does not mean you are on the wrong road. You may have been doing exactly what the Lord wanted you to do when the storm burst with all its fury. If in that storm you will look to Him and exercise your faith in Him, you will find that He is able to control even the storms that beset you and you will know that He is the Son of God. Then you can tell others about Him.

CLEAN HANDS VS. CLEAN HEARTS

> Then came to Jesus scribes and Pharisees, which were of Jerusalem, saying, Why do thy disciples transgress the tradition of the elders? for they wash not their hands when they eat bread. But he answered and said unto them, Why do ye also transgress the commandment of God by your tradition? For God commanded, saying, Honour thy father and mother: and, He that curseth father or mother, let him die the death. But ye say, Whosoever shall say to his father or his mother, It is a gift, by whatsoever thou mightest be profited by me; And honour not his father or his mother, he shall be free. Thus have ye made the commandment of God of none effect by your tradition. Ye hypocrites, well did Esaias prophesy of you, saying, This people draweth nigh unto me with their mouth, and honoureth me with their lips; but their heart is far from me. But in vain they do worship me, teaching for doctrines the commandments of men (Matthew 15:1-9).

One of the regulations which the Jewish religious leaders had set up was related to the washing of the hands. This was done not for sanitary reasons as much as for ceremonial reasons in keeping with the Old Testament law that you should eat with clean hands. Apparently the disciples of Jesus were not sufficiently careful about this to please the Pharisees, so they were accused of breaking the law.

The Lord Jesus did not respond directly to this loaded question, because the Pharisees were not really interested in an answer. All they wanted to do was to embarrass Jesus in front of the crowds.

They wanted to throw a monkey wrench into the works, as He was teaching the people about God.

So Jesus asked them a question concerning some of their own practices which openly worked contrary to the commandment of God. According to the law of Moses, a son was to honor his parents. This would be interpreted to include sharing in their support with his earnings or produce. In later times the rabbis had taught that if he gave part to the priest as an offering to God he no longer would need to give any of it to his parents. In this way, the parents did not receive anything, the priest got a small part and the young man could keep the rest for himself. It was a way of getting around a plain teaching of the Old Testament Scriptures. The Pharisees had devised a way to approve that which was obviously unlawful.

Because they were guilty of such tricky practices, Jesus said boldly, "Ye hypocrites." The word "hypocrite" comes from the idea of wearing another face over your own. It is like wearing a false face or being made up to act a role in a play. Many people do this in church. No matter how they live throughout the week, when they come to church on Sunday they put on their Sunday-go-to-meeting face. That is hypocrisy. God is not fooled by hypocrites.

Some hypocrites are so good at fooling others that they can even fool themselves. The Pharisees seemed to be this way. They seemed to have deceived themselves into thinking that they were good. By going to the temple regularly, by keeping strict regulations, they apparently felt they were pleasing God; after they had kept these practices, they seemed to think they could do anything they pleased. The Lord accused them of swindling widows and driving sharp practices in business (Matthew 23). But though they could fool every man on earth and though they might even fool themselves, they could not fool God. "Man looketh on the outward appearance, but God looketh at the heart."

What the Mouth Is For

And he called the multitude, and said unto them, Hear, and understand: Not that which goeth into the mouth defileth a man; but that which cometh out of the mouth, this defileth a man. Then came his disciples, and said unto him, Knowest thou that the Pharisees were offended, after they heard this saying? But he answered and said, Every plant, which my heavenly Father hath not planted, shall be rooted up. Let them alone: they be blind leaders of the blind. And if the blind lead the blind, both shall fall into the ditch. Then answered Peter and said unto him, Declare unto us this parable. And Jesus said, Are ye also yet without understanding? Do not ye yet understand, that what-

soever entereth in at the mouth goeth into the belly, and is cast
out into the draught? But those things which proceed out of the
mouth come forth from the heart; and they defile the man. For
out of the heart proceed evil thoughts, murders, adulteries, forni-
cations, thefts, false witness, blasphemies: These are the things
which defile a man: but to eat with unwashen hands defileth
not a man (Matthew 15:10-20).

Having dealt with the critics, Jesus examined the criticism.
It seems almost as if He did not discuss the criticism with the
scribes and Pharisees because they were not worthy, but He did
discuss the whole matter with the multitude. He did this so that
all might understand there had actually been nothing unworthy
nor improper in the conduct of His disciples.

Jesus began by talking about the mouth. The mouth is both
for eating and for speaking. It is both for the receiving of food
and for the expression of attitudes, thoughts and ideas. A man
is not defiled by what he eats, Jesus said, but rather by the expression of his attitudes, thoughts and ideas. A man is not defiled
by earthly environment, but rather by his own outlook.

This saying apparently offended the Pharisees even more. We
will remember they had already been offended. They had previously
talked about putting Christ to death. It hardly mattered, therefore,
if they became grieved again with Jesus for something else He said.
So the Lord answered, "Every plant, which my heavenly Father
hath not planted, shall be rooted up."

Nothing in this world is permanent except that which God
does. There is much in this world that God is not doing. You
certainly must not hold God responsible for everything. Certainly
He provides the strength with which men do whatever they do,
but that does not mean that God shares in a murder. God did not
inspire it, He did not direct it, and He is not responsible for it.
This applies to religion as well. The Pharisees were religious leaders, but God was certainly not responsible for their course of action.

Then came this word which sounds strange, coming from the
lips of Jesus, "Let them alone: they be blind leaders of the blind.
And if the blind lead the blind, both shall fall into the ditch."
The true servant of Christ is responsible to God for a great many
things. In fact, he has more in his hands than he can do. But one
of the things that he is not responsible for is the convincing of
those who have willfully turned their backs on God. A Christian
need not waste his time arguing with people who do not want
to know the truth. Many people have not heard the Gospel and
are willing to listen. There are many whose hearts are hungry for
the good news of salvation. It is to them the servants of Christ
must direct their energies and their time. There is far too much

to do that can be done, to waste time and energy on such as in their willful refusal to listen are turning their backs on God.

A Woman's "Great" Faith

Then Jesus went thence, and departed into the coasts of Tyre and Sidon. And, behold, a woman of Canaan came out of the same coasts, and cried unto him, saying, Have mercy on me, O Lord, thou son of David; my daughter is grievously vexed with a devil. But he answered her not a word. And his disciples came and besought him, saying, Send her away; for she crieth after us. But he answered and said, I am not sent but unto the lost sheep of the house of Israel. Then came she and worshipped him, saying, Lord, help me. But he answered and said, It is not meet to take the children's bread, and to cast it to dogs. And she said, Truth, Lord: yet the dogs eat of the crumbs which fall from their masters' table. Then Jesus answered and said unto her, O woman, great is thy faith: be it unto thee even as thou wilt. And her daughter was made whole from that very hour. And Jesus departed from thence, and came nigh unto the sea of Galilee; and went up into a mountain, and sat down there. And great multitudes came unto him, having with them those that were lame, blind, dumb, maimed, and many others, and cast them down at Jesus' feet; and he healed them: Insomuch that the multitude wondered, when they saw the dumb to speak, the maimed to be whole, the lame to walk, and the blind to see: and they glorified the God of Israel (Matthew 15:21-31).

She was a Gentile. As a Gentile, she did not belong among the Jews. She was not included in the Old Testament promises. But surprisingly, she called Him, "Lord, Son of David." Apparently she knew the Old Testament Scriptures, and so she asked Him for help. "But he answered her not a word."

This is one of those incidents that can easily be misunderstood, so you must be on the alert as you read it. The compassion of Jesus must have gone out to her. His gentle disposition must have been ready to reach her. But He paused. His disciples asked Him to send her away because she was bothering them. Finally He said, "I am not sent but unto the lost sheep of the house of Israel."

I believe the Lord Jesus said this to test His disciples, because this was the popular view. It was the common idea that salvation by the grace of God was to be only for the Jews; God's blessing would come only to the Jews. Although some of the Jews might stray, they were still God's sheep. So Jesus was quoting here the popular Jewish idea. The woman's response to this was to worship Him and to beg again for help. This time Jesus replied that it is not a good thing to take the children's bread and to cast it to dogs. The Jewish people thought of themselves as "the children" even

as they called all Gentiles "dogs." Jesus was drawing attention
to this common Jewish doctrine. Her humble and clever reply
was, "Truth, Lord: yet the dogs eat of the crumbs which fall from
their masters' table." Could not "drops of mercy" go beyond the
household of God?

This woman of Canaan, knowing the Old Testament, understood that anyone can come to God, even as Abraham first came
to God; and that the Jewish people themselves, the nation of Israel,
were to be the messengers to the whole world of this gospel story.
She may have known such promises as, "In his name shall the
Gentiles trust" (Matthew 12:21). She was a Gentile and she was
trusting in God. God is not the exclusive property of the Jews. He
belongs to the world.

Though God is God of the whole world, we must not get the
idea that He deals with different nations in different ways so that
whatever may be their national culture would be valid for them
in spiritual reality. God has only one way and that is Jesus Christ
who said, "I am the way, the truth, and the life. No man cometh
unto the Father, but by me" (John 14:6). In fact when any Gentile, anywhere, any time, comes to God and is accepted by Him,
it will be because that person came as a true child of Abraham.
He can be a child of Abraham because Abraham's children are
not biologically begotten. The children of Abraham are the people
who have the faith of Abraham.

Finally, Jesus told the woman, "O woman, great is thy faith;
be it unto thee even as thou wilt." Why did He say that she had
great faith? It was great faith because she along with Abraham
believed that promise of long ago, "In thee, and in thy seed, shall
all the nations of the earth be blessed" (Genesis 22:18). That included the Canaanites; that included this woman, and this includes
you and me.

FOUR THOUSAND MEALS

> Then Jesus called his disciples unto him, and said, I have com-
> passion on the multitude, because they continue with me now
> three days, and have nothing to eat: and I will not send them
> away fasting, lest they faint in the way. And his disciples say
> unto him, Whence should we have so much bread in the wilder-
> ness, as to fill so great a multitude? And Jesus saith unto them,
> How many loaves have ye? And they said, Seven, and a few little
> fishes. And he commanded the multitude to sit down on the
> ground. And he took the seven loaves and the fishes, and gave
> thanks, and brake them, and gave to his disciples, and the dis-
> ciples to the multitude. And they did all eat, and were filled:
> and they took up of the broken meat that was left seven baskets

full. And they that did eat were four thousand men, beside women and children. And he sent away the multitude, and took ship, and came into the coasts of Magdala (Matthew 15:32-39).

Perhaps you remember that Matthew had just described a miracle similar to this one. So it would be normal to skip over this account and say, "I know about that already." But this would be a mistake. It is the part of wisdom never to skip anything that the Scripture repeats, because repetition in the Bible usually has a purpose.

Long ago, my father-in-law, who greatly helped me in my understanding of the Scriptures, said to me, "It is a· good thing to follow along with the proportion that the Bible uses. When the Bible speaks of a thing seldom, then speak seldom of it. When the Bible speaks of a thing often, then speak often of it." There may be exceptions to this, but it is a good general rule to follow. It is important to get the balance of truth as it is written in the Scriptures.

The feeding of the four thousand differs from the feeding of the five thousand in several ways. In this case, the feeding of the multitude came by the initiative of the Lord Jesus Christ Himself. On the first occasion, the disciples came to Jesus and said, "Send them away so that they will be able to get something to eat." This time Jesus brought the matter up, saying "I have compassion on the multitude." The Lord Jesus Christ looks out upon a confused world with so much contention and conflict today. He still has compassion on the multitude.

Perhaps we should note that Jesus did not open up restaurants and feed all the poor people in Palestine. No, He fed the multitudes around Him only on occasion, and for specific purposes. Jesus was interested in practical needs. In fact, He gave Himself for the needs of the people. But He always taught that spiritual needs are the most important; physical needs are secondary. He used the physical to illustrate spiritual truth. In the same way that the Lord Jesus looked out upon the multitude who had been so long without food, He even now looks out upon many a church congregation that has been so long without spiritual food. There are doubtless many congregations today upon whom the Lord Jesus Christ looks with compassion, who do not have any food, and are fainting by the way.

Jesus did not give supernatural strength to the multitude, although He could have done it that way. He did not have some wind blow over the people and suddenly refresh them so that they did not need to eat for another thirty days. These people were hungry in an ordinary way, so He gave them ordinary bread. This procedure demanded no special faith on the part of the multitude, but it exemplified the grace of God before their eyes.

In supplying the needs of the people, He used what the disciples had – a few loaves and fishes. "Give it to me," He said, and the little they had was blessed and multiplied until everyone had all he needed and was filled. Once again there was more left afterward than when they started.

The person who has spiritual truth will come across others who need it, but may feel that he does not have much to give. When the Lord says, "What do you have?" he will say, "I have only this." The Lord will reply, "Give it to Me," and He will use it to bless. A person may feel he knows so very little of the Gospel even though it is enough to bring him to the Lord. That little he knows may be all he needs to be able to serve effectually in bringing the message of salvation to others.

Chapter 13

HOW TO BE A MEMBER OF THE TRUE CHURCH

What Is the Church?

Often you use the word "church" to refer to a denomination, such as the Presbyterian, Methodist or Baptist church. Sometimes you use it to refer to a local congregation, such as "the church down at the corner." Sometimes you are referring to an actual building. You say, "They are building a new church over there." Sometimes you refer to it as a social agency, such as when you say, "Well, the church will have to do something about that." In this case you mean that the organized group of people in that area who are worshiping together might be able to get something done by united action. For instance, when you say that the church favors education or opposes Sunday amusements, you are using the word "church" as a social factor.

But none of these things are what the Lord Jesus Christ had in mind when He said, "Upon this rock I will build my church." Jesus was speaking about *the body of believers* indwelt by the Holy Spirit of God. This is sometimes called "the true Church," the *Church* with the capital letter. This is the Church that is related to the Lord by faith and its members are related to one another in love. This is the Church which is drawn together by the Holy Spirit.

In the New Testament there are several illustrations which are used to describe the Church. The Lord said, "I am the vine, ye are the branches." Paul often talked of the Church as "the body of Christ." Christ, as the head, directs the body: the body has hands, feet, eyes and ears which do whatever the head directs. The New Testament also speaks of the Church as "the temple of the Holy Ghost." The Church is indwelt by the Holy Spirit and the individual believers are "living stones" which comprise the temple. Elsewhere the Church is called "the bride of Christ," indicating our personal commitment to Him.

Throughout Christian history we have developed some other

ways of characterizing the Church. Sometimes "the Church Visible" is distinguished from "the Church Invisible." "The Church Visible" refers to organizations such as the Methodist, Presbyterian or Baptist churches. This is the church that man sees; it is the church from man's point of view. "The Church Visible" is an organization with the limitations that any human organization has. But "the Church Invisible" is the Church from God's point of view. It is composed of all the people who belong to the Lord Jesus Christ. Some of its members are in heaven and some are living today. "The Church Invisible" is something that only God knows. It is an organism, an actual, living union and fellowship.

When the Lord said, "I will build my church," He was referring to the Invisible Church, whose members are known to God. In this section of Matthew, He sets forth certain distinctive aspects of this Church. The foundation of this Church is the heartfelt conviction that Jesus is the Christ. The fact that He refers to "my church" indicates that it belongs to Him. He is referring to a fellowship that is committed to Him. Furthermore, it is originated not by flesh and blood but by the Father Himself who takes the responsibility for bringing people to Himself. We are assured also that this Church will be triumphant, for "the gates of hell shall not prevail against it."

However there is a price to pay by each person who wants to belong to this Church. Jesus said, "If any man will come after me, let him deny himself and take up his cross, and follow me." This is the cost of membership. Even as Jesus Christ predicted His own suffering and death, He said that the candidate for membership in the Body of Christ must be willing to suffer and die.

Yet the function of the Church in the whole plan of salvation is so glorious that it is a most wonderful privilege to belong to it and to share in it. The Church is the means of evangelism for the whole world. What the Church does by way of making the Gospel known is significant. Souls that are won to Christ by the witness of the Church are set free by Him throughout all eternity; souls that are not won but continue in their sinful living by themselves will be left in everlasting bondage.

A Lesson From Leaven

The Pharisees also with the Sadducees came, and tempting desired him that he would shew them a sign from heaven. He answered and said unto them, When it is evening, ye say, It will be fair weather: for the sky is red. And in the morning, It will be foul weather to day: for the sky is red and lowring. O ye hypocrites, ye can discern the face of the sky; but can ye not discern the signs of the times? A wicked and adulterous generation seeketh after a sign; and there shall no sign be given unto it, but the sign of the prophet Jonas. And he left them, and departed. And when his disciples were come to the other side, they had forgotten to take bread. Then Jesus said unto them, Take heed and beware of the leaven of the Pharisees and of the Sadducees. And they reasoned among themselves, saying, It is because we have taken no bread. Which when Jesus perceived, he said unto them, O ye of little faith, why reason ye among yourselves, because ye have brought no bread? Do ye not yet understand, neither remember the five loaves of the five thousand, and how many baskets ye took up? Neither the seven loaves of the four thousand, and how many baskets ye took up? How is it that ye do not understand that 1 spake it not to you concerning bread, that ye should beware of the leaven of the Pharisees and of the Sadducees? Then understood they how that he bade them not beware of the leaven of bread, but of the doctrine of the Pharisees and of the Sadducees (Matthew 16:1-12).

The Pharisees delighted in emphasizing Scripture and tried to do exactly what the law required. Of course, the minute they had fulfilled the letter of the law, they stopped. The Sadducees, on the other hand, claimed all the benefits and blessings promised in Scripture, but doubted the reality of the supernatural even as recorded in the Scriptures.

Both the Pharisees and Sadducees came to test Jesus about giving a sign. It was another of their attempts to snare Him, to get Him to say something they could use against Him.

Jesus remarked to them that they could read the signs of the weather, but not the signs of the times. Since they had known the promises of the Old Testament, they should have been able to recognize Jesus Christ.

My father-in-law had been reared in the Jewish faith and was in training to be a rabbi. Although forbidden to do so, he was reading the New Testament to see what Christians believed and he noticed the description of Jesus of Nazareth. He wondered, "If Messiah were to come, how would he be different from Jesus of Nazareth?" Then as he read the New Testament account of Jesus, he realized, "That is exactly what Messiah would look like."

The Pharisees and Sadducees could have realized that too. Certainly, if they had been seeking the truth sincerely, they would have recognized that Jesus bore all the marks of the Messiah. But they did not really want to understand the truth. Because of this, Jesus left them and departed.

When they reached the other side of the lake, Jesus told His disciples to "beware of the leaven of the Pharisees and of the Sadducees." It took a while for the disciples to understand what

Jesus was saying, but finally they saw that He was not talking about actual bread, but of the doctrine of the Pharisees and Sadducees.

Here is a warning for us to take to heart. If we want to understand the life that is lived in Christ, we must be careful about two things:

1) Watch out for the legalistic frame of mind of the Pharisees, in which we think that by keeping regulations we are fulfilling God's will. Actually it is by yielding to the indwelling Holy Spirit of God that we become acceptable in God's sight. When Abraham believed God, it was counted to him for righteousness. This was not a mental assent, but an inward attitude. He committed himself to follow God wherever God directed. In response to the call of God Abraham went out, "not knowing whither he went." He went out by faith.

We should never reduce Christianity to certain Christian duties. Going to church, tithing, praying are important, but the legalistic attitude, wherein we over-stress regulation-keeping, kills off a deep spiritual relationship with God. Soon you would become a person who lives by the rules, rather than by the Spirit. As you don't do this, you don't do that, you become proud of your conduct, you become critical of others, selfish and vain.

2) The other danger is the leaven of the Sadducees. There are many Christians who try to explain everything in the Bible from a natural point of view. They take the supernatural Gospel and transform it into a human idea. They take what only God can do and transform it into something that any man could do. They do away with miracles, demons and angels, because they will not accept anything beyond what is to be known in this world.

Both the leaven of the Pharisees and the leaven of the Sadducees are dangerous. We need to be especially careful because these two misleading tendencies are so liable to appear in the thinking and the teaching of men who try to interpret the Gospel. The Lord Jesus warned His disciples to beware of both.

The Confession of the Church

When Jesus came into the coasts of Caesarea Philippi, he asked his disciples, saying, Whom do men say that I the Son of man am? And they said, Some say that thou art John the Baptist: some, Elias; and others, Jeremias, or one of the prophets. He saith unto them, But whom say ye that I am? And Simon Peter answered and said, Thou art the Christ, the Son of the living God (Matthew 16:13-16).

Here is the very center of Matthew's gospel. The Lord Jesus finally asked, "Whom do men say that I the Son of man am?" He did not ask, "What do people think about My philosophy? What do people say about My ethics? How will people support My program?" No, He asked, "Whom do men say that *I* the Son of man *am?*"

The Lord Jesus was concerned about what people thought about Him. What you think of Christ determines how you respond toward Him. You may believe that men are saved by faith in Christ, yet you will need to say, *"Who* is Christ?" If He is the Son of God to you, then God is working in you; but if He is only a man, you cannot expect divine help.

Some people thought that Jesus was John the Baptist returned from the dead. They were in accord with Herod's idea that Jesus of Nazareth was John the Baptist raised from the dead. John the Baptist was such a powerful preacher that all Jerusalem and Judaea went to hear him. Now the Lord Jesus was preaching and the fact that He was likened to John the Baptist indicates that He too must have been a preacher of great power.

Some said that He was Elias, the Greek name for Elijah, since the Bible promised that Elijah was to return before the coming of the Messiah. It is still customary for Jews to set an extra plate at their tables for Elijah on certain occasions, so that if he were to come he would have a place.

Others said He was Jeremias (Jeremiah). Jeremiah too was a great preacher. It was his lot to preach at a time when the city was dying and would soon be destroyed by Nebuchadnezzar. Those who compared Jesus with Jeremiah probably felt that in Christ's preaching there was a certain urgency, a certain note of warning telling people of the results of their sin.

But of course Jesus was none of these. When you try to place the Lord Jesus Christ, and you ask yourself, "Who is He?" never put His name in a list, not even at the top of the list. He does not belong in any list of men. These people all saw Jesus as a man, a good man, a great man, but nevertheless only a man. But Jesus was not only greater than all, He was also different from all. Of no other man could you say that He was God and man at the same time.

Then He turned to His disciples and asked, "But whom say ye that I am?" And Simon Peter gave expression to what we call *The Great Confession,* "Thou art the Christ, the Son of the living God." When Peter said, "Thou art the Christ," he meant that Jesus was fulfilling all the Old Testament predictions about the Messiah who would come and deliver God's people.

In the Garden of Eden God told Eve that the seed of the

woman would crush the serpent, and the serpent would bruise his heel. Moses prophesied, "There will come after me a prophet like unto myself, and he shall come up from among you. Hear him." To David the promise was given that one of his seed would sit on the throne forever. To Abraham the promise was given, "In thy seed all the nations of the earth shall be blessed." All these were taken to refer to the promised Messiah who should come to save the people of God.

These are the prophecies which Peter probably had in mind when he said, "Thou art the Christ." It is possible many of the disciples had wondered about these things for a long time; they may have discussed them together, and yet they apparently had never been absolutely convinced. But now when the Lord Jesus confronted them with this question, Peter's famous reply came forth, "Thou art the Christ, the Son of the living God." We may well understand that He spoke out what was the common conviction of the whole company of the apostles.

The Foundation of the Church

And Jesus answered and said unto him, Blessed art thou, Simon Barjona: for flesh and blood hath not revealed it unto thee, but my Father which is in heaven. And I say also unto thee, That thou art Peter, and upon this rock I will build my church: and the gates of hell shall not prevail against it. And I will give unto thee the keys of the kingdom of heaven: and whatsoever thou shalt bind on earth shall be bound in heaven: and whatsoever thou shalt loose on earth shall be loosed in heaven. Then charged he his disciples that they should tell no man that he was Jesus the Christ (Matthew 16:17-20).

After Peter's Great Confession comes this remarkable declaration of what the Lord Jesus will do to set up His Church. Jesus first blessed Peter and then said, "Flesh and blood hath not revealed it unto thee."

Human thinking, reasoning or argument can never bring to the heart of man a conviction that Jesus is the Christ, the Son of the living God. Man cannot really believe it until God Himself gives him the faith to believe. And God is willing to give to any soul faith to believe in the same way you received life when you were born. Where does a baby's life come from? It comes from God. Just as God gives life to the human body, so He gives life to the human soul. In other words, if you want to believe in the Lord Jesus Christ, God will give you faith to do so.

I once attended a students' convention in Chicago. One of the speakers gave several reasons for believing that Jesus Christ was the Son of God. His reasons were all good, but they were all flesh and blood reasons – observations of history, investigations of literature, impressions from the original languages, corroborations of archeology. Although God may use such human arguments to clear away intellectual difficulties one or another may have, the actual matter of faith is something that an individual can receive only from God. That speaker did not really believe in Jesus Christ because of those reasons. If he believed, it was because God enabled him to do so.

Jesus said to Peter, "And I say also unto thee, That thou art Peter, and upon this rock I will build my church." Originally Peter's name was Simon, which comes from an ancient word meaning "sand." But Jesus gave him the name of Peter, "petros," meaning "rock." The sand of the old Simon becomes the rock of the new Peter. This is the reverse of the natural order. In nature, rock is ground down into sand. But God by His regenerating power can turn sand into a rock. Because Jesus said, "Thou art Peter, and upon this rock I will build my church," some people think that Peter is the rock on which the church is built.

What then does it actually mean? In the Sermon on the Mount, do you remember the man who built his house on sand, and the man who built his house upon rock? "Upon this *rock*" or "on this *foundation*" Christ will build His Church. What foundation is this? Is it not the heartfelt conviction that Jesus is the Christ? This is the foundation of the Church. This is the basis for all true spiritual experience. Even to this day this is the one essential conviction necessary in becoming a Christian.

"The gates of hell" is a phrase that seems to have several possible true meanings. "Gates" in any city in that day were the signs of the city's military strength. You could say therefore that souls will not be kept under the power of Satan. The gates of hell would be like the gates of a prison in which men's souls are bound by Satan. Here Jesus promised that the power of the Church will deliver these souls. This phrase also may indicate that as the Church goes throughout the world, seeking to win people to God, the gates of hell shall not stand in its way. Jesus will deliver anyone who has this rock foundation of belief that He is the Christ, the Son of the living God.

"I will give unto thee the keys of the kingdom of heaven." In other words, Christ Jesus will empower the Church to open the door for people to come in. This is true of the Church as the whole company of all Christians, but also it is true of each member of the Church individually. You can open the kingdom of heaven to your friends and neighbors. As you witness and testify, those who respond to the message of the Gospel will be received both on earth and in heaven. By sharing with other people what you know and believe about Jesus Christ, you may be the very one who opens the door into eternal life for other human beings.

THE CONSECRATION OF THE CHURCH

From that time forth began Jesus to shew unto his disciples, how that he must go unto Jerusalem, and suffer many things of the elders and chief priests and scribes, and be killed, and be raised again the third day. Then Peter took him, and began to rebuke him, saying, Be it far from thee, Lord: this shall not be unto thee. But he turned, and said unto Peter, Get thee behind me, Satan: thou art an offence unto me: for thou savourest not the things that be of God, but those that be of men. Then said Jesus unto his disciples, If any man will come after me, let him deny himself and take up his cross, and follow me. For whosoever will save his life shall lose it: and whosoever will lose his life for my sake shall find it. For what is a man profited, if he shall gain the whole world and lose his own soul? or what shall a man give in exchange for his soul? For the Son of man shall come in the glory of his Father with his angels; and then he shall reward every man according to his works. Verily I say unto you, There be some standing here, which shall not taste of death, till they see the Son of man coming in his kingdom (Matthew 16:21-28).

The death of Jesus Christ was not an unfortunate accident, nor the inevitable result of the opposition of wickedness against the Gospel. The death of Jesus Christ was according to God's eternal plan of salvation, a plan that was formulated before the foundations of the world.

However, early in His ministry Jesus did not talk much of future suffering and death. No doubt He knew that His disciples were not ready as yet to accept such teaching. But now the time had come to prepare them for His death. After Peter had made his grand declaration, the right time had come to begin teaching the disciples what would happen on Calvary's cross.

After telling His disciples that He must die, Jesus was rebuked by Peter. The rebuke no doubt was meant kindly, for Peter was speaking as a friend. He said in so many words, "Don't let this happen to you. You don't have to stand for that." But Jesus turned to Peter and said, "Get thee behind me, Satan: thou art an offence unto me: for thou savourest not the things that be of God, but those that be of men."

This word "offence" indicates "You are a stumbling-block to me; you are a hindrance." Why? Because "thou savourest not the things that be of God, but those that be of men." That Old English word "savourest" really means "taste." In other words, "the flavor you have is not the flavor of God, but that of man. You are not thinking like God, but like man."

You see, Peter was saying, "Save yourself." Self-preservation is the first law of nature. But it is not the first law of the kingdom of God. The one thing that the Lord Jesus Christ would not do, indeed that He could not do, was to save Himself.

Then Jesus said, "If any man will come after me, let him deny himself, take up his cross, and follow me." Denying himself means that he is not going to do what he wants to do. He is not going to do his own will. Many people speak about crosses as if they were burdens. Any one of them might say, "I've got a certain man working with me in my office and he is one of my crosses." Another might have a physical disability, and he might say, "This is the cross I have to bear." But such things aren't crosses, they are burdens. To take up your cross means to deny yourself unto death. If any man wants to come after Jesus Christ, he must first of all deny his own ego, and then he must accept the program of God which calls for self-crucifixion.

"For whosoever will save his life shall lose it: and whosoever will lose his life for my sake shall find it." The purpose of losing your life is not so that Christ's work may advance, but rather that you may gain Christ. Any man who will lay down his life in order to gain Christ will find it again.

From the natural point of view this primary Christian procedure of total surrender of the self unto death is drastic, and shrinking back from such a procedure is easy to understand. Satan could certainly tempt any one of us to save ourselves from such complete committal to the will of God. But the response of the Lord Jesus is the pattern for us to follow. Enabled by His grace we are led by His Spirit to just this very action. "If any man will be my disciple let him deny himself, take up his cross, and follow me." This is the true consecration of ourselves into which we are called by our Lord Jesus Christ Himself.

THE GLORY OF THE MASTER

And after six days Jesus taketh Peter, James, and John his brother, and bringeth them up into an high mountain apart, And was transfigured before them: and his face did shine as the sun, and his raiment was white as the light. And, behold, there appeared unto them Moses and Elias talking with him. Then answered Peter, and said unto Jesus, Lord, it is good for us to be here: if thou wilt, let us make here three tabernacles; one for thee, and one for Moses, and one for Elias. While he yet spake, behold, a bright cloud overshadowed them: and behold a voice out of the cloud, which said, This is my beloved Son, in whom I am well pleased; hear ye him. And when the disciples heard it, they fell on their face, and were sore afraid. And Jesus came and touched them, and said, Arise, and be not afraid. And when they had lifted up their eyes, they saw no man, save Jesus only. And as they came down from the mountain, Jesus charged them, saying, Tell the vision to no man, until the Son of man be risen again from the dead. And his disciples asked him, saying, Why then say the scribes that Elias must first come? And Jesus answered and said unto them, Elias truly shall first come, and restore all things. But I say unto you, That Elias is come already, and they knew him not, but have done unto him whatsoever they listed. Likewise shall also the Son of man suffer of them. Then the disciples understood that he spake unto them of John the Baptist (Matthew 17:1-13).

The Lord Jesus has been stressing that He is going to build His church on the foundation of a heartfelt conviction that Jesus is the Christ. This will mean that He must die and must be raised from the dead. Any who would follow Him must also be willing to die in themselves, in order that they also might be raised in the Lord to live in Him. This is the cost of belonging to Him.

Though the cost of discipleship as pointed out above may seem high, it is worth it, because our Leader is no mere man, but the Son of God. Jesus had already said that "the Son of man shall come in the glory of his Father with his angels; and then he shall reward every man according to his works." This was an encouragement to those who would give up this world to gain another world. This was a promise of assurance that if you yield yourself to God and give up this world, it will not be in vain. You will be exchanging the glory of this world for the glory of God. What this means can be seen in this passage of Scripture.

The Lord Jesus had said, "Verily I say unto you, There be some standing here, which shall not taste of death, till they see the Son of man coming in his kingdom." I personally used to think this meant that He was predicting that some of His disciples would not die until the end of the world. But when I read the end of the 16th chapter with the beginning of the 17th chapter, it all becomes quite clear to me. As the 17th chapter begins, Jesus takes three disciples up a high mountain to be witnesses of His glory. Peter, James and John were the three men who did not taste death until they had seen the Son of man coming in His kingdom.

High atop a mountain, Peter, James and John saw Jesus in a way they had never seen Him before. He was glorious. His face and His clothes were beaming rays of light. Then suddenly Elijah and Moses were there talking with Him in His glory. Elsewhere we are told that they talked with Him about His coming death on the cross. Apparently they knew about Calvary and wondered about it. All heaven was aware of the fact that Jesus of Nazareth was the Son of God, and that He would soon give His life for sinful man.

Moses was the law-giver; Elijah was perhaps the greatest of the prophets. When the time came for Moses to die, he was taken up to Mount Nebo by God, and no man ever found his grave. Elijah, you will remember, rode up to heaven in a fiery chariot. In any case, these two Old Testament characters were on the Mount of Transfiguration talking with Jesus Christ. This was not any hallucination; they were actually there.

When Peter suggested that three tabernacles be built, one each for Moses, Elijah and Jesus, a voice from heaven said, "This is my beloved Son, in whom I am well pleased: hear ye him." At the sound of this voice, they fell on their faces, each indicating, "I am not worthy to look on these things."

Afterward, Jesus told them not to tell what had happened until after the Resurrection. It would be only then that people would be able to grasp the significance of this strange occurrence on the top of the Mount of Transfiguration.

As they returned, one of the disciples asked Jesus about the return of Elijah who, according to the prophet Malachi, was supposed to return before the Messiah came. Jesus then identified John the Baptist as Elijah, thereby intimating that what they had seen was another evidence of His identity: He really was the Christ promised in the Old Testament Scriptures.

It should give us all pause to think that as members of His Church we should be aware that even while He was here on earth as Jesus of Nazareth He was really the Son of God all the time. And He had come from glory to die for us that we might be brought into fellowship with God in all power and glory.

FAITH TO SERVE

And when they were come to the multitude, there came to him a certain man, kneeling down to him, and saying, Lord, have mercy on my son: for he is lunatick, and sore vexed: for ofttimes he falleth into the fire, and oft into the water. And I brought him to thy disciples, and they could not cure him. Then Jesus answered and said, O faithless and perverse generation, how long shall I be with you? how long shall I suffer you? bring him hither to me. And Jesus rebuked the devil; and he departed out of him: and the child was cured from that very hour. Then came the disciples to Jesus apart, and said, Why could not we cast him out? And Jesus said unto them, Because of your unbelief: for verily I say unto you, If ye have faith as a grain of mustard seed, ye shall say unto this mountain, Remove hence to yonder place;

and it shall remove; and nothing shall be impossible unto you.
Howbeit this kind goeth not out but by prayer and fasting (Matthew 17:14-21).

From the Mount of Transfiguration where they had seen Him
in His glory and had watched with awe, the disciples, Peter, James
and John, had come down with the Lord Jesus to be among men.
Those who worship Him in His glory can turn to serve others
with power.

Apparently, while Jesus and the three disciples were on the
mountain top, the remaining nine disciples were asked by a father
to heal his boy. But they could not. When the father told Jesus
of his disappointment, the Lord rebuked His disciples, "O faithless
and perverse generation, how long shall I be with you?" In
this comment He was saying they were operating without faith
and in what they had done they were going about their service in
the wrong way. It was as if He had said, "Will you never learn?"

What were they to learn? What had they missed? We get
some idea of this when Jesus says, "Bring him hither to me." In
that simple command may be the clue to the whole matter. Had
the disciples tried to heal this boy in their own strength? They
could have known where there was power available. Did they
think they had it in themselves? Had they forgotten that power
belongs to God and was available to them through Jesus their
Lord?

Faith is not something we can have in a tube that we can
squeeze out at will like toothpaste. Nor is it something that we
have in a shaker that we can shake out like salt. We don't walk
around with a big reservoir of faith in us. Faith is our response
to the living God. It is our yielding ourselves into the hand of
the Lord that He may work through us. Faith always involves
commitment to God. Though we may know that God has done
things for us in times past, it is quite possible for us now to undertake
something on our own. We may not now be exercising
faith in the Lord. We may be trying to do something for Him in
our own strength and we will find that nothing will happen of
any spiritual significance.

"Bring him hither to me." Should not this be the aim of every
service we conduct? Is not this what we should do every time we
speak in His name? Parents will bring their children to Sunday
school; families will send their young people to church; friends
will bring a loved one to an evangelistic service. What are they
looking for? What are they expecting? Are they not hoping that
something will happen in the life of this loved one? Perhaps they
have prayed for months and have spent much time preparing the
way for this one visit to church. Now when they bring this one to

church, what happens? Do the leaders in the church bring him to the Lord? Remember what the Lord Jesus said to the disciples, "Bring him hither to me." Is it possible that in our church activity we do not bring people to the Lord? Is this the reason for so much futility in Sunday school? Is this why more does not happen in your Sunday school classes? Are we trying to teach them in our own wisdom? In the Sunday worship services are we seeking to bring those who attend into the presence of the Lord? As far as our church work is concerned, are we organizing the church to accomplish what we can do, or are we seeking together to find out what the Lord would have done and to do what the Lord wants us to do? Would this be the reason why people come to our services and go home unchanged? Is it because we have not brought them to the Lord?

This incident should make it very clear to all Christians that power to do things belongs to the Lord Himself. It is for us as believers to remember this and to serve by bringing the needy to the Lord. On our part this is a matter of confidence in Him, and we exercise our faith by bringing those who come to us for help into direct relation with the living Lord, to whom alone has been given "all power in heaven and on earth."

PAYING TRIBUTE

And while they abode in Galilee, Jesus said unto them, The Son of man shall be betrayed into the hands of men: And they shall kill him, and the third day he shall be raised again. And they were exceeding sorry. And when they were come to Capernaum, they that received tribute money came to Peter, and said, Doth not your master pay tribute? He saith, Yes. And when he was come into the house, Jesus prevented him, saying, What thinkest thou, Simon? of whom do the kings of the earth take custom or tribute? of their own children, or of strangers? Peter saith unto him, Of strangers. Jesus saith unto him, Then are the children free. Notwithstanding, lest we should offend them, go thou to the sea, and cast an hook, and take up the fish that first cometh up; and when thou hast opened his mouth, thou shalt find a piece of money: that take, and give unto them for me and thee (Matthew 17:22-27).

In the first part of this chapter we saw the Lord Jesus in His glory on the Mount of Transfiguration. Certainly no man was ever like that. Then we beheld the Lord Jesus healing the afflicted son even after His disciples had failed. But now we are brought abruptly to this: He is to be betrayed. We are reminded at once that what happens in this world is not all of one piece. Events happen in a mixture and a conglomeration. Sometimes what happens is good, sometimes wonderful; sometimes what happens is bad, sometimes awful; and all in the same day. Even in the life of Jesus there were days like this, mixed with glory and grief, heights and depths. On the same day that He was transfigured in glory, powerful in service, He was aware of betrayal!

And now we are to see that He paid tribute money to the Roman government just as any other Jewish citizen. This was what you might call a head tax. Each person had to pay a certain amount to the government each year.

When Peter went to get the money to pay this tax, Jesus stopped him to talk to him about it. In a few words He set before Peter the relationship of the godly man to his earthly government.

Human government, strictly speaking, would be without jurisdiction over the spiritual man. It cannot control your spirit, so you might logically claim that it has no power over you. But the Lord Jesus taught a principle here that we should never forget. Simply put in four words it is, "Lest we offend them." The world would not understand our announcing to them that we do not belong to them. We would offend them (cause them to stumble) if we did not obey their orders as all citizens are expected to do.

Following this example of the Lord, the Christian principle would be "lest we offend them, we will do what they require us to do." This is profound. It means that in your community you will work along with your neighbors and fellow citizens. When community projects are presented, we will do our part. It could be argued by a Christian, "I am just a stranger here; heaven is my home. I don't want any part of this world." Such a view might cause you to feel you don't need to vote, or to pay attention to the Community Chest drive or to give to the Red Cross. You may feel further you don't have to concern yourself about juvenile delinquency or the social problems in your community. But these words of Jesus should remind you: "Give unto Caesar that which is Caesar's."

In the remarkable incident which followed in which Peter was told to catch a fish in whose mouth would be the Roman government's tribute money, there is another truth you might easily overlook. It is this: God providentially will provide what it will take to pay the tribute. If you need to give some time to the problems of the local community, the Lord will give you time. Give what those in the leadership ask you to give. Don't worry, the Lord has given you everything you have and He can supply all your needs in the future. Fulfill all requirements by His help. Sometimes you may feel reluctant to give money to public needs because the money may be used for various activities of which you do not approve. Do not assume responsibility for what others do. Your responsibility is to do your part. If you should be given an opportunity to serve in leadership, take it. Do whatever needs to be done, as the demands come to you as a citizen in the community. Your humble fulfillment of every local responsibility will adorn the Gospel you profess.

Chapter 14

CHARACTERISTICS OF THE CHRISTIAN

The Greatness of Humility

In this section of the gospel of Matthew Jesus holds up the virtue of humility as the outstanding characteristic of the member of the true church. We can understand how the world would be puzzled as to why the Son of God, who has the enormous power of creation in His hand, would submit Himself to the devices of wicked men and allow them to kill Him. Yet this is what He prophesied would happen. And it did. In this Jesus was demonstrating His great humility.

And again it is astonishing to see that after saying that He would willingly suffer and die, the King of kings and Lord of all paid a simple, ordinary tax to the Roman government that anyone would pay. He made Himself to be subject to men and their laws, as if He were no more than anyone else.

In Matthew 18 Jesus was asked, "Who is the greatest in the kingdom of heaven?" In reply, He took a little child and set him in the midst of the disciples. Then He said, "Except ye . . . become as little children, ye shall not enter into the kingdom of heaven."

Little children have certainly not attained success in life; they have no measure of greatness. They have neither fame nor fortune; they have no backlog of good works nor record of philanthropic giving. They are only children, sincere, genuine and completely dependent. They look to others for everything they need. And that is the way the followers of the Lord are to be – sincere, genuine and completely dependent. They won't claim that they know, they won't claim that they have, they won't claim that they can do. Instead they will turn to Him trusting in Him for help.

In Matthew 18:6-10 we find the stern warning that none should dare to harm these little ones. In giving this warning the Lord gives also the assurance "that in heaven their angels do always behold the face of my Father which is in heaven."

It is interesting to note that wherever humility is set forth as the characteristic of the kingdom, there is both this warning against hurting such little ones and this assurance that God Himself provides angelic messengers and protectors to take care of them. It is true that believers are to be humble, but they can be assured they will not be left unguarded. Each believer has One who is watching over him, who will take care of him.

Later in chapter 18 the humility of the Christian is further emphasized in his readiness to forgive others who do him wrong. When anything occurs to alienate brethren from each other, the Christian is concerned. The Lord instructs him how to do all he can to heal such a rift. Then comes the need to forgive others. In order to forgive, one must forsake the idea of retaliation. If others have harmed you and you act to retaliate, matters will only get worse. But if you forgive, you will release them from the obligation to make good the harm they have done, and you yourself will be given peace. This will actually make it possible for the group as a whole to be together in love. In this fellowship the presence of the Lord can be a blessing to all.

As a Little Child

At the same time came the disciples unto Jesus, saying, Who is the greatest in the kingdom of heaven? And Jesus called a little child unto him, and set him in the midst of them, And said, Verily I say unto you, Except ye be converted, and become as little children, ye shall not enter into the kingdom of heaven. Whosoever therefore shall humble himself as this little child, the same is greatest in the kingdom of heaven. And whoso shall receive one such little child in my name receiveth me. But whoso shall offend one of these little ones which believe in me, it were better for him that a millstone were hanged about his neck, and that he were drowned in the depth of the sea. Woe unto the world because of offences! for it must needs be that offences come; but woe to that man by whom the offence cometh! Wherefore if thy hand or thy foot offend thee, cut them off, and cast them from thee: it is better for thee to enter into life halt or maimed, rather than having two hands or two feet to be cast into everlasting fire. And if thine eye offend thee, pluck it out, and cast it from thee: it is better for thee to enter into life with one eye, rather than having two eyes to be cast into hell fire (Matthew 18:1-9).

What is really most important in Christian living?

"And Jesus called a little child unto him, and set him in the midst of them." It would appear from this incident that in the beginning as you come to know the Lord He does not tell you to go and do things. What He says is simply this: "Come and yield to me." He isn't telling you, "I want you to *do*." He is telling you, "I want you to *come*." It turns out that after you come to Him and He works in you, He will work through you to accomplish His purposes.

The expression, "a little child," refers to a nursling, a little child who is still nursing. In those days it would probably be a child not more than four years old, probably two or three. With this little child in front of them all, Jesus said, "Verily I say unto you, except ye be converted, and become as little children." When we use the word "converted," we usually refer to a man's salvation experience with God. But here the word refers more simply to the disciples' attitude. "Converted" means turned around, "changed." The attitude of the disciples about greatness had to be turned around. The natural mind will see things one way, but the spiritual mind will see things differently, in God's way.

What was the Lord Jesus actually saying? What would a little child of two or three be like?

For one thing, a young child would look to his parents for anything he needed. He wouldn't worry about providing for himself. He wouldn't go into the kitchen to prepare his own meal. He would go to his mother and say, "I'm hungry." A little child goes to his parents expecting them to do something for him. Such a child is totally dependent. Anyone who takes such an attitude toward God, an attitude of total dependence upon Him, will be great in the kingdom of heaven.

There is another remarkable truth revealed here. They asked, "Who is the greatest?" and He replied by talking about entering the kingdom. The truth seems to be that the very attitude that brings you into the kingdom is the same attitude which would make you great in it. As you start out by believing in the Lord Jesus Christ and trusting humbly in Him, this is exactly what you must continue to do.

The Lord went on to say, "Whoso shall receive one such little child in my name, receiveth me." Our attitude toward any young convert is our attitude toward the Lord Himself. In this way the Lord Jesus identified Himself with those who humbly, simply trust in Him. Just as anyone who would harm one of your own family is harming you, so anyone who would harm one of God's spiritual children is doing an injury to God.

In this connection the Lord gave stern warning. "Whoso shall offend one of these little ones which believe in me, it were better for him that a millstone were hanged about his neck, and that he were drowned in the depth of the sea." The word "offend" means "cause them to stumble." This seems to say plainly that if by any chance anyone cause one such little, new convert, who has a disposition and attitude like a little child, to stumble and stray spiritually, God will hold that man personally responsible. The Lord Himself is watching over His young followers and He will take drastic action against anyone who will mislead them or cause them any harm.

SETTLING ARGUMENTS

Take heed that ye despise not one of these little ones; for I say unto you, That in heaven their angels do always behold the face of my Father which is in heaven. For the Son of man is come to save that which was lost. How think ye? if a man have an hundred sheep, and one of them be gone astray, doth he not leave the ninety and nine, and goeth into the mountains, and seeketh that which is gone astray? And if so be that he find it, verily I say unto you, he rejoiceth more of that sheep, than of the ninety and nine which went not astray. Even so it is not the will of your Father which is in heaven, that one of these little ones should perish. Moreover if thy brother shall trespass against thee, go and tell him his fault between thee and him alone: if he shall hear thee, thou hast gained thy brother. But if he will not hear thee, then take with thee one or two more, that in the mouth of two or three witnesses every word may be established. And if he shall neglect to hear them, tell it unto the church: but if he neglect to hear the church, let him be unto thee as an heathen man and a publican. Verily I say unto you, Whatsoever ye shall bind on earth shall be bound in heaven; and whatsoever ye shall loose on earth shall be loosed in heaven. Again I say unto you, That if two of you shall agree on earth as touching any thing that they shall ask, it shall be done for them of my Father which is in heaven. For where two or three are gathered in my name, there am I in the midst of them (Matthew 18:10-20).

Recently I was asked about guardian angels. Do they exist? I believe they do. In the Bible angels appear in various forms, but they are always servants of the Lord. I don't know whether I should say there is one angel for each Christian, but I do know from this passage of Scripture that God Himself has His messengers watching and taking care of those who trust in Him.

Let me repeat, the Lord has a special interest in young Christians. This is why His warning is so stern toward those who might mislead them or otherwise harm them. As Jesus told the parable of the lost sheep, He said, "Even so it is not the will of your Father which is in heaven, that one of these little ones should perish." "The little one" in this parable points directly toward any member of the family of God. Even as Christ is concerned for the welfare of any who believe, so we should have a similar concern.

In our society, if a two- or three-year-old child wanders away from home and is lost, everyone in the community comes out to search the area until the lost child is found. We should have the same spiritual concern for those who may have strayed spiritually.

Sometimes we think that wandering away means a person has become involved in the things of the world. Such may not always be the case. In this passage Jesus speaks of those who stay within the church fellowship, and yet cause real trouble.

The Lord says, "Moreover if thy brother shall trespass against thee, go and tell him his fault between thee and him alone: if he shall hear thee, thou hast gained thy brother." This says quite plainly that if someone has wronged you, you are to take the initiative to try to smooth it out. If you can't work out the problem in dealing with that person directly, you are to bring some friends along and ask their help in seeking reconciliation. If that doesn't work, you are to explain it to the church. In other words, you are to ask them to share your concern that this alienation between you and your brother might be removed. "But if he neglect to hear the church, let him be unto thee as a heathen man and a publican." A heathen man is one with no relation to our Lord; a publican is one who is given over to wrong conduct. How would you act toward heathen and publicans? Would you go out and chase them with a shotgun? No, you would not. You would not hurt them in any way. But neither would you try to live with them in Christian fellowship.

"Again I say unto you, That if two of you shall agree on earth as touching any thing that they shall ask, it shall be done for them of my Father which is in heaven." Do you see what that implies? If Tom and Dick meet as believing brethren for prayer, Tom brings his prayer requests and Dick brings his. Some of Tom's prayer interests are not shared by Dick and some of Dick's are not shared by Tom. When Tom omits what Dick doesn't share, and Dick omits what Tom does not share, the chances are that Tom and Dick can get together and pray for what is really in God's will. United prayer is a great blessing, as two or more fellowshiping Christians approach the Lord together in "the tie that binds our hearts in Christian love."

Forgiving Always

Then came Peter to him, and said, Lord, how oft shall my brother sin against me, and I forgive him? till seven times? Jesus saith unto him, I say not unto thee, Until seven times: but, Until seventy times seven. Therefore is the kingdom of heaven likened unto a certain king, which would take account of his servants. And when he had begun to reckon, one was brought unto him, which owed him ten thousand talents. But forasmuch as he had not to pay, his lord commanded him to be sold, and his wife, and children, and all that he had, and payment to be made. The servant therefore fell down, and worshipped him, saying, Lord, have patience with me, and I will pay thee all. Then the lord of that servant was moved with compassion, and loosed him, and forgave him the debt. But the same servant went out, and found one of his fellowservants, which owed him an hundred pence: and he laid hands on him, and took him by the throat, saying, Pay me that thou owest. And his fellowservant fell down at his feet, and besought him, saying, Have patience with me, and I will pay thee all. And he would not: but went and cast him into prison, till he should pay the debt. So when his fellowservants saw what was done, they were very sorry, and came and told unto their lord all that was done. Then his lord, after that he had called him, said unto him, O thou wicked servant, I forgave thee all that debt, because thou desiredst me: Shouldest not thou also have had compassion on thy fellowservant, even as I had pity on thee? And his lord was wroth, and delivered him to the tormentors, till he should pay all that was due unto him. So likewise shall my heavenly Father do also unto you, if ye from your hearts forgive not every one his brother their trespasses (Matthew 18:21-35).

Often when the number seven is used in Scripture, it seems to imply the total amount of what is involved. So when the law says that you should forgive a man seven times, it probably means you should forgive him altogether. But Peter wanted to be sure. He asked the Lord how far one should apply this principle.

The Lord Jesus answered Peter, "I say not unto thee, Until seven times: but, Until seventy times seven." A person might be able to remember seven times, but no one could remember seventy times seven or 490 times. By the time you had forgiven a person 490 times, you might as well say that you would always forgive him. In this way Jesus was saying that a godly man should practice forgiveness all the time.

Then the Lord Jesus told a parable to emphasize this matter of forgiveness. Talents and pence are pieces of money that we may not know much about, but we can be sure that when one owed 10,000 talents, and the other owed 100 pence, it was as if you owed a man $10,000,000 and he forgave you, and someone else owed you $20 and you refused to forgive him. In this way the Lord Jesus was reminding His disciples that since God had forgiven them so much, they ought also to forgive the little owed to them by others.

It will help us to remember that to forgive does not mean to forget. It does not mean that you are going to overlook the wrong lightly. It does not mean that you will necessarily ignore it. And it certainly does not mean that you are going to approve it. If it is a real debt, then the amount is actually owed. But you are going to "forgive" it.

Then what does "forgiveness" mean? Look at the word "forgive." The main element in the word is "give." If you are going to forgive anyone, you must give them something. What are you going to give them? You are going to give them release from their obligation to make good what they owe you. Perhaps you have relatives or friends with whom there is a conflict because that person owes you something. What is the natural human reaction? The natural reaction is to withdraw from personal fellowship until you feel that person has paid up whatever he owes. If he does not pay up, you will feel that you ought to retaliate. Since he offended you, you will feel that he should somehow suffer. You will stay away from him until you feel that your withdrawal has brought him distress that would be equal to what he brought to you when he did not pay up.

But the Lord Jesus says, "Forgive." This means that you should forego that demand to be satisfied for the wrong done to you. You must not retaliate. You must not pay him back. You must let him go free. Why? Because God has let you go free. When you remember how the Lord has forgiven you, you should be able to forgive anyone. And when you thus forgive by giving up any idea of getting even, or retaliation, the fellowship of all the believers in the group can be promoted.

Chapter 15

ANSWER FOR MAN'S GREATEST PROBLEMS

MAN CAN BE CHANGED

The gospel of Matthew begins its message with my standing before God as a human being. It reveals me to be a sinner in need of repentance and shows Christ Jesus as my Saviour, promising that in Him I will receive forgiveness of sin and providing that through Him I will have reconciliation with God. The gospel continues by showing Jesus Christ as a worker of miracles. These miracles encourage me to expect that I can be saved by the grace of God and so changed that I can do the will of God.

If I have heard the Gospel and decide to turn to Jesus Christ, if I accept Jesus Christ as my Lord and Saviour and am received by God as one of His redeemed children, will anything further happen to me? Is it all over then? Or is there more to belonging to Christ and living in Him?

The answer is found in the 19th and 20th chapters of Matthew. These chapters teach that God's law doesn't change, since God never changes, but man can be changed. When I believe in the Lord Jesus Christ, I am enabled in His Spirit to want to do the will of God. As a Christian I have resources that I did not have before. I have access to the grace of God that I did not know before. I can appropriate the power of God in a way that was impossible before.

Jesus once again used children as an object lesson. Little children are welcome in the kingdom of God. Apparently God appreciates humility and dependence on Him. He wants every believer to act toward Him in the same way that little children act toward their parents.

In the incident of the Rich Young Ruler, Jesus taught that material assets are to be used to help others, rather than to be kept. By "material assets" we should understand more than money. Anything is an asset that gives you an advantage over your brother. Your assets include your abilities and opportunities for personal advantage. Your assets are what make you rich. You can be rich in money, in strength, in education, in power and in many other ways.

If you are rich in one way or another, what then should you do? Should you forsake your riches? No, Jesus taught that your riches should be used to help others. The rich young ruler was to sell what he had and give to the poor. The man who is strong should help the weak. The man who has much education should help the one who has little. Whatever your assets you should make use of them to benefit others.

After the rich man had turned away, Jesus said, "It is easier for a camel to go through the eye of a needle than for a rich man to enter into the kingdom of God." This does not mean it is impossible. It can be done, but it will be hard. The "eye of the needle" is the low, narrow side gate into a walled city. To get through, a camel would have to "humble himself" by getting down on his knees and with goods all unloaded, squeeze through the small gate into the city. Just so, a rich man *can* squeeze into the kingdom of God if he is willing to unload his goods and humble himself in order that he might come to Jesus.

Next the Lord Jesus is confronted by the mother of James and John who wanted her sons to sit alongside of Jesus in His kingdom. In response, Jesus said that they did not know what they asked for. Here is one request which Jesus did not grant. But He took the occasion to teach all the disciples about humility. "Whosoever will be great among you, let him be your minister, and whosoever will be chief among you, let him be your servant."

THE PROBLEM OF DIVORCE

And it came to pass, that when Jesus had finished these sayings, he departed from Galilee, and came into the coasts of Judea beyond Jordan; And great multitudes followed him; and he healed them there. The Pharisees also came unto him, tempting him, and saying unto him, Is it lawful for a man to put away his wife for every cause? And he answered and said unto them, Have ye not read, that he which made them at the beginning made them male and female, And said, For this cause shall a man leave father and mother, and shall cleave to his wife: and they twain shall be one flesh? Wherefore they are no more twain, but one flesh. What therefore God hath joined together, let not man put asunder. They say unto him, Why did Moses then command to give a writing of divorcement; and to put her away? He saith unto them, Moses because of the hardness of your hearts suffered you to put away your wives: but from the beginning it was not so. And I say unto you, Whosoever shall put away his wife, except it be for fornication, and shall marry another, committeth adultery: and whoso marrieth her which is put away doth commit adultery. His disciples say unto him, If the case of the man be so with his wife, it is not good to marry. But he said unto them, All men cannot receive this saying, save they to whom it is given. For there are some eunuchs, which were so born from their mother's womb: and there are some eunuchs, which were made eunuchs of men: and there be eunuchs, which have made themselves eunuchs for the kingdom of heaven's sake. He that is able to receive it, let him receive it (Matthew 19:1-12).

The Pharisees were not interested in solving the problem of divorce. They were interested in hearing how the Lord Jesus would answer their question. They knew what the Old Testament said, but because there was some confusion regarding the proper interpretation of the Old Testament on this matter, they thought they might trap Jesus into saying something that would offend someone. When they asked, "Is it lawful for a man to put away his wife for every cause?" the phrase "for every cause" meant "for any reason." The law of Moses provided that if the wife were guilty of any impurity her husband could divorce her.

In His reply, Jesus emphasized that God's plan was one man with one woman in one marriage as in the case of Adam and Eve. The Pharisees responded by asking why then did Moses give instructions for divorce. Jesus' answer indicated that while God's plan for the marriage relationship was that it should be permanent, sinful human beings sometimes caused this relationship to be broken by their conduct. If the marriage relationship had been broken and divorce seemed the only course to follow, Moses taught there was still a proper way to act and an improper way to act even in the matter of divorce.

This is like saying that the original plan was for a man to have two arms. But if a man were to lose one arm, would he be obliged to quit living? No, but living with one arm would cause his way of life to be changed drastically. No one encourages a person to cut off an arm, but there could be advice available as to how to act if such a sad circumstance were to happen.

Adultery is a case of breaking the marriage relationship in fact. If the marriage relationship is thus already broken in fact, the Scripture says one can put the other away, because this is only doing legally what has already taken place actually. But Jesus emphasized that although the law made it permissible for a man to put away his wife under certain conditions, this did not mean that God was condoning divorce. And certainly this did not mean that divorce could be granted for any reason whatever.

CHILDREN ARE IMPORTANT

Then were there brought unto him little children, that he should put his hands on them, and pray: and the disciples rebuked them. But Jesus said, Suffer little children, and forbid them not, to come unto me: for of such is the kingdom of heaven. And he laid his hands on them, and departed thence (Matthew 19:13-15).

Parents were bringing their little children to the Lord for His blessing. Once again, these little children were quite young, certainly not over four years old. The disciples apparently felt that these young children were too young to receive any benefit from the Lord Jesus. Even today many people have a similar idea. Many think that a six-, eight- or ten-year-old child is too young to consider seriously the claims of Jesus Christ upon his heart and life.

How easily we fall into the snare of thinking that the blessing of the Lord is to be earned. Since little children can't work, they can't earn and so we judge they are too young to be saved. We need to remember that men do not have to earn God's blessing; men need only to come to receive it. What Jesus came to give, even a child can receive.

Jesus said, "Let them come . . . for of such is the kingdom of heaven." Then He laid His hands on them. This does not necessarily mean that any mysterious spiritual power passed through His fingertips. Rather it seems to mean that these little children were to receive blessing from the heavenly Father in response to their faith in Jesus Christ. A parent can bless his child in much the same way. When he faithfully prays for his children, it is as if he is laying his hands upon them and dedicating them to the Lord.

How do we let little children come unto the Lord? First, we can arrange that they are in Sunday school and church every Sunday. Then when they do come, we can make sure that they hear about Jesus Christ by presenting the Gospel of Christ to them. It is up to us to show them the things of the Lord. Make no mistake, they can understand these things better than we can realize. Our responsibility is to set it before them, so that they will have the opportunity.

WHAT IS ETERNAL LIFE?

And, behold, one came and said unto him, Good Master, what good thing shall I do, that I may have eternal life? And he said unto him, Why callest thou me good? There is none good but one, that is, God: but if thou wilt enter into life, keep the commandments. He saith unto him, Which? Jesus said, Thou shalt do no murder, Thou shalt not commit adultery, Thou shalt not steal, Thou shalt not bear false witness. Honour thy father and thy mother; and, Thou shalt love thy neighbour as thyself. The young man saith unto him, All these things have I kept from my youth up: what lack I yet? Jesus said unto him, If thou wilt be perfect, go and sell that thou hast, and give to the poor, and thou shalt have treasure in heaven: and come and follow me. But when the young man heard that saying, he went away sorrowful: for he had great possessions (Matthew 19:16-22).

For a long time I thought that eternal life simply meant life that went on and on. While it does certainly mean that, its distinctive characteristic is not only its everlastingness. It is not so much a matter of duration, as it is a matter of kind. In other words, "eternal life" is the life of God, and it is to be distinguished from "life," which is the life of man. When Jesus said, "I am come that they might have life, and that they might have it more abundantly," He certainly referred to an ability to live fully and successfully while in this world. And this ability to live fully and successfully in this world would be possible because the life of God would have been made operative in man.

In your human nature, your consciousness is focused on self. You tend to be grasping. You reach out to take things to yourself. You want to get more than you have. At the same time you are fearful. You are afraid you will get hurt. You are afraid you will lose what you have. Yet consciousness is only temporary. It started when you were born and it ends when you die. Your life, so wrapped up in its own self-interest, is marked by unkindness to others. You have so much to do to look after yourself, you have no time for others. But because there is so much for you to do and so much you can't control, you become depressed. Watch the people who go by on the street. Look at their faces and notice how seldom you see a cheerful face. Most everyone seems to be downhearted and depressed. You are noticing exactly what characterizes the life of man.

Over against the life of man is the life of God, "eternal life." The life of God is not focused on self but on others. It is a life of generosity, of confidence instead of fear, and of eternity rather than of the things of time. Death will come, but even death won't interfere with your life in God. Your body may die, but your being with God won't be affected. It is also a life that is gracious. It is kind to others, because God is so kind to you. Instead of being depressed, it is buoyant. It is cheerful. Such is the life of the person who has the grace of God in his heart.

Evidently the young man had seen this "eternal life" in the Lord Jesus and had been attracted by what he saw. So he asked the question.

When the Lord Jesus said, "Why callest thou me good?" He was raising the question whether or not the young man actually recognized to whom he was speaking. Then Jesus told the young man to keep the commandments. When the young man responded that he had always kept the Ten Commandments, he meant that he had obeyed every one of them, and that in his heart and mind he had always recognized that was the right thing to do.

Jesus continued the conversation by saying, "If thou wilt be perfect [the word *perfect* in the New Testament means *mature* or *full grown*], go and sell that thou hast and give to the poor . . ." When you sell a piece of property, you transfer the ownership of it. You don't destroy it or throw it away. You turn over the ownership to someone else. Jesus was telling the young man to use what he had to help the less fortunate. ". . . and thou shalt have treasure in heaven . . . " That is a result of giving to the poor. This gives a new meaning to life. You can use your wealth to help those who are not as fortunate as you are, and you can have treasure in heaven. This is not yet eternal life, but it empties the heart so that attention can now be given to the matter of personal relation to God. It is a common principle that persons who are "rich" or "fortunate" in things of this world must set those things aside to be able to come to Christ (Philippians 3:7). The best way to set them aside is to use them in service to the poor. ". . . and come and follow me." Deny yourself and obey the will of God. Other accounts of this incident include the words "take up thy cross." Deny your own human interest, let the will of God be done in your heart. This is the way to eternal life.

The Problem of Being Rich

Then said Jesus unto his disciples, Verily I say unto you, That a rich man shall hardly enter into the kingdom of heaven. And again I say unto you, It is easier for a camel to go through the eye of a needle, than for a rich man to enter into the kingdom of God. When his disciples heard it, they were exceedingly amazed, saying, Who then can be saved? But Jesus beheld them, and said unto them, With men this is impossible; but with God all things are possible. Then answered Peter and said unto him, Behold, we have forsaken all, and followed thee; what shall we have therefore? And Jesus said unto them, Verily I say unto you, That ye which have followed me, in the regeneration when the Son of man shall sit in the throne of his glory, ye also shall sit upon twelve thrones, judging the twelve tribes of Israel. And every one that hath forsaken houses, or brethren, or sisters, or father, or mother, or wife, or children, or lands, for my name's sake, shall receive an hundredfold, and shall inherit everlasting life. But many that are first shall be last; and the last shall be first (Matthew 19:23-30).

When the Lord said that a rich man shall "hardly" enter into the kingdom of heaven, the word "hardly" does not mean it cannot be done. It just means it is difficult. He can get in, but it won't be easy. The disciples then asked, "Who then can be saved?" Who will ever be inclined to give up everything he has and humble himself in that way? Jesus answered, "With men this is impossible; but with God all things are possible." God can touch the heart.

Then Peter asked, "Behold, we have forsaken all and followed thee; what shall we have therefore?" Peter had forsaken his life as a fisherman to follow Christ. In His reply, Jesus said that those who believe in Him will reign with Him. Those who sacrifice to follow Him will receive much more than they gave up and shall in addition inherit everlasting life.

The Same Result for Everybody

For the kingdom of heaven is like unto a man that is an householder, which went out early in the morning to hire labourers into his vineyard. And when he had agreed with the labourers for a penny a day, he sent them into his vineyard. And he went out about the third hour, and saw others standing idle in the marketplace, And said unto them; Go ye also into the vineyard, and whatsoever is right I will give you. And they went their way. Again he went out about the sixth and ninth hour, and did likewise. And about the eleventh hour he went out, and found others standing idle, and saith unto them, Why stand ye here all the day idle? They say unto him, Because no man hath hired us. He saith unto them, Go ye also into the vineyard; and whatsoever is right, that shall ye receive. So when even was come, the lord of the vineyard saith unto his steward, Call the labourers, and give them their hire, beginning from the last unto the first. And when they came that were hired about the eleventh hour, they received every man a penny. But when the first came, they supposed that they should have received more; and they likewise received every man a penny. And when they had received it, they murmured against the goodman of the house, Saying, These last have wrought but one hour, and thou hast made them equal unto us, which have borne the burden and heat of the day. But he answered one of them, and said, Friend, I do thee no wrong: didst not thou agree with me for a penny? Take that thine is, and go thy way: I will give unto this last, even as unto thee. Is it not lawful for me to do what I will with mine own? Is thine eye evil, because I am good? So the last shall be first, and the first last: for many be called, but few chosen (Matthew 20:1-16).

This is one of the parables of our Lord which puzzles many readers. It would seem that the Lord is approving something that is unfair.

The Jews began counting hours at six o'clock in the morning. Consequently, the third hour of the day would be nine o'clock our time. The sixth hour would be noon, the ninth hour would be three o'clock in the afternoon, and the eleventh hour about five o'clock in the afternoon. Perhaps you have been puzzled by this parable. A natural question would be, why did all these people who worked different hours receive the same pay?

One of the first things to remember is that the benefits we receive from God through the Lord Jesus Christ are not wages. They are not earned by our efforts. Our relationship with God is not an employer-employee relationship. It is a father-son relationship. The father gives and the son serves. The son serves as he can, the father gives as he will.

Another lesson we see in this parable is that some people may be saved early in life and some may be saved late in life. When you believe in Jesus Christ, you receive eternal life. If you live only five days after you receive Him, you have eternal life. If you live fifty years after you receive Him, you have eternal life. Suppose a peasant girl married a king. The moment she is married, she is queen. If she lives for three days, she is queen just as much as if she lived for thirty years. She can't be queen any more than she is at the moment she marries the king.

There is yet another lesson we can see here. If you are thinking only of the rewards of faithful service, that will mean that your whole relationship is that of a hired servant. You would be trying to live the Christian life for what you can get out of it. In other words, you would not really belong to God as His child. He would not own you and you would not own Him, as belonging in the same family. All you would be looking for would be your fair wages for your labor.

Suppose you were to fill several glasses of different sizes with water. If you fill a pint glass, that is all it will hold. If you fill a quart jar, that is all it will hold. If you fill a gallon jug, that is all it will hold. Each one is given all it can hold. The pint is just as full as the gallon. By comparison, one is bigger than the other, but by experience each is full.

Something like that happens with Christians. We should not compare ourselves with others. Rather, in turning myself over to the Lord and receiving from Him, He will fill me with all I can hold, so that I will be fully satisfied in Him.

SPECIAL PRIVILEGE

And Jesus going up to Jerusalem took the twelve disciples apart in the way, and said unto them, Behold, we go up to Jerusalem; and the Son of man shall be betrayed unto the chief priests and unto the scribes, and they shall condemn him to death. And shall deliver him to the Gentiles to mock, and to scourge, and to crucify him: and the third day he shall rise again. Then came to him the mother of Zebedee's children with her sons, worshipping him, and desiring a certain thing of him. And he said unto her, What wilt thou? She saith unto him, Grant that these my two sons may sit, the one on thy right hand, and the other on the left, in thy kingdom. But Jesus answered and said, Ye know not what ye ask. Are ye able to drink of the cup that I shall drink of, and to be baptized with the baptism that I am baptized with? They say unto him, We are able. And he saith unto them, Ye shall drink indeed of my cup, and be baptized with the baptism that I am baptized with: but to sit on my right hand, and on my left, is not mine to give, but it shall be given to them for whom it is prepared of my Father. And when the ten heard it, they were moved with indignation against the two brethren. But Jesus called them unto him, and said, Ye know that the princes of the Gentiles exercise dominion over them, and they that are great exercise authority upon them. But it shall not be so among you: but whosoever will be great among you, let him be your minister; And whosoever will be chief among you, let him be your servant; Even as the Son of man came not to be ministered unto, but to minister, and to give his life a ransom for many (Matthew 20: 17-28).

The mother of James and John wanted a place of personal prestige for her children. She wanted them to be right next to the Lord Himself in heaven. But Jesus told her that she didn't realize what she was asking. He then asked James and John, "Are you willing to endure the suffering that you might be called on to endure?"

By their answer James and John claimed that they would be willing to endure anything to have such a privilege. Jesus then told them that eager willingness to suffer is not the qualification for eminence. Besides they had no idea of how He was to suffer.

When the other disciples heard of this request they were angry. Their indignation however was almost the same piece of cloth from which the request had come. The ten were provoked because apparently they really wanted for themselves what James and John had requested first.

Then Jesus taught them once more about humility. In the world, the big man is the one who is in charge. He shows he is in charge by putting you in your place. But among the followers of Christ, the mark of greatness is humility and willingness to serve. You are to be a servant, "even as the Son of man came not to be ministered unto, but to minister, and to give his life a ransom for many" (Mark 10:45).

This is a wonderful revelation of the nature of Jesus Christ.

It is also a revelation of what should characterize the lives of His followers. As you are in His will, you will not think of yourself, but of others. The person who is great in God's sight is the humble person. "Whosoever will be chief among you, let him be your servant" is the principle to follow. The only way you can do that is by denying yourself. If the Spirit of God is moving in your heart, you will not be so interested in getting things for yourself; you will rather be interested in helping others.

Chapter 16

CRUCIAL DAYS IN JERUSALEM

THE TIME HAD COME

For months Jesus had been teaching, preaching and performing miracles, but He had avoided being hailed as a king by the multitudes. He had even avoided announcing Himself as the Messiah. There came a time, however, when He had to step forward and present Himself as the fulfillment of the Old Testament prophecies. Though opposition had been increasing continually, Jesus determined to go to Jerusalem where the temple was located. This was the point from which the whole country was ruled. There is no doubt that He knew what would happen there.

While He was on His way to the most crucial test of His life on earth, indeed while He was walking directly toward the most important event of all history, as great crowds thronged about Him, He stopped to help two blind men. They called and Jesus stood still. He interrupted a public demonstration to attend to their personal needs. To Him one single soul mattered more than any public demonstration.

After this He entered triumphantly into Jerusalem on what we now call Palm Sunday. In this incident you see the humility of the Lord. Riding a donkey was a poor man's transportation. The King of kings and Lord of all, at whose name every knee will one day bow, came as a poor man even as He presented Himself as the King. In His coming He was ignored by human leaders. The scribes and Pharisees, the Sadducees and high priests were nowhere to be seen. None of the important people of the world were there. But those two blind men whom Jesus had healed were doubtless there. And so were many, many others whose names are known only to God. He was acclaimed by the common people, the lowly, the children.

The first act that the Lord Jesus performed after the Triumphal

Entry into Jerusalem was to cleanse the temple. This seems to teach that when He comes into your heart, the first thing He does is to affect your worship of God.

In the temple He found businessmen who were interested only in personal gain. They had made the situation around the worship of God into something from which they could profit. Jesus overturned their tables and put them out. When you go to the Lord's house to worship, do not seek things for yourself. Go to worship God, humbly seeking to honor Him.

"And when he had cast them out, the blind and the lame came to him in the temple." Apparently they did not come until the others were cast out; but when the cleansing had taken place, they came and were healed. Not only does this suggest profound truth for our public worship services, but there is a sober message to each one of us for our own personal devotional life. In a very real sense our first interest in coming to God should be to praise Him and to worship Him. "Seek ye first the kingdom of God . . . and all these things shall be added unto you."

Two Blind Men Near Jericho

And as they departed from Jericho, a great multitude followed him. And, behold, two blind men sitting by the way side, when they heard that Jesus passed by, cried out, saying, Have mercy on us, O Lord, thou son of David. And the multitude rebuked them, because they should hold their peace: but they cried the more, saying, Have mercy on us, O Lord, thou son of David. And Jesus stood still, and called them, and said, What will ye that I shall do unto you? They say unto him, Lord, that our eyes may be opened. So Jesus had compassion on them, and touched their eyes: and immediately their eyes received sight, and they followed him (Matthew 20:29-34).

Immediately before this incident happened, a certain request had been presented to the Lord Jesus Christ, which was not granted. The mother of James and John had asked Jesus for special privilege for her two sons. It was a request for eminence: this was denied.

As Jesus moved toward Jerusalem, surrounded by the usual multitudes, two men cried out, "Have mercy on us, O Lord, thou son of David." They wanted to be able to see, and their request was granted. The request of James and John had been for personal advantage. Receiving this would not benefit anyone but themselves. But these blind men were asking for the ability to see. In their blindness they were handicapped in living normal lives. Receiving their request would only enable them to live as their Maker had originally intended they should live.

Being called "Lord" by the two blind men would not be so

significant, for "Lord" was the common term used in speaking to masters and teachers. But when they coupled the word "Lord" with the phrase "son of David," it meant that they believed that Jesus was the One of whom the prophets had spoken. He was the fulfillment of Old Testament prophecy.

We may note further they did not say, "Jesus of Nazareth, come and help us," but rather "son of David." "Jesus of Nazareth" was His earthly name. "Son of David" signified His relation to the promises of God in the Old Testament. When we pray to Jesus the Lord now, we should remember we are not praying to "the Babe of Bethlehem," nor to "the Carpenter of Nazareth." We are praying to the One who is raised from the dead and is seated now at the right hand of God the Father. He can answer prayer, not because He was a good man, but because He is the only begotten Son of God.

Though the multitude tried to silence them, the blind men continued crying. "And Jesus stood still." He was walking toward the great city of Jerusalem, where He would present Himself as the promised Messiah. He would soon take a colt, the foal of an ass, and ride on it to fulfill Old Testament Scripture. The crowds would soon be shouting, "Hosanna to the Son of David." But here two blind men were calling and Jesus stood still! "What will ye that I shall do unto you?"

Their cry had been, "Have mercy upon us." But they needed to be more specific in their praying. General ideas are proper — we need to have trust in God in all things – but specific requests are essential. Much of our praying is too indefinite. We could do more than merely mention the names of friends, relatives and missionaries. We could think about their specific needs. Are they facing a particular problem? Even when you pray for yourself and ask, "Lord, be with me today," what is it that you really need? Be specific. What one thing do you need this day? The blind men made a definite request: "That our eyes may be opened." Faith becomes operative when it is exercised about definite things.

"Immediately their eyes received sight." There were definite results.

"And they followed him." These two blind men were probably not planning to go anywhere. They were seated by the wayside, perhaps only waiting, until Jesus came. When He came and took away their blindness, enabling them to move about as other people do, these men did not go about matters of their own. Evidently more happened to them than the opening of their eyes. Now they wanted to be with Him, and to serve Him. Answers to prayer always bring so much other blessing to those who receive them.

THE FIRST PALM SUNDAY

And when they drew nigh unto Jerusalem, and were come to Bethphage, unto the mount of Olives, then sent Jesus two disciples, Saying unto them, Go into the village over against you, and straightway ye shall find an ass tied, and a colt with her: loose them, and bring them unto me. And if any man say ought to you, ye shall say, The Lord hath need of them, and straightway he will send them. And this was done, that it might be fulfilled which was spoken by the prophet, saying, Tell ye the daughter of Sion, Behold, thy King cometh unto thee, meek, and sitting upon an ass, and a colt the foal of an ass. And the disciples went, and did as Jesus commanded them, And brought the ass, and the colt, and put on them their clothes, and they set him thereon. And a very great multitude spread their garments in the way; others cut down branches from the trees, and strawed them in the way. And the multitudes that went before, and that followed, cried, saying, Hosanna to the son of David: Blessed is he that cometh in the name of the Lord; Hosanna in the highest. And when he was come into Jerusalem, all the city was moved, saying, Who is this? And the multitude said, This is Jesus the prophet of Nazareth of Galilee (Matthew 21:1-11).

This significant incident was carefully done by Jesus. He had come into Jerusalem in exactly this way to fulfill Old Testament Scripture. Over and over again the Old Testament had predicted the coming of the King. He was to be the Messiah, God's chosen anointed One, who would do God's will on earth and thereby would save His people and establish His kingdom. In this very presentation of Himself as the King, His humility was plainly to be seen. A rich man might come with horses and chariot, whereas a poor man's beast of burden was the donkey. Here was the Son of God, come to rule as King, and yet He rode on a lowly donkey.

This is like His birth in Bethlehem. Into a little town, an obscure place among poor people, came the One before whom angels fall down to worship.

So when He came as the long-awaited King, He did not come belligerently to overpower by force, but He came in humility to save by His grace.

The people were so stirred that they thronged about Him, spreading their garments in the way, cutting down branches of trees and throwing them in the streets.

Another gospel says that this was a colt "upon which never man sat." If a man were to undertake to ride a colt on which no one ever sat before, he could expect to have some trouble. Because this animal was not trained to being ridden, you could expect that when this colt was taken into a city, in front of a noisy crowd, he would become unmanageable. But the Lord Jesus rode on that colt as if the colt were accustomed to Him. Anyone acquainted with donkeys would recognize this as a miracle of control. There is a lesson suggested here for us. When the Lord Jesus comes into the heart, He comes to control and rule. He will control our natural dispositions, even as He controlled that colt. This riding of the colt in the streets of Jerusalem, and the enthusiastic popular reception by the common people fulfilled the Old Testament prophecies about the coming of the King.

CLEANSING THE TEMPLE

And Jesus went into the temple of God, and cast out all them that sold and bought in the temple, and overthrew the tables of the moneychangers, and the seats of them that sold doves, And said unto them, It is written, My house shall be called the house of prayer; but ye have made it a den of thieves. And the blind and the lame came to him in the temple; and he healed them. And when the chief priests and scribes saw the wonderful things that he did, and the children crying in the temple, and saying, Hosanna to the son of David; they were sore displeased. And said unto him, Hearest thou what these say? And Jesus saith unto them, Yea; have ye never read, Out of the mouth of babes and sucklings thou hast perfected praise? (Matthew 21:12-16).

We have already noted that this was the first action of Jesus Christ as King. When He came into the city and received such a royal welcome from the crowds singing His praises, He went straight to the temple. The temple, of course, was the place to worship God. So the Lord's first concern in Jerusalem was to see that God was worshiped properly. When He saw what was going on He knew that the temple needed to be cleansed.

In Christian experience, spiritual trouble often begins just this way. A person may greet the Lord Jesus as King, and yet may fail to worship Him in purity. Human desires, the inner longings of the human heart and good spiritual intentions may be all mixed up. Even while we say we are seeking to serve God, we may yet be seeking our own advantage. It is when we seek our own desires that we are led into sin of all kinds.

Jesus found the temple cluttered with moneychangers and those who sold animals and birds for sacrificial use. This need not mean that the temple was being turned into an ordinary market. Actually it could be noted there was probably quite a practical purpose in what was being done.

Jews came from long distances to worship in Jerusalem. They would not be expected to bring animals with them for sacrifice. Since they wanted to worship God in the temple, they needed to buy an animal for sacrifice when they arrived in Jerusalem. It was therefore convenient to have these animals sold nearby, and quite naturally there would be merchants who would be desirous of making the most of such a business opportunity. The cattle salesmen who had their stalls nearest the temple, of course could expect the most business. Evidently those who set up their business inside the temple compound would have the best location of all.

The presence of the moneychangers can be understood in the same way. When the Jews came from far away countries, they had money of various currencies which was different from the coinage used in Jerusalem. So when they wanted to make a purchase in the temple, they had to exchange their money for local currency. The moneychangers provided this service, and of course they received a handsome profit in the rendering of this service. So worshipers brought their own money with them, got it changed by the moneychangers, and purchased a sacrificial animal from the merchants in order to make their sacrifice. The convenience of doing all this in the temple grounds would be obvious to everyone.

But although these businesses in the temple may have been established in connection with worship, the truth of the matter was that these merchants were interested not in worship but in making money. This is why Jesus threw them out. They were profiting from the worship of God. The love of the Lord Jesus for His Father in heaven was such that He could not tolerate the presence in the temple of those who were using the temple worship for their own selfish personal advantage.

After He had cleansed the temple, the blind and the lame came into the temple to Him, and He healed them. What a contrast! He was so stern and severe in driving out the moneychangers, yet He was so tender and loving as He healed the unfortunate. We need to see both of these elements in His love.

This whole incident, however, displeased the chief priests and scribes. The singing of the children at the Triumphal Entry had irritated them from the very first. Now Jesus Christ was disturbing the status quo of the temple. And here we see the strange perversity of the human heart, even when it is religious. The priests did not object to the selling of animals and the moneychanging in the temple, but they did object to the actions of Jesus and the response of the children as being something unseemly.

Apparently it was this frame of mind which was judged to be evil by the Lord Jesus when He answered, "Have ye never read, Out of the mouth of babes and sucklings thou hast perfected praise?" It almost sounds like what we have heard Jesus say before, "Except ye become as little children, ye cannot enter the kingdom of heaven."

This whole incident teaches us that we should be ready to cleanse our personal attitude toward the public worship of God.

We need to keep in mind that He should be praised, that His name should be lifted up, that He should be glorified. Let us be willing to let Him rule in all that we do in His name, that He may cast out those things that are displeasing in His sight.

THE WITHERED FIG TREE

And he left them, and went out of the city into Bethany; and he lodged there. Now in the morning as he returned into the city, he hungered. And when he saw a fig tree in the way, he came to it, and found nothing thereon, but leaves only, and said unto it, Let no fruit grow on thee henceforward for ever. And presently the fig tree withered away. And when the disciples saw it, they marvelled, saying, How soon is the fig tree withered away! Jesus answered and said unto them, Verily I say unto you, If ye have faith, and doubt not, ye shall not only do this which is done to the fig tree, but also if ye shall say unto this mountain, Be thou removed, and be thou cast into the sea; it shall be done. And all things, whatsoever ye shall ask in prayer, believing, ye shall receive (Matthew 21:17-22).

The next morning as He was on His way into the city of Jerusalem, Jesus was hungry. He saw a fig tree, but when He came to it, He found nothing on it but leaves. Then He passed judgment on it, "and presently the fig tree withered away." "Presently" doesn't necessarily mean the next few minutes. Another gospel tells us that the disciples first noticed the withering of the fig tree the next day. But when they noticed it, they were astonished at such a display of power. Then our Lord taught them a lesson about faith.

Most people are aware that there is a reference to "moving mountains" in the Bible, but like many other passages of Scripture, this reference isn't understood by the natural mind.

What Jesus said was that you can move mountains, "if ye have faith." Faith is the key. This faith is not some strength you have in yourself. It is not some degree of will power. Actually, faith is our response to the revealed will of God.

The classic example of faith is Abraham, the man who believed God and it was counted to him for righteousness. Abraham believed God about the birth of Isaac, but was this his own idea? Was it that Abraham thought he needed a son to perpetuate his family and so he turned on his will power and produced the child? No, that isn't what faith is. Messengers from God came to Abraham with a message which seemed so incredible that Sarah laughed at it. Yet Abraham, when he received that message, considered not his own body, now as good as dead, neither yet the barrenness of Sarah's womb, but gave glory to God believing that what God had promised, he was able also to perform. This is true faith that achieves wonders.

To exercise faith, then, you must first know God's will, but, as Paul wrote, "We know not what to pray for as we ought." It may well be that you must pray, as Jesus did in the Garden of Gethsemane: "Not my will but thine be done." Then you may ask of God, "What do you want me to do? What is Thy will?" And when you know what is God's will for you to do, you can exercise faith in God to accomplish His will through you. If such revealed promise means moving mountains, God is able to do it through you, as your faith responds to God's will.

Chapter 17

OPPOSITION INCREASES

FACING UP TO JUDGMENT

Everything Jesus did had significance. His entry into Jerusalem was significant for it predicted His coming as King. His cleansing of the temple and His cursing of the fig tree were also significant, for these predicted His coming as Judge.

When the Lord Jesus showed by throwing the moneychangers out of the temple that the conduct of such people was subject to His judgment, some naturally came to Him and asked, "Who gave You this authority?" Judgment of the conduct of men properly belongs only to God who made man and keeps him.

We read that when God looked out upon the world that He had created, He saw that it was good. That means that He judged it. And judgment has been going on ever since. He is not waiting for a distant day in order to judge. There is a special day of judgment coming, to be sure, but God's judgment is going on all the time.

In the same way our Lord Jesus judged and His judgment was true. This was Biblically-based judgment, for He said, "It is written, My house shall be called the house of prayer."

In answering this question regarding His authority, Jesus asked, "How do you feel about John's baptism? Was it from heaven, or was it of men?" John's baptism had to do with repentance. In other words Jesus was asking, "How do you feel about repentance? How do you feel about judging yourself as unworthy?" When they were unwilling to accept that repentance was a call of God, no further light was offered.

Then Jesus told a parable which helps toward an understanding of His attitude in rejecting these critics. This is the parable of the two sons in which one of then said to his father, "I'll do what you say," but did not do it; the other one said, "No, I will not," but then did his father's will anyway. In this way Jesus pointed to the importance of repentance. The one who repented and actually did what the father wanted him to do was the one who was accepted. No amount of religious activity will make up for lack of repentance. No matter how much you may go to church and no matter how hard you strive to serve in church functions, if you are not willing to repent, your efforts will be of no avail.

It will be helpful for anyone to realize that what the Lord Jesus did as He came to Jerusalem on this occasion, can well be taken to indicate what He will do when He comes into our hearts. He comes as King, expecting to rule. We should not be misled by His humble, meek manner. He is the King of kings, the Lord of all. He is to be received with praise. When He comes, He comes in judgment. Our personal worship of God is to be cleansed of any selfish interest, and our lives are expected to be fruitful. It is a sobering thought to see that He does not tolerate fruitless lives. That we can be barren is human enough, but in that case we should be repentant before Him.

THE UNWILLING WILL NEVER LEARN

And when he was come into the temple, the chief priests and the elders of the people came unto him as he was teaching, and said, By what authority doest thou these things? and who gave thee this authority? And Jesus answered and said unto them, I also will ask you one thing, which if ye tell me, I in like wise will tell you by what authority I do these things. The baptism of John, whence was it? from heaven, or of men? And they reasoned with themselves, saying, If we shall say, From heaven; he will say unto us, Why did ye not then believe him? But if we shall say, Of men; we fear the people; for all hold John as a prophet. And they answered Jesus, and said, We cannot tell. And he said unto them, Neither tell I you by what authority I do these things (Matthew 21:23-27).

Whenever truth is presented, there will always be some who will resist. Whenever authority is exerted, there will always be some who will question. Often Jesus was criticized for the claims He made. Often His authority was questioned. When He entered Jerusalem, the multitudes cried, "Hosanna to the son of David." He accepted their praise. Then He went immediately to the temple to cleanse it. He threw out those who were in the temple for personal gain and insisted that it be used for the worship of God. For this the chief priests and the elders criticized Him. They questioned His right to act with such authority. "What right do you have to do this?" they asked.

Jesus could have told them by what authority He did these things. But instead He answered with another question. This is a procedure that Jesus followed during His ministry. Sometimes questions were asked of Him not in good faith. Some questions were asked to embarrass Him or belittle Him. The Lord exercised His own will in answering as it would serve His purpose. Here He asked them, "What about the baptism of John? Was it from God or was it from men?"

The chief priests refused to give a direct answer. They reasoned like politicians. "What answer will do us the most good? If we say that it comes from God, He'll say, 'Why didn't you respond to it?' If we say it comes from man, the people won't like it. The safe thing is to say nothing." So they refused to answer. They took the "Fifth Amendment." Their response to His question showed they were not ready to receive the revelation from the Lord about Himself.

The Lord Jesus replied, "Neither tell I you."

Often sincere people have become entangled in endless, fruitless controversy because they have in good will answered questions that were asked of them for devious purposes. In dealing with the questions of others, it is well to study them carefully, consider them wisely, and to answer only those that will be edifying. Asking questions is proper enough. It is the motive with which the question is asked that matters. People who ask questions only to confuse or to embarrass the presentation of the Gospel need not expect to learn anything from the Lord.

Two Sons and a Vineyard

But what think ye? A certain man had two sons; and he came to the first, and said, Son, go work today in my vineyard. He answered and said, I will not: but afterward he repented, and went. And he came to the second, and said likewise. And he answered and said, I go, sir: and went not. Whether of them twain did the will of his father? They say unto him, The first. Jesus saith unto them, Verily I say unto you, That the publicans and the harlots go into the kingdom of God before you. For John came unto you in the way of righteousness, and ye believed him not: but the publicans and the harlots believed him: and ye, when ye had seen it, repented not afterward, that ye might believe him (Matthew 21:28-32).

This parable begins with a definite command. "Son, go work today in my vineyard." This calls for obedience. Whatever else the son had in mind to do that day, he was to set it aside. There was no doubt as to what he was asked to do. He was to work in the vineyard belonging to his father. He was not to work in his own or in the vineyard of a neighbor.

The son's first response was "No." Afterward he repented. In other words, he changed his mind. Though at first he had said he would not, now he went, doing what his father wanted him to do.

The second son received the same command, but his initial response was different. He said he would go, but for some reason he decided later that he would not go.

Which of the two did his father's will? Of course, the chief priests and the elders had to admit that the first one did. Jesus then said, "The publicans and the harlots go into the kingdom of God before you."

Jesus was talking to the religious leaders of Jerusalem, men whose lives would seem above reproach to the average man. Yet He said that publicans who lived worldly lives and harlots who lived sinful lives would go into the kingdom of God before them. This does not mean that worldly, sinful people will go to heaven because of their worldliness and sinfulness. No, it is not because of their past record of sinfulness, but because with such records of past conduct they may more readily recognize themselves as sinners and repent humbly before God than the highly moral priests and elders.

Jesus explained: "John came unto you in the way of righteousness, and ye believed him not." Believing is more than accepting a statement as factually correct. Believing implies obeying. In other words, when John preached repentance, the chief priests refused to do it. They always applied the message of John to publicans and harlots and never to themselves. But the publicans and harlots could believe John's message was for them. Many of them repented because of his preaching and they obeyed God.

Those who were worldly and sinful judged themselves unfit for God, and so received God's forgiveness. Those who were morally upright and religious thought they were good enough for God as they were and did not repent. Consequently the latter would not be forgiven. Those who receive God's forgiveness may enter into the kingdom. Those who do not receive it will not enter in.

This is most sobering. Today our church rolls are crowded with people who live fairly good lives, but who have never really accepted Christ Jesus as Saviour. Like the chief priests, they do not question their personal relationship with God. This is a sad thing, for Jesus' words are still true. Such unrepentant persons will miss the salvation of Christ because they are satisfied to think they are all right as they are.

THE REJECTED STONE

Hear another parable: There was a certain householder, which planted a vineyard, and hedged it round about, and digged a winepress in it, and built a tower, and let it out to husbandmen, and went into a far country: And when the time of the fruit drew near, he sent his servants to the husbandmen, that they might receive the fruits of it. And the husbandmen took his servants, and beat one, and killed another, and stoned another. Again, he sent other servants more than the first: and they did unto them likewise. But last of all he sent unto them his son, saying, They will reverence my son. But when the husbandmen saw the son, they said among themselves, This is the heir; come, let us kill him, and let us seize on his inheritance. And they caught him, and cast him out of the vineyard, and slew him. When the lord therefore of the vineyard cometh, what will he do unto those husbandmen? They say unto him, He will miserably destroy those wicked men, and will let out his vineyard unto other husbandmen, which shall render him the fruits in their seasons. Jesus saith unto them, Did ye never read in the scriptures, The stone which the builders rejected, the same is become the head of the corner: this is the Lord's doing, and it is marvellous in our eyes? Therefore say I unto you, The kingdom of God shall be taken from you, and given to a nation bringing forth the fruits thereof. And whosoever shall fall on this stone shall be broken: but on whomsoever it shall fall, it will grind him to powder. And when the chief priests and Pharisees had heard his parables, they perceived that he spake of them. But when they sought to lay hands on him, they feared the multitude, because they took him for a prophet (Matthew 21:33-46).

This parable of the vineyard was told to reveal certain truths to the children of Israel. God is represented as Lord of His vineyard. He had given the workers all that they needed to prosper bountifully. Then "he went into a far country." This doesn't mean that He forsook His people. Rather, it would indicate that He put an opportunity for service in their hands.

When the time came to expect results from what had been done, "he sent his servants." One after another, His servants were shamefully treated by the very people to whom He had given privileges.

The Jews who were listening to Jesus knew very well how the Old Testament prophets had been sent to speak God's Word to His people and how they had been rejected and shamefully treated by the people to whom they had been sent. Lastly, Jesus predicted that they would even kill God's Son.

Whenever the Jewish people are mentioned in New Testament records, the passage can be applied to many in the church today. Many have been brought up in the church. Many have been initiated into the Christian community by their parents. Parents may actually dedicate children to the Lord, and then consider them as belonging to Him. Yet like these Jews who listened to Jesus, such children belong to God only halfway. It seems quite possible that some people will be trying to accept the blessings of living in the Christian community, while at the same time persisting in rejecting Jesus Christ as Saviour and Lord.

The Lord taught very clearly that He would reject those who reject Him. It did not matter then if they were scribes or Pharisees and it does not matter today if they are twentieth-century church members – God looks on the heart. The Lord Jesus gave this warning, "The kingdom of God shall be taken from you and given to a nation bringing forth the fruits thereof." In other words, persons may have had an opportunity to know the Gospel; their parents may have been fervent believers; there may have been an open Bible in the home; there may have been family devotions. But if such persons do not respond humbly and penitently to the Gospel, the blessings of the kingdom may be taken from them.

"Whosoever shall fall on this stone shall be broken, but on whomsoever it shall fall, it will grind him to powder." The stone is Jesus Christ. The person who falls on the stone is the one who comes to Christ with a broken, penitent heart trusting in Jesus Christ. But the person on whom the stone falls is the one who turns his back on Christ, the one whom the Lord will judge severely. This parable soberly warns us there may be such persons among believers.

INVITATION TO A WEDDING

And Jesus answered and spake unto them again by parables, and said, The kingdom of heaven is like unto a certain king, which made a marriage for his son, And sent forth his servants to call them that were bidden to the wedding: and they would not come. Again, he sent forth other servants, saying, Tell them which are bidden, Behold, I have prepared my dinner: my oxen and my fatlings are killed, and all things are ready: come unto the marriage. But they made light of it, and went their ways, one to his farm, another to his merchandise: And the remnant took his servants, and entreated them spitefully, and slew them. But when the king heard thereof, he was wroth: and he sent forth his armies, and destroyed those murderers, and burned up their city. Then saith he to his servants, The wedding is ready, but they which were bidden were not worthy. Go ye therefore into the highways, and as many as ye shall find, bid to the marriage. So those servants went out into the highways, and gathered together all as many as they found, both bad and good: and the wedding was furnished with guests (Matthew 22:1-10).

This parable points out clearly that salvation is a gift provided for those who will receive it. The parable also brings to mind that the church is often called the bride of Christ. God arranged that the Lord Jesus Christ should have a church, His bride, with whom

He would have fellowship. "He sent forth his servants to call them that were bidden to the wedding." Jesus seems to be referring to those in Israel who were brought into a covenant relationship with God by their parents. They had been circumcised and identified as belonging to God. They were called the Lord's people. These people were now being called to turn to God by the Lord Jesus.

This may well remind us of the average church congregation. Many of the members have never had a personal experience with God. They belong to a church because their parents belonged to the church. In this relationship they have the advantage of hearing the Gospel preached, but it will be necessary that they as individuals accept Jesus Christ as their personal Saviour and Lord if they are to enter into the permanent blessing of God.

After the parable goes on to say, "They would not come," there is the record of what the king did next. "He sent forth other servants, saying, Tell them which are bidden, Behold, I have prepared my dinner: my oxen and my fatlings are killed, and all things are ready: come unto the marriage." This is a gracious explanation of the urgency of the invitation, and a warning against ignoring it. "But they made light of it." They had other things to do; they had their businesses to take care of and their farms to tend. This is followed by a record of the king's anger. In all of this it is easy to see the warning to those who neglect to receive the Gospel. You can be sure that people who turn down the invitation of God will not escape divine wrath either in this world nor in the world to come.

Finally, the king sent his servants to find strangers on the highways and invite them to the wedding feast. Sometimes, people who are brought up in a Christian home do not experience a personal relationship with Jesus Christ, while someone else with no Christian background at all becomes a committed Christian. In the history of the Christian church this has happened over and over again. God reaches out beyond the old group and brings in new people. The Jews were the people who had the blessings of the Gospel, but they rejected God's gracious invitation in Jesus Christ. So God opened salvation to the Gentiles. And in our day those who have the privilege of hearing the Gospel should not treat the invitation lightly. They should be wise to accept and participate in what God offers in Christ, otherwise God will bypass them and turn to the strangers on the highways, who may never have had the opportunity of church attendance or Sunday school instruction.

A Special Wedding Garment

And when the king came in to see the guests, he saw there a man which had not on a wedding garment: And he saith unto him, Friend, how camest thou in hither not having a wedding garment? And he was speechless. Then said the king to the servants, Bind him hand and foot, and take him away, and cast him into outer darkness; there shall be weeping and gnashing of teeth. For many are called, but few are chosen (Matthew 22: 11-14).

At a wedding feast in those days the host provided garments for his guests. The special wedding garments were bright and colorful, in keeping with the gay occasion. Some guests may not have been able to afford suitable clothes of their own and so could not come satisfactorily dressed for a wedding, unless their clothing were provided for them. In our day the custom has changed although we can see evidence of the same idea even now. The bride may provide gowns for the bridesmaids and the groom may rent tuxedos to be worn by his attendants.

Now suppose for a moment that you lived back in the time of Jesus of Nazareth. Can you imagine how startling it would be if one of the bridesmaids appeared at a wedding wearing a house dress? It would show an utter lack of respect for the bride. It might be a very nice informal garment, but it would be totally out of keeping with the spirit of a wedding.

In this parable, when the king came to see his guests, he noticed one man without a wedding garment. He said what might be comparable in our day to, "Whatever gave you the nerve to come in here without being dressed for the wedding?" When the guest failed to answer, the king ordered his servants to throw the man out. The Lord Jesus told this parable to teach us a truth. When we come before God He will look to see how we are clothed. Do we have the kind of clothing that is acceptable in His sight? The Bible speaks repeatedly about the righteousness of the saints as fine linen, but it is clearly shown that the only way one could ever have garments of righteousness is to accept those provided by the Lord Jesus Christ Himself. Isaiah wrote, "All our righteousnesses are as filthy rags" (64:6). To anyone who thinks he can come to God in his own righteousness, God's Word would say: "Take him, bind him and throw him out."

It is never a question as to whether a man is as good as anyone else. The question is always how does he compare to the Lord Jesus Christ. If any man compared his righteousness with the righteousness of his neighbor, he might stand a chance, but when he compares himself to Jesus Christ, he falls far short. How then can a man please God? The answer is this: by accepting the righteousness of Jesus Christ as his own. When you receive the Lord Jesus Christ as your Saviour, He covers you with His righteousness. This means that when you stand in the presence of God, you are clothed in the garments of Jesus Christ.

Many people seem to want the benefits and blessings of Christian living without accepting Jesus Christ. When they read that the fruit of the Spirit is love, joy, peace, longsuffering, goodness, gentleness, meekness, self-control, faith, they try in themselves to imitate these things. Since the fruit of the Spirit is love, they attempt to act in love toward others. If they have come from a good Christian home, they may be able to accomplish a reasonably good imitation of Christian virtues. But God knows it is just an act. He looks into the heart. If a man were to come into the presence of God in his own righteousness, no matter how well he might compare with others, he would be cast out, for God demands spotless righteousness. This is provided only by the Lord Jesus Christ.

Chapter 18

FOUR QUESTIONS

In Matthew 22 we can see four different attitudes which people have toward life, reflected in the questions they ask.

The first was shown by the Herodians who came to Jesus and asked Him whether or not they should pay taxes. Their question was, "Is it right?" Now if you are going to live your life on the basis of what is right, you must first define what you mean by right. One of the problems is that often what is right may depend upon circumstances. Something may be right to do at one time, but wrong to do at another time. This is not true of everything, but it is true about many things. "Is it right?" is a good question. It uncovers a good principle for living, but in itself it is not good enough. Circumstances are so different in different places that one often has difficulty in deciding what is right. Also such emphasis upon outward form of conduct leads some people into pride and conceit because by comparison they think they are better than others.

The second attitude was shown by the Sadducees who raised a question about the Resurrection. Their question was, "Is it reasonable? Is it logical?" It is always good to act reasonably if it is possible, but this also is not good enough. Reason, you see, cannot reveal anything beyond one's own experience. You can reason only within the limits of what you have seen and heard. Jesus answered, "Ye do err, not knowing the Scriptures nor the power of God." In other words, reason could be very helpful after you have experienced the grace of God, but it would not be helpful before you came to God, because God is supernatural, outside the realm of human experience, and no man by reason could find out about God.

The third attitude was shown by a lawyer, a student of the Scriptures. He came with the question, "What is the great commandment?" In other words, what is most important? What is best? (What is good?) But here again we need help. In order to know what is good, one must know God's Word. Without a thorough knowledge of the Source of all good, it is folly to try to determine what is good for you. But if the Holy Scriptures are known to you in mind and heart, you have an adequate basis for determining what is good.

The fourth attitude was shown by the question which Jesus Christ Himself asked. He turned to His questioners and asked, "What think ye of Christ? whose son is he?" No one but the Son of God could have met the standards which the Old Testament prophecies had set up. Therefore the only logical answer would be that Christ is the Son of God.

If you want to get right with God, the real thing for you to settle in your heart is the answer to this question. If you know Jesus Christ as divine Lord and Saviour, you will know the answer to the question, "What is right?" The Holy Spirit indwells you as a Christian and will guide you into all truth. He will aid you in the interpretation of Scripture. If you have the Lord Jesus Christ in your heart, you will know the answer to the question, "What is reasonable?" What is reasonable must be in accord with the divine plan of God who created our reasoning abilities. If you know the Lord, you will also know the answer to the question, "What is good?" God alone is good, and you have been adopted as a dearly loved son into His family.

What think ye of Christ? whose son is he?" Answer this question properly and all the rest will become clear.

CAESAR'S IMAGE ON A COIN

Then went the Pharisees, and took counsel how they might entangle him in his talk. And they sent out unto him their disciples with the Herodians, saying, Master, we know that thou art true, and teachest the way of God in truth, neither carest thou for any man: for thou regardest not the person of men. Tell us therefore, What thinkest thou? Is it lawful to give tribute unto Caesar, or not? But Jesus perceived their wickedness, and said, Why tempt ye me, ye hypocrites? Shew me the tribute money. And they brought unto him a penny. And he saith unto them, Whose is this image and superscription? They say unto him, Caesar's. Then saith he unto them, Render therefore unto Caesar the things which are Caesar's; and unto God the things that are God's. When they had heard these words, they marvelled, and left him, and went their way (Matthew 22:15-22).

Notice the reputation which the Lord Jesus Christ had even with the Pharisees and the Herodians. As they addressed Him, they acknowledged four things about Him· (1) He was honest;

(2) He was a reliable teacher; (3) He was not a flatterer; (4) He did not trim what He had to say on account of the people who were standing before Him.

Those who asked the question were disciples of the Pharisees, zealous Jews eager to rid their country of Roman domination, who would think paying taxes to the Romans was wrong. Standing by were the Herodians, who were cooperating with the Roman government, and who would think paying taxes was right. Obviously, Jesus was being put on the spot in front of these two opposing groups. No matter what He said, one group would be offended.

In this setting came the question: "Is it Scriptural to pay taxes to Caesar?" After all, the government was a Roman government, a worldly government. Should Israel pay money to support a pagan government? Today we could ask, should a Christian pay taxes to a worldly government, not knowing what such a government will do with the tax money? Perhaps Christians should reserve everything for God, since they are stewards of all they have! Such was the question which they pushed at Jesus.

It is easy to see what different answers could be given. He could say that the things of God were so important that nothing else really mattered, and therefore taxes should not be paid. Then the Herodians would report him to the authorities. Or He might say that the Roman government was entitled to receive the taxes. That would infuriate the Pharisees and most of the Jewish people.

But Jesus saw through their trickery and said, "Why tempt ye me, ye hypocrites?" Then looking at a coin, He asked them whose image was on it. When they replied, "Caesar's," He said, "Render therefore unto Caesar the things which are Caesar's; and unto God the things that are God's."

In other words, the legal coinage we use for money belongs to the local society in which we live. We live in a community with others; we share in a society. We use the streets and the sidewalks. We depend on the police and the fire department. Since we derive benefit from them and they protect our life and property, it is right for us to share in the responsibility financially.

I was born and reared in Canada. In those days, as a Canadian citizen, I paid taxes, I served in the Canadian army and I voted in the Canadian elections. Later I came to the United States. After living here several years, I realized I probably would not return to Canada and so I became a citizen of the United States. As a citizen I assumed certain privileges and responsibilities. Now I pay my taxes, cast my vote and obey the laws of the United States. I am to render unto the United States government the things that belong to it and render to God the things that belong to Him.

What are some of the things that are God's? I am a man and I have a life. The United States government did not make me a man nor give me my life. God did. God watches over my life and provides for me. He gives me air to breathe and water to drink and food to eat. I am responsible unto God for the life I live. Once God held me responsible to obey His law, but I failed. I sinned, but God in His love provided a sinless Saviour, through whom my sin has been forgiven. Now as a Christian I expect to enter the presence of God without judgment for my sins. All these blessings I receive from God.

If I am to render unto Caesar the things that are Caesar's, I will pay my taxes. If I am to render unto God the things that are God's I will worship Him and serve Him with all my heart. My money may bear the image of Caesar, but my soul has the image of God stamped upon it. I was created in His image and I belong to Him.

WHOSE WIFE SHALL SHE BE?

The same day came to him the Sadducees, which say that there is no resurrection, and asked him, Saying, Master, Moses said, If a man die, having no children, his brother shall marry his wife, and raise up seed unto his brother. Now there were with us seven brethren: and the first, when he had married a wife, deceased, and, having no issue, left his wife unto his brother. Likewise the second also, and the third, unto the seventh. And last of all the woman died also. Therefore in the resurrection whose wife shall she be of the seven? for they all had her. Jesus answered and said unto them, Ye do err, not knowing the scriptures, nor the power of God. For in the resurrection they neither marry, nor are given in marriage, but are as the angels of God in heaven. But as touching the resurrection of the dead, have ye not read that which was spoken unto you by God, saying, I am the God of Abraham, the God of Isaac, and the God of Jacob? God is not the God of the dead, but of the living. And when the multitude heard this, they were astonished at his doctrine (Matthew 22:23-33).

After the Herodians had been silenced, the Sadducees came to question Jesus. As we have noted before, the Sadducees did not believe in heaven, angels, nor the resurrection of the dead. So when they came to Jesus, they tried to show that His teaching about heaven and eternal life was ridiculous. They invented a story that was intended to reveal the foolishness of life after death. Eternal life, they endeavored to point out, was utterly illogical. Since they had confidence only in things that could be considered as rational, they rejected anything that could not be proven rationally.

Jesus responded boldly, "You are wrong. You don't know the Bible." Jesus went to the Bible to establish spiritual truth. We believe in heaven, the soul and eternal life, because the Bible says so. Nowhere else do we find such ideas. Nowhere else do we find such clear teaching of resurrection from the dead. It should be real guidance to us to note that when men asked about spiritual things the Lord Jesus referred all men to the Bible.

Not only were the Sadducees ignorant of the Bible, but they were also ignorant regarding the power of God. If they had known the power of God, they could have believed the Resurrection.

If you have ever wondered whether or not some loved one of yours will live again, read God's Word. If you have ever wondered whether or not there is life for you after this world, read God's Word. Don't try to build up your hope on your feelings or on what someone else said or even on logic. Build your hope for eternal life on the Scriptures.

Jesus said, "Have ye not read that which was spoken unto you by God?" The Bible is God's Word, not man's, and the truth of the Resurrection is based upon what God said and not on what man said.

God said, "I am the God of Abraham, the God of Isaac, and the God of Jacob?" Jesus observed that God did not say, "I *was,*" but "I *am.*" In other words, Abraham was still alive, because God is not the God of the dead, but the God of the living. This whole teaching of Christ is based on the tense of the verb and shows us how important even single words of Scripture really are.

Most Important Commandment

But when the Pharisees had heard that he had put the Sadducees to silence, they were gathered together. Then one of them, which was a lawyer, asked him a question, tempting him, and saying, Master, which is the great commandment in the law? Jesus said unto him, Thou shalt love the Lord thy God with all thy heart, and with all thy soul, and with all thy mind. This is the first and great commandment. And the second is like unto it, Thou shalt love thy neighbour as thyself. On these two commandments hang all the law and the prophets (Matthew 22:34-40).

In Jerusalem there were several schools of thought, each with its own group of enthusiastic adherents. The group with whom Christ was most often in conflict was the group called the Pharisees, who thought that the best way to please God was by keeping the many rules and regulations which they had developed to obey the law.

Although these various groups opposed each other vigorously, they agreed in that all opposed the claims of Jesus Christ. This is why the Pharisees were able to get the Herodians and the Sadducees to cooperate in a scheme to trap Jesus. But the Herodians had failed, and so had the Sadducees.

Then a "lawyer" came with a question to Jesus. This "lawyer" was not a lawyer in our sense of the word; rather, he was an expert in the law of God, the five Books of Moses. His question was really a matter of comparative ethics. Of all the various possibilities in conduct, which is the best? It was a question asked mostly for argument's sake, for it is impossible to prove which commandment is the greatest, by any comparison or reason.

Sometimes in Bible classes people want discussion, and they think up questions to start an argument. Usually they are questions that can't be answered definitely. There may be some value in such questions. They may cause some people to study the Bible, even if they are studying it for argument's sake. And, of course, Bible study is always of value. But there is so much in Scripture that is clear and unquestionable, that it is foolish to waste time pondering unanswerable questions.

Jesus answered the lawyer, "Thou shalt love the Lord thy God with all thy heart, and with all thy soul, and with all thy mind." The first four commandments in the Ten Commandments deal with loving God. Jesus could have argued about the comparative value of the first, the second, the third or the fourth, but He put them all together, and said, "Thou shalt love God."

"The second is like unto it, Thou shalt love thy neighbour as thyself. On these two commandments hang all the law and the prophets." Jesus avoided a lot of useless, endless discussion and came to the real root of the matter. All Biblical guidance rests on two things: first, your heart should be right with God; second, your heart should be right with your fellow man.

When you go into an orchard and look at an apple tree, you go to pick apples. You don't debate whether the roots are more important than the branches, or which branch is best. The whole tree was involved in producing the apples.

As Jesus pointed out, the important thing is to love God. If your heart is right with God, other things will take care of themselves.

Whose Son Is He?

While the Pharisees were gathered together, Jesus asked them, Saying, What think ye of Christ? whose son is he? They say unto him, The son of David. He saith unto them, How then doth David in spirit call him Lord, saying, The Lord said unto my

Lord, Sit thou on my right hand, till I make thine enemies thy footstool? If David then call him Lord, how is he his son? And no man was able to answer him a word, neither durst any man from that day forth ask him any more questions (Matthew 22:41-46).

You will remember that the Herodians had come and asked Him, "Is it all right for us to pay taxes?" Then the Sadducees came to Him and said, "What you say about heaven does not make sense." Then a lawyer, an expert in the Scriptures, came and asked, "What is the greatest commandment?" When they were all finished asking their questions, Jesus asked them a question.

Jesus' question was the most crucial question that could be asked: "What think ye of Christ? Whose son is he?"

Since the Old Testament had stated that the Messiah would be a descendant of David, the Pharisees naturally answered, "The son of David." Of course, such an answer implies that the Messiah was only a human, because David was human.

Then Jesus replied by quoting from one of the Psalms in which David referred to the Messiah as Lord. In those days especially it was unthinkable for a man to call his son, "Lord." Obviously then, the Messiah must have been more than an ordinary son of David.

"And no man was able to answer him a word, neither durst any man from that day forth ask him any more questions."

What do you think of Jesus Christ? Who is He? This is the real question.

Some people emphasize, "He was so meek and mild. He was so loving and helpful. We ought to teach others to try to imitate His example."

But this is not the real issue. The question is not, "What is He like?" The question is, "Who is He?" Who is this Person who was born in Bethlehem, lived in Galilee and died in Jerusalem? Who is this One who taught in the temple, who opened the eyes of the blind, who walked on the water and who finally died on the cross? Who is He?

If you only say that He is the Son of David, the Son of Mary, the Man of Galilee or the Babe of Bethlehem, you have not said enough. He is Lord! He is the Lord who sits on the throne! "Sit thou on my right hand, till I make thine enemies thy footstool." David called Him, "Lord." We should not stop short of that.

If you say, "He became a man in order that I could see Him and understand God," you are right to a certain extent. But don't forget that He became a man in order to die. The outstanding event in the life of Jesus was His death on Calvary's cross and His Resurrection three days later from the grave. He came to give His life a ransom for many. And now He is living in the presence of God, able to save to the uttermost those who come unto God by Him. Our salvation depends upon the fact that Jesus of Nazareth was the Son of God, and He is now in heaven interceding for us as the Son of God.

Chapter 19

THE PRETENDERS ARE EXPOSED

GOOD EXAMPLES MAKE A DIFFERENCE

At birth your consciousness is without definite images. As you live and participate in affairs, pictures form of every experience in your life. What you are today is largely the result of the pictures your mind has developed in the previous years of your life. Actually, the experiences of all men are basically quite similar. Yet, we all are different and have different ideas. Why is this? It is because we give our various experiences different meanings and interpretations as we prefer. We develop these interpretations from parents, teachers and others with whom we associate.

Our interpretation of God may well come from parents, Sunday school teachers and ministers. Consequently, it is a great blessing to grow up in a home where the Gospel is believed and in a church where a personal relationship with Jesus Christ is emphasized. A child brought up in such surroundings will have little trouble in receiving the Lord Jesus Christ as his Saviour.

Consider what a great lack it is to grow up where God is not honored. In some places people do not believe in God and do not act in the home as if God existed. Even in homes where parents are church members, people might live that way. They eat their meals, they dress, they go to school, they work, they play; from morning until night there is no evidence that they have any thought about God. They talk about people, about friends, about politics, about the communists, about the weather, but never about God. Think of a child growing up in a home like that! What do you think will be filling that mind? It would be easy for such a child to grow up with the idea that God, if He does exist, doesn't matter very much.

For such conditions, God holds leaders responsible. Teachers are responsible, parents are responsible, ministers are responsible. God will judge also every church and every home where pastors, teachers, and parents promote lip service to God; where they say things about God that they do not actually live out in their daily lives.

In Matthew 23 Jesus pointed His finger at the leaders of the Jews. He warned His disciples about such pretenders. What they taught was often true, but what they did was false. Jesus sternly rebuked these leaders, these scribes and Pharisees, who foolishly failed to perform the very things they professed. Jesus called them false teachers. They were false teachers not because they taught error, but because they lived a lie. Though they said all the right things, they did not do those things themselves.

Then Jesus warned Jerusalem, because its citizens were responsible for allowing such leadership to guide their minds and hearts. But if the Lord Jesus could sit and weep over Jerusalem, He could certainly weep over His church today. Because the Jews had repudiated the truth, "your house is left unto you desolate." With pathos He warned them that it would soon be too late. Men cannot play fast and loose with God and get away with it. Christians need to take soberly this warning as to their personal actions to make sure they act in ways that would show they actually believe that God is real.

Don't Do As They Do

Then spake Jesus to the multitude, and to his disciples, Saying, The scribes and the Pharisees sit in Moses' seat: All therefore whatsoever they bid you observe, that observe and do; but do not ye after their works: for they say, and do not. For they bind heavy burdens and grievous to be borne, and lay them on men's shoulders; but they themselves will not move them with one of their fingers. But all their works they do for to be seen of men: they make broad their phylacteries, and enlarge the borders of their garments, And love the uppermost rooms at feasts, and the chief seats in the synagogues, And greetings in the markets, and to be called of men, Rabbi, Rabbi. But be not ye called Rabbi: for one is your Master, even Christ; and all ye are brethren. And call no man your father upon the earth: for one is your Father, which is in heaven. Neither be ye called masters: for one is your Master, even Christ. But he that is greatest among you shall be your servant. And whosoever shall exalt himself shall be abased; and he that shall humble himself shall be exalted (Matthew 23:1-12).

In the synagogue the teacher's desk was called Moses' seat. It would be comparable to the preacher's pulpit in our churches. The teacher was to present the law of Moses faithfully. The Jews came to the synagogue to learn from the one who sat in Moses' seat. This was usually a scribe or a Pharisee.

Jesus told His followers to do what the scribes and Pharisees who sat in Moses' seat instructed from the law of Moses, but not to follow their deeds. They were to do as the Pharisees said, but not as they did.

Teachers are always in danger of assuming too much authority. Some people just love to be important. They love to walk in front. They love to boss. They love to teach others what to do, but such persons often do not follow their own advice. They love to be greeted "in the markets," that is, out on the street, and be known as "the Bible teacher." They like to receive honor because of their position. But Jesus warned His disciples not to grasp after the title of "Rabbi" nor "Father," for Jesus Christ is our Master and God in heaven is our Father. This is a stern warning not to give anyone absolute control over our spirits. Absolute control should be given only to God.

We are to listen to Scripture as it is taught by men, but we are not to permit the teacher to dominate our hearts for only God is the Lord of our souls.

These straightforward words were spoken in connection with religious leaders. Too often those who would lead us in spiritual things become such masters that they want to dominate us. They want us to do just what they say and accept just what they teach, because it is right in their estimation.

Throughout this chapter Jesus put His finger on the sore spots of the scribes and Pharisees. They had repeatedly tried to embarrass Him in the preceding chapter, but they had no success. Now He turned the tables on them. So He said sternly about such teachers, "There is nothing the matter with what they say; it is with what they do." May we ever be kept from falling into this arrogant snare of self-fancied importance.

BEHIND THE MASKS

But woe unto you, scribes and Pharisees, hypocrites! for ye shut up the kingdom of heaven against men: for ye neither go in yourselves, neither suffer ye them that are entering to go in. Woe unto you, scribes and Pharisees, hypocrites! for ye devour widows' houses, and for a pretence make long prayer: therefore ye shall receive the greater damnation. Woe unto you, scribes and Pharisees, hypocrites! for ye compass sea and land to make one proselyte, and when he is made, ye make him twofold more the child of hell than yourselves. Woe unto you, ye blind guides, which say, Whosoever shall swear by the temple, it is nothing; but whosoever shall swear by the gold of the temple, he is a debtor! Ye fools and blind: for whether is greater, the gold, or the temple that sanctifieth the gold? And, Whosoever shall swear by the altar, it is nothing; but whosoever sweareth by the gift that is upon it, he is guilty. Ye fools and blind: for whether is greater, the gift, or the altar that sanctifieth the gift? Whoso therefore shall swear by the altar, sweareth by it, and by all things thereon. And whoso shall swear by the temple, sweareth by it, and by him that dwelleth therein. And he that shall swear by heaven, sweareth by the throne of God, and by him that sitteth thereon. Woe unto you, scribes and Pharisees, hypocrites! for ye pay tithe of mint and anise and cummin, and have omitted the weightier matters of the law, judgment, mercy, and faith: these ought ye to have done, and not to leave the other undone. Ye blind guides, which strain at a gnat, and swallow a camel. Woe unto you, scribes and Pharisees, hypocrites! for ye make clean the outside of the cup and of the platter, but within they are full of extortion and excess. Thou blind Pharisee, cleanse first that which is within the cup and platter, that the outside of them may be clean also. Woe unto you, scribes and Pharisees, hypocrites! for ye are like unto whited sepulchres, which indeed appear beautiful outward, but are within full of dead men's bones, and of all uncleanness. Even so ye also outwardly appear righteous unto men, but within ye are full of hypocrisy and iniquity. Woe unto you, scribes and Pharisees, hypocrites! because ye build the tombs of the prophets, and garnish the sepulchres of the righteous. And say, If we had been in the days of our fathers, we would not have been partakers with them in the blood of the prophets. Wherefore ye be witnesses unto yourselves, that ye are the children of them which killed the prophets. Fill ye up then the measure of your fathers. Ye serpents, ye generation of vipers, how can ye escape the damnation of hell? (Matthew 23:13-33).

"Woe" means just the opposite of "blessed." "Blessed" implies that you are rich, happy and fortunate. "Woe" means you are poor, distressed and unfortunate.

The scribes were the educated students of the Old Testament. The Pharisees, scrupulously orthodox in their conduct and life, were the guardians of what they thought was the letter of the law. Yet the lives of both these groups actually hindered people from coming into a relationship with God. All their knowledge of the written Scripture, and their zeal for exact observance of the requirements left them cold in heart.

"Hypocrite" means two-faced. The old word actually meant a man with a mask on his face. The Pharisees put on an outward form, but it was not really what they were inside. "Hypocrite" refers to insincere pretenders.

"Devouring widows' houses" means that the Pharisees took gifts from poor widows and squandered the money on themselves. As they received the widows' money, they made long prayers to keep up the act. "Therefore ye shall receive the greater damnation." They were condemned not only because they did not trust in the Lord, but more so because they acted as if they did.

The Pharisees were very active in recruiting people for their party, but by their intense indoctrination their converts became even more superficial than they were.

"Woe unto you, ye blind guides, which say, Whosoever shall swear by the temple, it is nothing; but whosoever shall swear by the gold of the temple, he is a debtor!" These people guided others in their teaching, and set themselves up as experts in interpretation. However, their own interpretations were based on petty distinctions which completely twisted the original meaning. The Pharisees were so concerned with the letter of the law that they completely missed the spirit of it. The fine distinctions which those teachers tried to emphasize, Jesus said, do not matter. The big things, the important things, are what count. The Pharisees made a big to-do about small regulations, but neglected the major matters of judgment, mercy and faith. They had no real sense of proportion.

"Woe unto you, scribes and Pharisees, hypocrites! for ye are like unto whited sepulchres, which indeed appear beautiful outward, but are within full of dead men's bones, and all uncleanness." The Pharisees were like a mausoleum in a cemetery. The outside looked lovely, but the inside was rotten. Despite their rigid code of outward conduct, inwardly they were not right with God.

In addition, the Pharisees pretended to be great believers in the prophets, because they would read the prophets, quote the prophets, and preach from the prophets. But though they said kind words about the prophets who were dead, they persecuted the prophets who were still alive.

This is a stern indictment. It indicates that God abhors hypocrisy. He wants men to be sincere, to be honest, to be true. Those who come with a humble and contrite heart He will receive, but the proud He will despise. And this is just as true with religious instructors as with anyone else.

Who Killed the Prophets?

Wherefore, behold, I send unto you prophets, and wise men, and scribes: and some of them ye shall kill and crucify; and some of them shall ye scourge in your synagogues, and persecute them from city to city: That upon you may come all the righteous blood shed upon the earth, from the blood of righteous Abel unto the blood of Zacharias son of Barachias, whom ye slew between the temple and the altar. Verily I say unto you, All these things shall come upon this generation. O Jerusalem, Jerusalem, thou that killest the prophets, and stonest them which are sent unto thee, how often would I have gathered thy children together, even as a hen gathereth her chickens under her wings, and ye would not! Behold, your house is left unto you desolate. For I say unto you, Ye shall not see me henceforth, till ye shall say, Blessed is he that cometh in the name of the Lord (Matthew 23:34-39).

The human heart has always been hostile toward the things of God. Man has always turned his back on God. The Lord Jesus came to His own, but His own received Him not.

Nevertheless God has continued to send His prophets, wise men and scribes. The prophets are those who declare the Word of God, wise men are those who understand and interpret it, and the scribes are those who dig deeply into it and study it. But Jesus said, "Some of them ye shall kill and crucify, and some of them shall ye scourge in your synagogues, and persecute them from city to city."

This may be shocking to think about, but it is true. When a man of God presents the Word of God to unregenerate men, he is certain to suffer persecution of some kind. The natural heart is enmity against the law of God. "It is not subject to the law of God, neither indeed can be."

Servants of God have always been persecuted since the time of Abel. Opposition to the Word of God is like the opposition of Cain to Abel. "Zechariah, son of Barachiah, whom ye slew between the temple and the altar," was a more recent prophet who preached the Word of God to Israel.

"O Jerusalem, Jerusalem, thou that killest the prophets, and stonest them which are sent unto thee." In this passage God is speaking to His people who have actually killed His servants and stoned those that were sent unto them. Again and again, God in His grace and mercy was willing to gather them together to save them, comfort them and keep them, as a hen gathers her chickens under her wing. "And ye would not."

Though God is longsuffering, slow to anger and plenteous in mercy, He can be provoked; He can become indignant. Because Jerusalem had repeatedly provoked Him, "behold, your house is left unto you desolate." This is a way of saying, "God is going to turn away from you." God dealt with His people in mercy and grace, but His people ignored Him and were unthankful. God had warned the Jews through the various prophets. Now He was warning them through His Son, the Lord Jesus Christ. When Christ came to Jerusalem to present Himself, there was an air of finality about it. This was their last chance.

What was true of Jerusalem may also be true of us. If we repeatedly neglect Jesus Christ, our house "will be left desolate" too. Then we can expect to meet Him only as Judge and King.

"For I say unto you, Ye shall not see me henceforth, till ye shall say, . . . Blessed is he that cometh in the name of the Lord."

This was the greeting given to a king. In other words, Jesus was saying, "You shall not see me until you say, 'Blessed be the King.'" It is a sobering thing to realize that when He comes as King, the day of grace and mercy will be past. He will then come to judge. Even as He did when He came to Jerusalem riding on the colt, He will come in fulfillment of prophecy about the King.

Chapter 20

WHAT DOES THE FUTURE HOLD?

He Is Coming Again

Many people ask, "How did this world get started? How did man get to be here?" Some people offer various theories, but no one can give you a definite answer unless he accepts the Scriptures, which say simply and profoundly, "In the beginning God created the heaven and the earth."

Other people look around them and wonder, for example, about all the power necessary to keep the natural processes functioning. They may ask, "Where does the energy come from? What keeps everything going?" The Bible says that God holds all things by the word of His power, and by Him all things consist.

Still other people become confused about life when things seem to happen without rhyme or reason. They may ask, "Is there any purpose in it all? Is everything a great big confusion?" The Bible says to them that God is still on the throne and that He will bring His own will to pass.

Others are disturbed by the increasing crime rate and general lawlessness. They may ask, "Can anyone do anything he wants to do and get away with it?" The Bible says to them that God is the Judge of all the earth, and at the end of time every man will come before his Creator to give an account of himself. Every question about man and the universe leads us directly to God.

The disciples of Jesus Christ also asked many questions like these. In Matthew 24 the disciples had just shown the Lord the new temple under construction. No doubt they expected Him to be greatly impressed by the big magnificent structure that Herod was building. But instead, Jesus said, "Not one stone will be left upon another."

This startling statement provoked three serious questions from the disciples: (1) "When shall these things be?" (2) "What shall be the sign of thy coming?" (3) "What shall be the sign of the end of the world?"

These three are by no means identical questions. For instance, when they asked, "When shall these things be?" they were probably referring to the destruction of the temple. I think they were asking, "When do you think the city of Jerusalem will be destroyed?"

Jesus began His answer to these three questions by saying that there would be wars and rumors of wars, and famine, pestilence and earthquakes in various places. Saints will be persecuted, believers will quarrel with each other. False doctrine and heresies will arise. Iniquity shall abound. But in spite of all this, the Gospel will be preached to the ends of the earth. We may recall that all this has been going on ever since the Lord Jesus Christ was on earth. These happenings were not to be the end of the world, rather, they precede the end of the world.

Jesus also taught that there would be a time of great tribulation. People who study the Scriptures differ on when the Great Tribulation will be, but regardless of the differing views, all agree the Scriptures teach there will be a time of tribulation. Jesus also taught that there would be a great catastrophe of natural events. This might be called a cosmic eruption. The sun, moon and stars will all be affected. When this universal calamity occurs, this age will come to an end.

No man knows when the end of this world will be. In fact, Jesus said that He Himself did not know and that the angels did not know. God the Father alone knows. This does not necessarily mean that God has a calendar, and He has marked that date on it. God is not working on a railroad timetable; He is working according to His will. He is not as interested in *when* as He is in *what*. He is not as interested in time as He is in people and events. One day is with the Lord as a thousand years, and a thousand years is as one day.

However, even though we do not know when it will occur, we should certainly be ready for the end of the world. When should we get ready? The only answer for that is "Today." Jesus Christ may come back today, and so we should be ready today.

When someone says, "Oh, I know the Lord will come back, but it will be sometime later," this is dangerous. When someone says, "Oh, I don't think Jesus will ever return," this is wrong.

You will remember on that Ascension day when He went up in full view of them all the angels said, "Ye men of Galilee, why stand ye gazing up into heaven? this same Jesus, which is taken up from you into heaven, shall so come in like manner as ye have seen him go into heaven" (Acts 1:11). There is no possible way of understanding that statement without admitting that the early church was actually taught by the Word of God to expect His coming in due time.

Spiritual blessings will come to those who believe that His coming is imminent. The belief in the imminent coming of Christ means that there is no reason why He could not come back today. There is no big event in God's program which has to happen before He can return. But even this wise attitude toward the time of His coming is not as important as the simple conviction: "Jesus Christ is coming back!"

THE BEGINNING OF THE END

And Jesus went out, and departed from the temple: and his disciples came to him for to shew him the buildings of the temple. And Jesus said unto them, See ye not all these things? verily I say unto you, There shall not be left here one stone upon another, that shall not be thrown down. And as he sat upon the mount of Olives, the disciples came unto him privately, saying, Tell us, when shall these things be? and what shall be the sign of thy coming, and of the end of the world? And Jesus answered and said unto them, Take heed that no man deceive you. For many shall come in my name, saying, I am Christ; and shall deceive many. And ye shall hear of wars and rumours of wars: see that ye be not troubled: for all these things must come to pass, but the end is not yet. For nation shall rise against nation, and kingdom against kingdom: and there shall be famines, and pestilences, and earthquakes, in divers places. All these are the beginning of sorrows. Then shall they deliver you up to be afflicted, and shall kill you: and ye shall be hated of all nations for my name's sake. And then shall many be offended, and shall betray one another, and shall hate one another. And many false prophets shall rise, and shall deceive many. And because iniquity shall abound, the love of many shall wax cold. But he that shall endure unto the end, the same shall be saved. And this gospel of the kingdom shall be preached in all the world for a witness unto all nations; and then shall the end come (Matthew 24:1-14).

When the Lord Jesus lived on earth, the temple in Jerusalem used for worship was the one which had been built in the days of Ezra, Haggai and Zechariah. They had built it when they had returned from Babylon about 400 years earlier. King Herod, however, was working on a new temple. When Jesus came to Jerusalem, it had already been under construction for many years, but it was still unfinished. This new temple was very elaborate, much more ornate than the existing temple.

As already noted the disciples were evidently quite impressed with the new temple and expected Jesus to be also. But instead of being impressed, Jesus immediately announced that this temple would be completely destroyed.

Jesus' announcement prompted questions on the part of the

disciples. These questions pertained to the destruction of the temple, the time of Christ's return, and the end of the world.

Jesus began His lengthy reply, which is often called the Olivet Discourse, by warning, "Be very careful when you listen to people predicting things about the future. Don't let anyone fool you. Many will claim to be the Messiah. They will make promises to the people about how they can lead you out of trouble into the will of God. But don't be fooled."

In addition, there will be almost constant wars and rumors of wars. But war is not a sign of the end of the world. Besides war, which is a social calamity, there will be famine, which is an economic calamity; pestilence, a health calamity; and earthquakes, a natural calamity. These, Jesus said, are the beginning of sorrows, but they are not yet the end of the world.

The Lord Jesus went on to describe conditions which could be expected. Believers will be persecuted more than ever before. Many false ideas will be popular and will spread rapidly. There will be so much iniquity, immorality and offense against God and against man, that even believers will be affected by it. But the person who will not be shaken by these things will continue in his faith and will find assistance from God to help him through these difficult days.

"And this gospel of the kingdom shall be preached in all the world for a witness unto all nations, and then shall the end come." Missionary activity will continue in spite of wars and pestilence, persecution, heresy and immorality. Apparently this is to continue until all nations have heard the Gospel.

You remember that Jesus was speaking some 1900 years ago. Yet in what He said you can see a picture of all church history unto this day. These things are not the end of the world, Jesus said, but will precede the end of the world.

It is helpful to remember the Lord Jesus gave no hint as to the length of time these conditions would continue. From the point of time, when He stood on the Mount of Olives, looking forward to the end of the world and answering the question as to the signs which could be expected to appear, He described conditions which would be experienced *before* the end. How long such conditions would continue was not mentioned. Their occurrence in the world even now is a clear reminder that the end of the world is next in God's plan. The time of its coming is known only to God.

The Heavens Shall Be Shaken

When ye therefore shall see the abomination of desolation, spoken of by Daniel the prophet, stand in the holy place, (whoso readeth, let him understand:) Then let them which be in Judea flee into the mountains: Let him which is on the housetop not come down to take any thing out of his house: Neither let him which is in the field return back to take his clothes. And woe unto them that are with child, and to them that give suck in those days! But pray ye that your flight be not in the winter, neither on the sabbath day: For then shall be great tribulation, such as was not since the beginning of the world to this time, no, nor ever shall be. And except those days should be shortened, there should no flesh be saved: but for the elect's sake those days shall be shortened. Then if any man shall say unto you, Lo, here is Christ, or there; believe it not. For there shall arise false Christs, and false prophets, and shall shew great signs and wonders; insomuch that, if it were possible, they shall deceive the very elect. Behold, I have told you before. Wherefore if they shall say unto you, Behold, he is in the desert; go not forth: behold, he is in the secret chambers; believe it not. For as the lightning cometh out of the east, and shineth even unto the west; so shall also the coming of the Son of man be. For wheresoever the carcase is, there will the eagles be gathered together. Immediately after the tribulation of those days shall the sun be darkened, and the moon shall not give her light, and the stars shall fall from heaven, and the powers of the heavens shall be shaken: And then shall appear the sign of the Son of man in heaven: and then shall all the tribes of the earth mourn, and they shall see the Son of man coming in the clouds of heaven with power and great glory. And he shall send his angels with a great sound of a trumpet, and they shall gather together his elect from the four winds, from one end of heaven to the other. Now learn a parable of the fig tree: When his branch is yet tender, and putteth forth leaves, ye know that summer is nigh: So likewise ye, when ye shall see all these things, know that it is near, even at the doors. Verily I say unto you, This generation shall not pass, till all these things be fulfilled. Heaven and earth shall pass away, but my words shall not pass away. But of that day and hour knoweth no man, no, not the angels of heaven, but my Father only. But as the days of Noe were, so shall also the coming of the Son of man be. For as in the days that were before the flood they were eating and drinking, marrying and giving in marriage, until the day that Noe entered into the ark. And knew not until the flood came, and took them all away; so shall also the coming of the Son of man be. Then shall two be in the field; the one shall be taken, and the other left. Two women shall be grinding at the mill; the one shall be taken, and the other left (Matthew 24:15-41).

The prophet Daniel had predicted that "an abomination of desolation" would be found standing in the holy place. In other words, the holiest part of the temple would be desecrated. As this abomination of desolation would be put into the holy place, a great calamity would befall the city.

In a few words Jesus graphically described this calamity. This would also be the time when some would claim to have special knowledge of the Lord's return. "Don't pay any attention to them," Jesus said, "for when I return, everyone will know it."

It is hard to imagine such a great astronomical disturbance as Jesus describes, with the stars falling from heaven and the powers of the heaven shaken. But this is what Jesus said. After intense tribulation and after cosmic disturbances the Son of man will come in the clouds of heaven with power and great glory. He spoke of this to Pilate and to the Jewish Sanhedrin, as well as on other occasions.

"Heaven and earth shall pass away, but my words shall not pass away." What Jesus was talking about will actually occur, although it seems fantastic. No matter how it comes to pass, we can always count on His words as being true.

As mentioned before, we do not know when all this will happen. The time is unannounced, but the event is sure. Often we get so absorbed in the affairs of this world that we forget this future event in God's plan. Jesus is coming again.

WATCHING AND WAITING

Watch therefore: for ye know not what hour your Lord doth come. But know this, that if the goodman of the house had known in what watch the thief would come, he would have watched, and would not have suffered his house to be broken up. Therefore be ye also ready: for in such an hour as ye think not the Son of man cometh. Who then is a faithful and wise servant, whom his lord hath made ruler over his household, to give them meat in due season? Blessed is that servant, whom his lord when he cometh shall find so doing. Verily I say unto you, That he shall make him ruler over all his goods. But and if that evil servant shall say in his heart, My lord delayeth his coming; And shall begin to smite his fellowservants, and to eat and drink with the drunken; The lord of that servant shall come in a day when he looketh not for him, and in an hour that he is not aware of, And shall cut him asunder, and appoint him his portion with the hypocrites: there shall be weeping and gnashing of teeth (Matthew 24:42-51).

Life on this earth is temporary and will not go on forever. God made this world and holds it in His hand. But there is a time limit on it. The time is coming when this world will come to an end.

My father-in-law knew the Scriptures very well. Once I asked him about the coming of the Lord and the end of the world. He replied something like this: "No one knows when that will be; no one knows the day nor the hour. It might be in 100 years; it might be in 1,000 years. Already it has been close to 2,000 years. But, remember this, if the Lord Jesus returns in your lifetime, all that would happen to you would be that you would see Him. As far as you would be concerned, He would be coming just for you. But if He does not come back to this earth for a thousand years, you can be sure that you will see Him long before that."

Then he continued, "You can go to a life insurance agency and they can tell you about how long you can expect to live. On the basis of what they tell you, you can be sure that if the Lord does not return for another 100 or another 1,000 years, you will see Him a lot sooner than that, and it will be just as real. And remember this, everything that the Scripture has to say about being ready for the coming of the Lord applies to your being ready to meet him in death, too. The Bible says, 'Teach us to number our days that we may apply our hearts unto wisdom.'"

The Lord Jesus warned His disciples to be ready. "Watch therefore; for ye know not what hour your Lord doth come." His coming will be unannounced and unexpected. We would do well to keep this in mind. Each day as we do our work, we would be wise to keep in mind that He may come that day. Each week, as we make plans, we should bear in mind that He may come that week. To live in this world as though we were going to be down here forever is just plain foolish. Just because the time is unknown should not make us careless or indifferent. In fact since we do not know the time we should remember the Lord might return at any time, even today or tonight.

Five Foolish Virgins

Then shall the kingdom of heaven be likened unto ten virgins, which took their lamps, and went forth to meet the bridegroom. And five of them were wise, and five were foolish. They that were foolish took their lamps, and took no oil with them: But the wise took oil in their vessels with their lamps. While the bridegroom tarried, they all slumbered and slept. And at midnight there was a cry made, Behold, the bridegroom cometh; go ye out to meet him. Then all those virgins arose, and trimmed their lamps. And the foolish said unto the wise, Give us of your oil; for our lamps are gone out. But the wise answered, saying, Not so; lest there be not enough for us and you: but go ye rather to them that sell, and buy for yourselves. And while they went to buy, the bridegroom came; and they that were ready went in with him to the marriage: and the door was shut. Afterward came also the other virgins, saying, Lord, Lord, open to us. But he answered and said, Verily I say unto you, I know you not.

Watch therefore, for ye know neither the day nor the hour wherein the Son of man cometh (Matthew 25:1-13).

This well-known parable, commonly called "The Ten Virgins," has one major point. It is this: He is coming even though the time is not known. You can interpret His coming to refer to the end of the world or to His coming on the day you die. Like so many portions of Scripture, these verses can have both an immediate application and an ultimate application. Many times a passage will be so written that it will fit two or more different interpretations equally well. But one thing is certain: He is coming, and He is coming for me.

This parable of the ten virgins is to be understood as taking place in a city where the streets were not lighted. When guests came to a wedding or another gala occasion, girls would go out to meet them with torches which lit up the pathway. When the bridegroom came, all the road would be lit up by the torches carried by such girls. In this parable we are told of ten virgins. First the Lord tells of five who were ready. Then we are told about five foolish virgins who had no oil in their lamps.

"They that were foolish took their lamps, but took no oil with them." This would show they apparently did not expect to light their lamps. It would mean they had decided he was not coming that night. This is what the foolish virgins did. On the other hand the five wise virgins took oil in their lamps and were prepared to act; they expected the bridegroom might possibly come.

It is a sobering fact that in some ways all ten virgins were alike. They all had lamps and they all slumbered and slept. As a matter of fact they all expected him to come sometime. When the bridegroom finally came, they all awoke. Until now you could not see any difference between them. They all had acted alike. But five had neglected to put oil in their lamps. They had shared in all the arrangements but had made the mistake of thinking "not tonight." That was the foolish part. Sharing in all the activity of real believers, while actually thinking that nothing will happen, is foolish.

There is an important lesson here for each of us. When it comes to personal obedience to the Lord, buy for yourself! The good members of your family can't help you in this. The believing members of your congregation can't serve the Lord for you. When it comes to making sure there is oil in your lamp, that is your very own business. You cannot borrow the faith of anyone else, no matter how close that person may be to you.

It is a tragic story: "While they went to buy, the bridegroom came." How easily we could sympathize with them! Actually, they went to do the right thing. But when they tried to make up for wasted time, they found it was too late. "They that were ready went in with him to the marriage." What a wonderful privilege! But that privilege is available only to those who actually respond to the gospel message and truly expect things to happen as promised.

It is true some people don't care at all about the Gospel. They do not care about salvation, about God or about any spiritual matters. When such people do not respond we can understand. There are others, however, who do believe in God, the soul and heaven, who yet have not done what is necessary to get themselves right with God. They have accepted the Gospel as true, but they have not actually gotten right with God. These people may hope some time to walk with the Lord, but like the five foolish virgins, they will miss their opportunity because they do not commit themselves in expectation to the call of the Gospel now.

The truth of the matter is that a person can trifle away the time by not turning to God today. If you feel called in your heart to come to the Lord, do it. Tomorrow may be too late. The Lord Jesus said, "Watch, therefore, for ye know neither the day nor the hour wherein the Son of man cometh."

TALENTS AND JUDGMENT

For the kingdom of heaven is as a man travelling into a far country, who called his own servants, and delivered unto them his goods. And unto one he gave five talents, to another two, and to another one; to every man according to his several ability; and straightway took his journey. Then he that had received the five talents went and traded with the same, and made them other five talents. And likewise he that had received two, he also gained other two. But he that had received one went and digged in the earth, and hid his lord's money. After a long time the Lord of those servants cometh, and reckoneth with them. And so he that had received five talents came and brought other five talents, saying, Lord, thou deliveredst unto me five talents: behold, I have gained beside them five talents more. His lord said unto him, Well done, thou good and faithful servant: thou hast been faithful over a few things, I will make thee ruler over many things: enter thou into the joy of thy lord. He also that had received two talents came and said, Lord, thou deliveredst unto me two talents: behold, I have gained two other talents beside them. His lord said unto him, Well done, good and faithful servant; thou hast been faithful over a few things, I will make thee ruler over many things: enter thou into the joy of thy lord. Then he which had received the one talent came and said, Lord, I knew thee that thou art an hard man, reaping where thou hast not sown, and gathering where thou hast not strawed: And I was afraid, and went and hid thy talent in the earth: lo, there thou hast that is thine. His lord answered and said unto him, Thou wicked and slothful servant, thou knewest that I reap where I sowed not, and gather where I have not strawed: Thou oughtest therefore to have put my money to the exchangers, and then at my coming I should have received mine own with usury. Take therefore the talent from him, and give it unto him which hath ten talents. For unto every one that hath shall be given, and he shall have abundance: but from him that hath not shall be taken away even that which he hath. And cast ye the unprofitable servant into outer darkness: there shall be weeping and gnashing of teeth (Matthew 25:14-30).

This well-known parable of the talents emphasizes our responsibility for the opportunities each of us has. God gives to every believer certain opportunities for service. Some of these God has given to you and some to me. Of course, there are individual differences. Some believers may have five talents, some two and some only one. But the important question is, "What do you do with the opportunities you have?"

There is another lesson in this parable. It teaches plainly that Christ Jesus is coming back again. This time when He comes, He will not be as a Babe in Bethlehem, but as a mighty Ruler. He will not come to die; He will come to judge. It is a striking thing to note that in the parable the servant with only two talents received the same commendation as the one with five: "Well done, thou good and faithful servant." Each was told: "Thou hast been faithful over a few things, I will make thee ruler over many things." Apparently it is not a matter of how much, but a matter of how faithful the servant was.

You may not be prominent in this world, but you can be faithful. If you are faithful, your faithfulness is just as big in the eyes of the Lord as the faithfulness of an important person. If each is faithful, each will receive similar praise from the Lord. But there is sharp judgment coming upon the one who neglects the opportunity which he has. In the parable this servant was not only called wicked and slothful, but that which he had was taken away from him, and he himself was cast out to share the fate of the enemies of the Lord.

Separating Sheep from Goats

When the Son of man shall come in his glory, and all the holy angels with him, then shall he sit upon the throne of his glory: And before him shall be gathered all nations: and he shall separate them one from another, as a shepherd divideth his sheep from the goats: And he shall set the sheep on his right hand, but the goats on the left. Then shall the King say unto them on his right hand, Come, ye blessed of my Father, inherit the kingdom prepared for you from the foundation of the world: For I was an hungred, and ye gave me meat: I was thirsty, and ye gave me drink: I was a stranger, and ye took me in: Naked, and ye clothed me: I was sick, and ye visited me: I was in prison, and ye came unto me. Then shall the righteous answer him, saying, Lord, when saw we thee an hungred, and fed thee? or thirsty, and gave thee drink? When saw we thee a stranger, and took thee in? or naked, and clothed thee? Or when saw we thee sick, or in prison, and came unto thee? And the King shall answer and say unto them, Verily I say unto you, Inasmuch as ye have done it unto one of the least of these my brethren, ye have done it unto me. Then shall he say also unto them on the left hand, Depart from me, ye cursed, into everlasting fire, prepared for the devil and his angels: For I was an hungred, and ye gave me no meat: I was thirsty, and ye gave me no drink: I was a stranger, and ye took me not in: naked, and ye clothed me not: sick, and in prison, and ye visited me not. Then shall they also answer him, saying, Lord, when saw we thee an hungred, or athirst, or a stranger, or naked, or sick, or in prison, and did not minister unto thee? Then shall he answer them, saying, Verily I say unto you, inasmuch as ye did it not to one of the least of these, ye did it not to me. And these shall go away into everlasting punishment: but the righteous into life eternal (Matthew 25:31-46).

Do you remember the parable of the wheat and the tares in Matthew 13? Do you remember how they both grew together until the time of the harvest? The servants wanted to go and separate them, but the master said, "No, let them both grow together until the harvest." When the harvest comes, the separation will be made. This parable in Matthew 25 shows the scene at harvest time.

The people described in this parable did not come to this judgment and then become transformed suddenly into sheep and goats on the basis of their works. No, they were already sheep and goats, wheat and tares.

While this parable refers to social actions, this does not mean that this is the only conduct which God judges. He also judges faithfulness to Him; He judges actions toward those in authority; He judges attitudes toward other people; He judges obedience to His laws.

In this parable the conduct (visiting the sick, those in prison, etc.) which made the difference between the sheep and the goats was apparently quite ordinary and not at all spectacular. It was an ordinary deed being done as unto the Lord. This is what Paul meant when he said, "Whatsoever ye do in word or deed, do all in the name of the Lord Jesus." It is possible to do each day's work as unto the Lord. If you do, you are a sheep. But it is also possible to do each day's work for yourself; if you do this, you are one of the goats.

The kingdom into which the sheep entered was prepared for them before the foundation of the world. But the kingdom which the goats entered into was one of "everlasting fire prepared for the devil and his angels." It was not prepared for people. Nowhere in the Bible does it say that God created man to be lost. Some souls will certainly be lost, but they are lost in spite of all that the Lord has done to prevent it. This everlasting fire was not prepared for sinners. It was prepared for the devil and his angels. Sinners will be there only because they persisted in their sinful neglect of opportunities to turn to God.

Chapter 21

WORSHIP, BETRAYAL AND DENIAL

WHAT ARE YOU LOOKING AT?

In Matthew 26 we can see various responses of the followers of Christ. We can see various degrees of faithfulness and foolishness. But while we look at these followers of Christ, let us remember that we are like them. Their weaknesses may be our weaknesses; their strengths can be our strengths.

We may well wonder what made the difference in their responses? Perhaps the simple truth is that the difference depended on what they looked at. Each looked at a different thing, and because they were looking at different things, they had different frames of mind.

Why does a good man do good? He does it because he is thinking of something that moves him in that direction. In order to do good, a man must think of something other than himself. Just as surely as he thinks of himself, he is not going to be doing good.

In this chapter we first see Mary coming to the Lord Jesus Christ with a precious box of ointment. Breaking it, she used it to anoint Him. Her action implied that nothing was too good for her Lord. What caused Mary to do this? Who was Mary looking at? She was looking at the Lord Jesus and saw Him as her Saviour. Her heart and mind were focused on Him in His saving work. She was looking on Jesus who would soon die for her. Remember the Lord Jesus said, "For in that she hath poured this ointment on my body, she did it for my burial."

Apparently Mary understood what would soon happen to Jesus. And why did she have this insight? Because this is the woman who sat at Jesus' feet. She had chosen that good part to sit at His feet rather than to be distracted by other things. Because she was looking at the Lord Jesus Christ, she came to understand His mission here upon earth. She realized He would be put to death and she knew He was dying for her. In her response to Him she felt nothing was too good for Him.

You and I might be inclined to praise her. I am not sure that she would be especially interested in our praise. She did this not for praise, but because in her heart she loved Him.

Immediately after this incident involving Mary is the record of the sin of Judas, who betrayed his Lord for thirty pieces of silver. How could he do such a thing? Judas was obviously not a degenerate person. Yet the record is clear enough. This is a man who loved money. His eye was so much on money that he lost sight of other things. You can take a dime and hold it so close to your eye that you cannot see the sun. That is the way it is with anything. You can hold things so close to your heart that you can't even see the Gospel of Jesus Christ.

If Mary had been looking at money, she would not have poured out the precious ointment on Jesus. If Judas had been looking at the Lord, he would not have betrayed Him.

When the disciples gathered to eat the Last Supper, the Lord Jesus told them, "One of you shall betray me." Immediately one after another of the disciples asked Jesus, "Lord, is it I?" The statement had focused attention upon themselves and each man looked at his own heart. As he did this, each one was moved to uncertainty about himself. Looking into one's own heart can bring no assurance or comfort to anyone.

Reading the account of the Lord's Supper you will note how He took the cup and said, "This is my blood of the New Testament, which is shed for many for the remission of sins." Here your attention is once again focused on the death of Christ.

Possibly the most wonderful experience we can have is to reflect on the thought that Jesus Christ, God Incarnate, loved us so much that He died for us. There is no time when our whole Christian experience can be so richly blessed as when we come into the presence of the Lord Jesus Christ. And the sacrament of the Lord's Supper is designed to bring us face to face with Jesus Christ.

Following the Last Supper, the Lord Jesus said to His disciples, "All of you shall be offended because of me this night." They all began to say, "No, we will not." Peter most emphatically said, "Lord, if everybody else should, I won't." Only a short time before, when the Lord Jesus said that one disciple would betray Him, Peter had asked, "Lord, is it I?" But this time Christ placed the emphasis on the group, rather than the individual. He said "all" not "one." This time the disciples looked at each other rather than at their own individual hearts. When you look at the group, you feel how different you are from others. Others may turn away, but strangely enough you feel in your heart you will never turn away. Often you question the faith of others, but you are confident you are not like them. Here we can see the possible danger of presenting a message to the public at large. When that is done the individual heart at once takes refuge in self-esteem and self-assurance.

Turn your eyes upon Jesus,
Look full in His wonderful face,
And the things of earth will grow strangely dim,
In the light of His glory and grace.

A BROKEN BOX OF PERFUME

And it came to pass, when Jesus had finished all these sayings, he said unto his disciples, Ye know that after two days is the feast of the passover, and the Son of man is betrayed to be crucified. Then assembled together the chief priests, and the scribes, and the elders of the people, unto the palace of the high priest, who was called Caiaphas, And consulted that they might take Jesus by subtilty, and kill him. But they said, Not on the feast day, lest there be an uproar among the people. Now when Jesus was in Bethany, in the house of Simon the leper, There came unto him a woman having an alabaster box of very precious ointment, and poured it on his head, as he sat at meat. But when his disciples saw it, they had indignation, saying, To what purpose is this waste? For this ointment might have been sold for much, and given to the poor. When Jesus understood it, he said unto them, Why trouble ye the woman? for she hath wrought a good work upon me. For ye have the poor always with you; but me ye have not always. For in that she hath poured this ointment on my body, she did it for my burial. Verily I say unto you, Wheresoever this gospel shall be preached in the whole world, there shall also this, that this woman hath done, be told for a memorial of her (Matthew 26:1-13).

The Lord Jesus knew that the time was drawing nigh for Him to be crucified and He told His disciples that things were moving rapidly toward the end of His ministry on earth. Even then the Jewish leaders were consulting with the high priest on the best method of capturing Jesus in order to put Him to death.

But while this act of enmity was in progress, one of the sweetest incidents in the earthly life of our Lord took place in Bethany in the house of Simon a leper. It happened when Mary came and anointed Him with a precious ointment. Anointing with spices was a way to show deference and honor to someone. What Mary did was done as a gift of love. She did it not for publicity nor fame. She did it just for her Lord.

It seems that Mary anticipated that the Lord Jesus would soon be killed. Jesus said that while she was putting this ointment on His body now, she did it actually because she knew that His body would soon be dead. It was customary to anoint a dead body with perfumes since they had no process of embalming a corpse as we have today.

This woman was criticized by the disciples. She was very foolish, they thought, to spend so much for the Lord. But Jesus took a different view of it. He appreciated it. "She hath wrought a good work upon me. . . . For in that she hath poured this ointment on my body, she did it for my burial. Verily I say unto you, wheresoever this gospel shall be preached in the whole world, there shall also this, that this woman hath done, be told for a memorial of her."

Do you realize that this is the only deed done to the Lord Jesus Christ personally that He ever asked anyone to repeat? Everything He taught, He did Himself. Every illustration He gave, He gave Himself, except this one. This one He presents to us because it is an example of what anyone can do to serve the Lord. When you think about the Gospel being preached you realize there is only one thing that Christ cannot illustrate Himself: that is, how a person should act toward Him. He can illustrate obedience, faithfulness and humility, but He could not illustrate a believer's response to the Son of God.

So he took this one incident and gave it to us for our understanding. If you really want to know how to serve the Lord, this is it. This woman took something very precious, and brought it to the Lord personally and gave it to Him as a gift.

How did Mary know that this act would be so pleasing to the Lord? Why should we think that she knew? She didn't do this to have her name spoken of everywhere. She did it because she loved Him.

Are you trying to be faithful to Him in your home? Would you like to be well-pleasing in His sight? If you will do what you do for Him, everyone in your home will be blessed. Give Him your precious box of ointment, the very best that you have and bring it to Him as a gift.

Thirty Pieces of Silver

Then one of the twelve, called Judas Iscariot, went unto the chief priests, And said unto them, What will ye give me, and I will deliver him unto you? And they covenanted with him for thirty pieces of silver. And from that time he sought opportunity to betray him (Matthew 26:14-16).

We are now to consider the most tragic incident in the career of the Lord Jesus. One of His own chosen disciples betrayed Him.

How could he do it? Judas had been with the Lord Jesus for three years. He was not just one of the crowd. He was not one of 500 men following the Lord, nor even one of the 120 disciples. He was one of Twelve, chosen from among the disciples to be His apostles, to be with Him, to receive of His power, to cast out demons, to heal the sick, to preach the Gospel.

Judas was the treasurer of the apostolic company. Evidently they had one common fund which they all shared and which they used for the purchasing of supplies. We should not think of Judas as a crude, vulgar man. We should not think of him as a shifty, sneaky thief. He was so highly regarded among the apostles that they trusted him with the money. We may well remember that these apostles were not foolish men when it came to business. They were laymen by vocation. Some had their own fishing business; one was a tax collector. Consequently, whoever was their treasurer would have to have their confidence. This was a man who, by any conceivable standard, would have been counted a good man, a competent man, and a faithful man.

Actually, the idea of betraying the Lord Jesus Christ came into Judas' heart only shortly before the betrayal. In John 13 we read, "The devil having now put into the heart of Judas Iscariot, Simon's son, to betray him." The translation "put into" is too mild; it really means that Satan hurled the idea into his heart. It was an impulsive idea that struck him; he could make some money. Perhaps the idea came into his mind when he saw Mary anointing Him with precious ointment. Strange as it may seem, holy conduct can even be used by Satan to prompt some people to sin. Does that mean that holiness is wrong? No, it simply means that sin, buried in the heart of man, will eventually come out.

In this case, it was Judas' love for money which appealed to him in a weak moment and he fell victim to it. The real sin of Judas, in exchanging his loyalty to the Lord Jesus for thirty pieces of silver, was a sin that he had been committing a long time before. It was when he gave himself over to the love of money, when he esteemed money so highly that it was more important to him than anything else in the world: it was then he began his sin of betrayal.

Judas had a love for money and it was this that made him a thief, as the gospel of John intimates. Any time you are covetous you are a thief. Any time you try to get something that you are not willing to pay for, you are a thief. You may never steal, because you may not have the opportunity or because you may fear the consequences, but still you may be a thief at heart. There are many poor people whose hearts and minds are filled with the love of money. You don't have to be rich to love money. And he who loves money may become a thief, for the Bible says, "The love of money is the root of all evil" (I Timothy 6:10). The actual betrayal is what men see and condemn, but the inward sin of covetousness was undoubtedly the source of the evil deed.

"Is It I?"

Now the first day of the feast of unleavened bread the disciples came to Jesus, saying unto him, Where wilt thou that we prepare for thee to eat the passover? And he said, Go into the city to such a man, and say unto him, The Master saith, My time is at hand; I will keep the passover at thy house with my disciples. And the disciples did as Jesus had appointed them; and they made ready the passover. Now when the even was come, he sat down with the twelve. And as they did eat, he said, Verily I say unto you, that one of you shall betray me. And they were exceeding sorrowful, and began every one of them to say unto him, Lord, is it I? And he answered and said, He that dippeth his hand with me in the dish, the same shall betray me. The Son of man goeth as it is written of him; but woe unto that man by whom the Son of man is betrayed! it had been good for that man if he had not been born. Then Judas, which betrayed him, answered and said, Master, is it I? He said unto him, Thou hast said (Matthew 26:17-25).

There is always something dramatic about a final scene. If you have been visiting loved ones and the day comes when you must leave, everything you do on that day takes on new significance. The closing of your suitcase for the last time, and the putting on of your clothing, the last meal you share together, the parting words you say – all seem to be so significant.

So it was with the Lord Jesus Christ. He was about to leave His disciples, so He arranged to eat a meal, the Jewish Passover feast, with them. It was at this "last supper" that Jesus told His disciples, "One of you is going to betray me."

The first reaction of the disciples was sorrow: "They were exceeding sorrowful." In that sorrow may have been different elements. One element would certainly be sorrow because of the hurt to the Lord Jesus. It is a tragedy to think that anyone would ever betray Him. Perhaps they were also sorrowful to think that any one of them could be so weak.

The statement brought out their realistic appraisal of themselves. Each disciple seemed to feel that he was the weakest link. "Lord, do you mean me?" Each one thought he was more likely to betray Christ than any of the others. As each was struck with his own weakness and waywardness, his uncertainty about himself came to the surface. Each counted himself lower than the others. It did not occur to any of them to point the finger at someone else. It would have been the natural tendency to put the blame on others. But the disciples did not do this. Apparently they did not suspicion that Judas would be the guilty party. It seems they faced the statement personally. In their hearts they admitted, "If anyone could do it, I could. If anybody would be that weak, it would be I."

"He that dippeth his hand with me in the dish, the same shall betray me." The Lord Jesus told John, "It is the one to whom I give the piece of bread," and then He gave it to Judas. Judas was seated that near to Jesus.

Then He gave this sober warning: "Woe unto that man by whom the Son of man is betrayed! It had been good for that man if he had not been born." Think of it! A person can foolishly do something which is worse than if he had never been alive at all. This betrayal was not unexpected. Jesus knew it would happen, for it had been prophesied. But even though it had been predicted, this did not place any less responsibility on Judas. His action was still his own responsibility.

As we think of this heart-breaking incident we must ask ourselves, "Is it possible that I might betray the Lord?" The fact that it was an apostle that betrayed Him should be a salutary warning to each one of us. Just because we are in the company of believers, even as members of the church, does not mean we might not fail the Lord because of some secret sin that has long remained out of sight.

The Last Supper

And as they were eating, Jesus took bread, and blessed it, and brake it, and gave it to the disciples, and said, Take, eat; this is my body. And he took the cup, and gave thanks, and gave it to them, saying, Drink ye all of it; For this is my blood of the new testament, which is shed for many for the remission of sins. But I say unto you, I will not drink henceforth of this fruit of the vine, until that day when I drink it new with you in my Father's kingdom. And when they had sung an hymn, they went out into the mount of Olives (Matthew 26:26-30).

Friendship is a wonderful thing, but friendship is something that must be maintained. We keep letters that our friends write. We keep gifts they give us. We keep their pictures to remind us of them. These memorials are far more important to us by their associations than a particular gift in itself. Someone may give you a fountain pen, and that pen means far more to you than just something with which you write.

You may remember a friend vividly, but your friendship would become even more vivid if you called him on the telephone and talked with him. You might appreciate a friend very much, but if you go to see him, you will appreciate him even more. Visit him, sit down and chat with him. Such things strengthen, maintain and revive memories that build a long-lasting friendship.

In Scripture we have the record of many memorials. Some altars were set up as a memorial. The Sabbath day was to be kept holy as a memorial. The Lord's Supper is given to Christians as a memorial.

As you observe the sacrament, your relationship to Christ is strengthened. When you take the bread of the Lord's Supper and eat it, you are reminded that the Lord Jesus Christ gave Himself for you and is to be personally received. He died for you, His blood was shed for you, He was raised from the dead for you, He now appears in heaven for you. It is all for you, just as the bread you eat is for you. In using bread to eat, the sacrament of the Lord's Supper is designed to refresh your memory that Calvary was for you personally.

The Lord Jesus Christ came as a man and died as a man. One man, Christ, died for one man, you. And this one man, the Son of God, who died on Calvary, bought and paid for you. In just the way you eat bread, you are to reach out and receive Him. There may be ten others present or a hundred others present, but that makes no difference. It wouldn't help you if 1,999 others partook of the Lord's Supper and you did not. You must personally take for yourself. Take, eat; He is for you.

The same is true of the cup. The blood is for the remission of your sin. You are to receive God's forgiveness. By eating the bread and drinking the cup you will receive His blessing.

When you sit down to the sacrament of the Lord's Supper you are remembering that His body was broken and His blood was shed for you. You will never qualify by being good or perfect. That is not the promise you make. That would not be realistic. You could never achieve the perfection. What you do have in mind is that He died for you, and He will provide blessing for you in Himself.

Before the Cock Crows

Then saith Jesus unto them, All ye shall be offended because of me this night: for it is written, I will smite the shepherd, and the sheep of the flock shall be scattered abroad. But after I am risen again, I will go before you into Galilee. Peter answered and said unto him, Though all men shall be offended because of thee, yet will I never be offended. Jesus said unto him, Verily I say unto thee, That this night, before the cock crow, thou shalt deny me thrice. Peter said unto him, Though I should die with thee, yet will I not deny thee. Likewise also said all the disciples (Matthew 26:31-35).

Sometimes at a church service as the Holy Spirit seems to move the entire congregation close to God, you may feel that you will never again falter nor fail in the Christian life. This was exactly the way the disciples felt after the Last Supper. Yet Jesus told them that they would all be offended. This word "offended" does not mean a personal hurt. Rather it has the meaning that they would be disturbed or confused, that they would have difficulty following Him in what He commanded them to do.

Peter affirmed what the other disciples later declared also, "Though I should die with thee, yet will I not deny thee." They were all sure they would never forsake Him.

On the way to this passover feast, Jesus was very sorrowful and He said, "One of you shall betray me." Now, after the feast, He said, "All of you shall be offended." We may remember that before the feast each man wondered whether he would be the one to betray the Lord. But afterward all the disciples said with Peter, "I will never be offended." When the attention was focused on the individual, there was real heart-searching and a humble realization that any one of them might falter. When the attention was on the group as a whole, all said, "No, not I. It might be everyone else, but it would never be me."

Let us take one more look at this truth. As long as I stand before the Lord individually, I can be humble and realistically conscious of my own shortcomings. But as soon as attention is focused on the group, I feel strong. I feel better than some, more faithful than others. This is very important to have in mind, because what we all want is honest, sincere and realistic response to the Lord Jesus.

In Peter there was full self-confidence. He felt he was ready to stand alone. "Though all men forsake thee, I won't." He was comparing himself with the average man and this made him confident. Perhaps he had a low estimate of the average man.

This may be true in any of us. We may have a false image of our own faithfulness. Perhaps we feel that we would never fail Him as Peter did. Perhaps we can think of many others in our church who could expect to deny Him, but we feel sure we would never do that because we would be the last person in our church to act that way. Here we must be careful. We must make sure our confidence is not in ourselves but in the Lord. As long as our confidence is in ourselves, we will surely fail.

Chapter 22

THE GREATEST TRIAL IN HISTORY

AGONY AND ANGUISH

We see in the cross of Calvary the most cruel event in history. "He came unto his own, and his own received him not" (John 1:11). But that's putting it mildly. They rejected Him, they abused Him, they tortured Him. Beginning at Gethsemane, through the betrayal by Judas, the arrest by the Roman soldiers, the trials before Caiaphas and Pilate and then the horrors of the crucifixion, Jesus underwent agony that no man has ever experienced.

But throughout the horrible hours, Jesus was obedient to do His Father's will. His desire to please the Father is evidenced in the Garden of Gethsemane where He prayed, "If it be possible, let this cup pass from me: nevertheless, not as I will, but as thou wilt."

The full significance of the Garden of Gethsemane will probably be forever beyond our grasp. We can walk in there softly and tiptoe around. We can see Christ agonizing on the ground in prayer. But every time we try to understand it, we realize there is so much more to it that we can never fully understand. The anguish He endured was such that He may have died in the Garden if an angel had not strengthened Him. In Gethsemane was perhaps the final struggle between the natural and the spiritual, between earth and heaven, between body and soul.

In all history, the betrayal of Jesus by Judas is the classic case of contemptible conduct. Jesus was betrayed into the hands of His enemies by one whom He had treated as a friend. After the betrayal, Peter tried to defend the Lord by using his sword. Here one man was trying to attack an entire army. Whatever else one may think about Peter, he had courage. He would risk anything for the Lord. But Jesus warned him that "they that take up the sword shall perish by the sword." For the Lord Jesus there is no human defense. No one would ever have been able to help

Him to avoid the sacrificial death to which He was called by His Father.

Should we allow people to reject the Lord Jesus Christ? The name of Christ is used in profanity every day. The day of the Lord, Sunday, is used for everything that men want to do. The house of God, the church, is ignored and avoided in many ways. The Word of God, the Bible, is ridiculed and contradicted. When Jesus told Peter not to fight in His defense, is that a lesson for us? The way of God may well be that we do not fight in defending Him or His Word. God knows what is taking place, and in His own good time He will vindicate those who put their trust in Him, and will judge those who reject Him.

After His betrayal and arrest, the Lord Jesus Christ was tried before the Jewish Council. In order to request the Roman government to put Him to death, the Jewish leaders first had to sentence Him in their own court. The Jewish court administered their own laws over their own people, and the Romans gave them authority to do that. However, this Jewish court did not have the right to impose the death penalty. If anyone were to be put to death, that person would first have to be tried in a Roman Court for breaking a Roman law. So, first of all, Jesus had to be charged with some crime for which death was the punishment in the Jewish law. The law of Moses prescribed the death penalty for blasphemy. Jesus of Nazareth would be guilty of blasphemy when He made Himself equal with God, if He were only a man.

When Jesus stood on trial, diligent search was made for witnesses who would say that He blasphemed God, but they could locate no damaging testimony. Finally Jesus was openly asked by the high priest if He were the Messiah and Jesus admitted it. Then He went on to say, "Hereafter shall ye see the Son of man sitting on the right hand of power, and coming in the clouds of heaven." That was an Old Testament description of the Messiah. Their condemnation of Him then was based upon His use of Scripture which was used to refer only to the Messiah. He was condemned because He claimed to be the Christ. What makes this so tragic is that He was actually telling the truth! He really was the Son of God!

And so it turned out that He was not condemned because He was a friend of sinners. He was not condemned because He taught the people. He was condemned because He claimed to be the Messiah, and this would make Him equal with God.

Then we have the sad story of Peter's denial. What Judas did was deliberate; what Peter did was impulsive. What Judas did was planned; what Peter did was done unawares. What Judas did affected the Lord's fate; what Peter did affected only himself. What

Judas did remained unforgiven; what Peter did was forgiven. It is not so much the act as it is the intention which really qualifies our conduct.

Why did Peter deny Christ? Perhaps because Peter was "following afar off," he was not close to the Lord. Instead he was with the enemies of Christ, associating with the soldiers in the courtyard. We should be very careful with whom we associate. We too could be tricked into denying the Lord if we don't stay close to Him. It is always safer up front. There is a safety in zeal. It is tragic to think how much is lost by a lukewarm response to the call of God. "Hunger and thirst" arouse strong persistent efforts to find "food and drink." Here we can remember the words of our Lord, "Blessed are they which hunger and thirst after righteousness: for they shall be filled" (Matthew 5:6).

THE BITTER CUP

> Then cometh Jesus with them unto a place called Gethsemane, and saith unto the disciples, Sit ye here, while I go and pray yonder. And he took with him Peter and the two sons of Zebedee, and began to be sorrowful and very heavy. Then saith he unto them, My soul is exceeding sorrowful, even unto death: tarry ye here, and watch with me. And he went a little farther, and fell on his face, and prayed, saying, O my Father, if it be possible, let this cup pass from me: nevertheless not as I will, but as thou wilt. And he cometh unto the disciples, and findeth them asleep, and saith unto Peter, What, could ye not watch with me one hour? Watch and pray, that ye enter not into temptation: the spirit indeed is willing, but the flesh is weak. He went away again the second time, and prayed, saying, O my Father, if this cup may not pass away from me, except I drink it, thy will be done. And he came and found them asleep again: for their eyes were heavy. And he left them, and went away again, and prayed the third time, saying the same words. Then cometh he to his disciples, and saith unto them, Sleep on now, and take your rest: behold, the hour is at hand, and the Son of man is betrayed into the hands of sinners. Rise, let us be going: behold, he is at hand that doth betray me (Matthew 26:36-46).

As Jesus entered the Garden of Gethsemane with His band of disciples, He told the group as a whole, "Sit ye here, while I go and pray yonder." All of them were not equally ready to enter into close personal communion with God. This is the way it always is. Some people will just sit, as others go yonder to pray. This does not mean they are not Christians. It just means that they are not yet ready to enter into close communion with the Father.

Then Jesus singled out three disciples, Peter, James and John, the inner circle, to accompany Him further. Today there are some Christians who are in the inner circle and others who are not.

But every child of God should have the ambition to join this inner circle.

In the Garden, Jesus "began to be sorrowful and very heavy." He was in distress. If the Lord Jesus suffered this way, you can be sure that the Christian life for you will not always be one of sweetness and light.

"Then saith he unto them, . . . Tarry ye here, and watch with me." They were not going to do the praying, but they could have fellowship in prayer. You can share in prayer without actually doing the talking.

"He went a little farther and fell on his face." The entire world outside was unconcerned, the city of Jerusalem was unconcerned. Only one group was concerned about what He had predicted: He would soon be separated from them. Of that group, only three belonged to the inner circle and accompanied Him into the Garden's interior. Of these three there was not one who stayed with Him to pray.

Jesus prayed, "O my Father, if it be possible, let this cup pass from me: nevertheless not as I will, but as thou wilt." Another gospel adds the words, "Father, all things are possible unto thee." Some things God could do if He would, but He will not do them because they are contrary to His will. While God is omnipotent, He will do only those things that His holy, wise and just will prompts Him to do. So Jesus prays, "If it be possible"; that is, if the Father had liberty to do this. The actual request came later in His praying and was this: "Not as I will, but as thou wilt."

When any believer comes before God, he comes with a mixture of spiritual feelings and human feelings. In like manner, the Lord Jesus came before the Father. "Father, if it be possible [from a natural point of view], let this cup pass from me: nevertheless [I want only what is spiritual] not as I will, but as thou wilt." We may have wishes in our hearts which we never voice because they may not fit the plans of God.

When He returned after praying one hour, Peter, James and John were sleeping. Jesus again left them and prayed, committing Himself into the will of His Father. A third time He went to pray, and as He returned to find His disciples still asleep, He said, "Behold, the hour is at hand, and the Son of man is betrayed into the hands of sinners."

Sometimes when you wonder whether you need to pray for a thing a second time, remember that the Lord Jesus Christ prayed for something three times, spending perhaps as much as three hours in prayer.

There may be those who would say that the praying of Jesus

here actually did not affect the outcome. We need to consider *what did* Jesus *pray* for? Apparently it was *not* to save *Himself.* It seems clear that He prayed that the will of God should be done.

A KISS AND A SWORD

> And while he yet spake, lo, Judas, one of the twelve, came, and with him a great multitude with swords and staves, from the chief priests and elders of the people. Now he that betrayed him gave them a sign, saying, Whomsoever I shall kiss, that same is he: hold him fast. And forthwith he came to Jesus, and said, Hail, master; and kissed him. And Jesus said unto him, Friend, wherefore art thou come? Then came they, and laid hands on Jesus, and took him. And, behold, one of them which were with Jesus stretched out his hand, and drew his sword, and struck a servant of the high priest's, and smote off his ear. Then said Jesus unto him, Put up again thy sword into his place: for all they that take the sword shall perish with the sword. Thinkest thou that I cannot now pray to my Father, and he shall presently give me more than twelve legions of angels? But how then shall the scriptures be fulfilled, that thus it must be? In that same hour said Jesus to the multitudes, Are ye come out as against a thief with swords and staves for to take me? I sat daily with you teaching in the temple, and ye laid no hold on me. But all this was done, that the scriptures of the prophets might be fulfilled. Then all the disciples forsook him, and fled (Matthew 26:47-56).

Judas betrayed Christ with a kiss, an act of friendship. He had to betray Him in this way, so that the soldiers would know whom to arrest. Apparently the Lord Jesus was not unusual in appearance. No doubt He looked much the same as His eleven apostles. Of course it was at night and very possibly the only light was the light of the torches. So it became necessary for an "insider" to betray Him. Judas identified Him by saying "Hail, Master," and kissing Him. Kissing in those days would be very much like shaking hands today; it was a social greeting.

When Jesus asked, "Friend, wherefore art thou come?" He was not asking for information, but He was seeking to keep the record straight and maybe to open the eyes of Judas even then.

When Peter saw them take the Lord Jesus to arrest Him, he could not stand it. He drew his sword and attacked the company, cutting off a soldier's ear. His natural impulse was to defend and he was ready to do it at any cost. But that was not the way to do the will of God. As already stated we do not need to defend the Lord Jesus Christ with human ingenuity and human strength. Nor do the Scriptures need human defense. All we need to do is to witness about our faith. The fact that Peter wanted to defend

Christ was natural enough, but the Lord Jesus was not looking for such a defense. The Lord Jesus was expecting to be betrayed, tried and killed. If fighting had been the way to serve the Lord, God could have sent a multitude of angels to protect Him. But He didn't. He called these weak human creatures who believed in Christ Jesus, and who had been blessed, to be His witnesses.

WHEN CAIAPHAS RENT HIS CLOTHES

And they that had laid hold on Jesus led him away to Caiaphas the high priest, where the scribes and the elders were assembled. But Peter followed him afar off unto the high priest's palace, and went in, and sat with the servants, to see the end. Now the chief priests, and elders, and all the council, sought false witness against Jesus, to put him to death; But found none: yea, though many false witnesses came, yet found they none. At the last came two false witnesses, And said, This fellow said, I am able to destroy the temple of God, and to build it in three days. And the high priest arose, and said unto him, Answerest thou nothing? what is it which these witness against thee? But Jesus held his peace. And the high priest answered and said unto him, I adjure thee by the living God, that thou tell us whether thou be the Christ, the Son of God. Jesus saith unto him, Thou hast said: nevertheless I say unto you, Hereafter shall ye see the Son of man sitting on the right hand of power, and coming in the clouds of heaven. Then the high priest rent his clothes, saying, He hath spoken blasphemy; what further need have we of witnesses? behold, now ye have heard his blasphemy. What think ye? They answered and said, He is guilty of death. Then did they spit in his face, and buffeted him; and others smote him with the palms of their hands, Saying, Prophesy unto us, thou Christ, Who is he that smote thee? (Matthew 26:57-68).

Two different natural groups were interested in the Lord Jesus Christ. The Jews were interested in Him from a religious point of view. The Romans were interested in Him from a political point of view. The court of the Jews was called the Jewish Council and it was presided over by the high priest. They tried the Lord Jesus on the basis of His teaching, to see whether the Jewish religious law had anything against Him. The Governor presided over the Roman court which tried Jesus of Nazareth for the public disturbance He had caused.

The Jews, led by the high priest, Caiaphas, took the initiative against the Lord Jesus Christ. Caiaphas wanted to destroy Jesus and arranged to have Him tried before the Jewish Council and condemned for blasphemy. The punishment for blasphemy was death and so the Jewish Council condemned Him to death. But, as has been noted before, at that time the Jewish Council did not have the authority to put a man to death. In its police supervision of the city of Jerusalem, the Roman government reserved this right of capital punishment for itself. Thus in order to have the Lord Jesus condemned to death, He would have to be found guilty by a Roman court of something that would be worthy of the death penalty. We remember that when He was brought before Caiaphas He was charged with blasphemy, which was a crime against God in the Jewish law, punishable by death; but when He was brought into the court of Pilate, the Roman court, blasphemy was not a sufficient charge because the Roman law did not allow a death penalty for this reason. So before Pilate, Jesus was charged with treason. Needless to say, in each case from the point of view of justice the charge was false, the procedure was faulty, and the conclusion was prejudiced.

"Peter followed him afar off unto the high priest's palace, and went in, and sat with the servants, to see the end." The ground plan of the buildings of the temple help to understand what happened to Peter. The "palace" was not one big building, but rather a group of buildings where the high priest lived and worked. It resembled the buildings on a modern university campus, rather tightly grouped together around a courtyard. The rooms out from this courtyard were used for the court proceedings. On this occasion the soldiers and others stood in this area. And it was in this area, which was yet "in the palace," that Peter denied the Lord.

The chief priests, elders and all the council tried to find anyone who would accuse Jesus of a crime that was punishable by death. Such would have to be a false witness because He really had done nothing wrong in the eyes of the law. But they could not find anyone. (Different ones came forward to witness against Christ, but upon examination what they had to say did not amount to anything.) "At last came two false witnesses, and said, This fellow said, I am able to destroy the temple of God, and to build it in three days." We remember that when the Lord Jesus began His ministry, He was shown the buildings of the temple and then He had said, "You destroy this building that I am in [meaning His body], and I will rebuild it in three days." But they twisted the meaning of what He had said when they reported this in court.

The Lord Jesus did not answer the charges. He held His peace. The high priest became impatient with finding no satisfactory witnesses against Jesus and so he finally asked Him plainly "that thou tell us whether thou be the Christ, the Son of God. Jesus saith unto him, Thou hast said." That expression is similar to our slang expression, "You said it." Then Jesus added, "Nevertheless I say unto you, Hereafter shall ye see the Son of man sitting on the right hand of power, and coming in the clouds of heaven." He made it as plain as possible that He was the Son of God. The high priest tore his clothes, in a gesture of despair and grief and said, "He hath spoken blasphemy; what further need have we of witnesses?" They answered and said, "He is guilty of death." Then they surrounded Him, slapped His face, hit Him, and spat on Him.

The whole scene was one of crude and vulgar brutality toward One who had been patient, meek and kind and had not hurt a single one of them. But this can happen when people's prejudices are aroused. They had brought Him to their court according to their regulations, and had declared Him guilty, and sentenced Him to receive the death penalty.

Denial in the Courtyard

Now Peter sat without in the palace: and a damsel came unto him saying, Thou also wast with Jesus of Galilee. But he denied before them all, saying, I know not what thou sayest. And when he was gone out into the porch, another maid saw him, and said unto them that were there, This fellow was also with Jesus of Nazareth. And again he denied with an oath, I do not know the man. And after a while came unto him they that stood by, and said to Peter, Surely thou also art one of them; for thy speech bewrayeth thee. Then began he to curse and to swear, saying, I know not the man. And immediately the cock crew. And Peter remembered the word of Jesus, which said unto him, Before the cock crow, thou shalt deny me thrice. And he went out, and wept bitterly (Matthew 26:69-75).

Let us look again at this astonishing denial of Jesus Christ by the Apostle Peter. It all began while Peter was sitting outside the courtroom. He may have been in the courtyard with the soldiers and other observers of the trial. Here they could witness the proceedings of the court through an open doorway in an adjoining building.

First, a young girl came to Peter and said that he was a follower of Christ. Peter denied it before them all. "I don't know what you are talking about." He denied knowing the Lord!

Then Peter went into the porch, farther away from the room in which the Lord Jesus was being tried. On the porch another girl saw him, and accused him of being with Jesus of Nazareth. This time he denied it with an oath. He had said he did not know what the first girl was talking about, but now he came out more directly and said, "I do not know the man." And this he affirmed with an oath.

Then a third person came to Peter and identified him as a follower of Jesus of Nazareth. "Thy speech bewrayeth thee." Quite often when a person is in the wrong, he tries to cover it over with talk. At any rate, Peter had been talking and someone identified his accent as from Galilee. Then began he to curse and to swear, "I don't know what you are talking about. I don't know the man at all."

"Immediately the cock crew." Earlier that evening the Lord Jesus had told him, "Before the cock crow, thou shalt deny me thrice." Peter had been so sure that he would never deny the Lord, but now he had denied Him three times! Then Peter went out and wept bitterly.

Again we may ask:

"How could he do it?" Peter was a follower of the Lord Jesus Christ. He had known Him at least three years. He had heard the teachings, he had seen the miracles. If any man knew the Lord Jesus it was Peter. How could a thing like this happen? Do you remember when the Lord Jesus first told the disciples that He would be crucified? At that time Peter rebuked Jesus and said, "Lord, be this far from thee." And the Lord Jesus answered, "Get thee behind me, Satan: thou art an offence unto me: for thou savourest not the things that be of God, but those that be of men." Peter was thinking like a man. Filled with human thoughts he felt that Jesus did not need to go to Jerusalem.

And again when the Lord Jesus told the disciples that they were going to forsake Him, Peter spoke up and said, "I will never forsake thee." When the Lord Jesus told him that before the morning he would deny Him thrice, Peter said, "If they were to kill me, I will not forsake thee. I will never deny thee." In his self-confidence he fooled himself. Because things happened just as Jesus Christ knew they would, Peter had the humiliating experience of realizing his own human weakness.

In the Garden of Gethsemane we can have another insight into Peter. This time he was sleeping when he should have been praying. You can sympathize with him, for he was tired. Yet he did not watch and pray as the Lord had told him, and this was dangerous. Here we can see one reason why Peter denied the Lord. He was not prepared to identify himself with Christ. He had been thinking like a man. He had been filled with self-confidence instead of confidence in God. When the soldiers came to arrest Jesus, he took out his sword and attacked them. At this time Peter was fighting when he should have been yielding. It takes a stronger man to yield than it does to fight. He was sleeping when he should have been praying, fighting when he should have been yielding and denying when he should have been confessing. As long as Peter depended on himself he failed in a sad way. But the record later shows that Peter became one of the greatest servants of Christ.

Chapter 23

THE MIDDLE CROSS AND THE EMPTY TOMB

WHAT MAKES THE CROSS BEAUTIFUL?

The death of Jesus of Nazareth on Calvary's cross considered with His Resurrection is undoubtedly the most significant event that ever occurred in the history of man. The entire gospel of Matthew seems to move between the borderline of earth and heaven. True, it all took place in Palestine almost 2,000 years ago. And yet as you read, you feel that you are close to the very presence of God. It is as though you were walking along a long hall with curtains, and every now and again the curtain parts and the light of heaven itself shines through. In this gospel you see truth about man, about God and about salvation. If you read it on the surface, it is a simple account, but when you look more deeply into it, you open your heart to the truth that God Himself will show.

When you come to the cross you come to the climax of the entire Gospel. The record of what happened in the crucifixion is written in language that is simple and direct. Underneath this simplicity is profound truth.

As the Lord Jesus Christ stood in Pilate's courtroom, He was falsely accused, unjustly condemned and cruelly treated. But Pilate was on trial, too. His ruthless decision is an eternal illustration of knowing better but doing what is against one's own good judgment. He knew that there was nothing wrong with Jesus of Nazareth, and he had no desire to hurt him. His wife sent him advice: Do nothing against Jesus of Nazareth. Yet he turned his back on Jesus Christ, because he had political interests; he wanted to advance himself. When someone suggested to him that this Jesus of Nazareth had called Himself a king, he realized that this would not sound very good in the ears of Caesar. Pilate knew, of course, that Jesus was not talking about a political kingdom. He even tried to wash his hands of the whole thing.

We give various names to our children. We name people John, Peter, James and Joseph; these names are common. But no one ever calls a child by the name of Pilate. It is a name that is treated with contempt all over the world. "What did he do that was so contemptible?" When he knew better, for the sake of personal reasons, he turned his back on Jesus. From what is written it appears he knew there was no justice being shown in this trial. When Pilate reached the conclusion that the only thing he could do was to condemn Jesus of Nazareth, he actually condemned himself.

Jesus Christ was placed on the cross by Roman soldiers. This scene of the death of Christ is so vulgar and crude that many people think we should not talk about it. Yet this scene has been so powerful for good that it has again and again effected release from sin.

Beautiful scenes are to be found in every continent. Africa is perhaps the most beautiful continent in the world. But in the midst of that beauty, people live in misery, darkness and fear. The Himalaya Mountains of India are grander than anything man has ever seen, but on the slopes of those mountains people live beset by fear of all kinds. They have all that beauty in front of them but it does not help them any.

The scene in Matthew 27 is not beautiful from a human point of view. The cross was just a big post in the ground with a crossbar. On it a man was killed by an ugly mob. But this picture has brought peace to countless hearts and minds. In the presence of this picture, men's lives have been changed, people have been set free from sin, homes have been reunited, friendships have been restored. "The Old Rugged Cross, so despised by the world, has a wondrous attraction for me."

The moment that the Lord Jesus Christ died, the whole tone of the account changes. Not only was there an earthquake, but the veil of the temple was rent from the top to the bottom. Even the centurion said, "Truly this was the Son of God!" The women of Galilee, Mary Magdalene and Mary, the mother of James and Joseph, stood with many other women, looking on at His agony with breaking hearts. He whom the leaders rejected is now being worshiped by a faithful few.

Then Joseph of Arimathea came forward to acknowledge His Lord, to ask for His body that he might prepare it for burial. Satisfied upon examination that He was really dead, Pilate gave His body to Joseph. Joseph wound the corpse in linen clothes and put Him in his own new tomb. All the while the faithful women watched in the tragic pathos of the world's darkest hour.

THE PRICE OF BLOOD

When the morning was come, all the chief priests and elders of the people took counsel against Jesus to put him to death: And when they had bound him, they led him away, and delivered him to Pontius Pilate the governor. Then Judas, which had betrayed him, when he saw that he was condemned, repented himself, and brought again the thirty pieces of silver to the chief priests and elders, Saying, I have sinned in that I have betrayed the innocent blood. And they said, What is that to us? see thou to that. And he cast down the pieces of silver in the temple, and departed, and went and hanged himself. And the chief priests took the silver pieces, and said, It is not lawful for to put them into the treasury, because it is the price of blood. And they took counsel, and bought with them the potter's field, to bury strangers in. Wherefore that field was called, The field of blood, unto this day. Then was fulfilled that which was spoken by Jeremy the prophet, saying, And they took the thirty pieces of silver, the price of him that was valued, whom they of the children of Israel did value; And gave them for the potter's field, as the Lord appointed me (Matthew 27:1-10).

The action of Judas in betraying Jesus of Nazareth has long fascinated students of human nature as a deep puzzle. You have probably heard various explanations for Judas' action. Some people say that he did not really think that the Lord Jesus would actually be harmed. Others think that since Jesus was going to be arrested anyway, Judas felt he might as well collect the thirty pieces of silver as not. Still others say that he had become disappointed in the Lord Jesus: the Lord Jesus had not done what he had expected Him to do. Perhaps he just saw thirty pieces of silver available and the love of money was so strong that for the time being it overcame him. The truth is that this man who had walked with the Lord turned against Him, and was used by Satan to turn the Lord Jesus over to His enemies.

After Jesus was condemned by the Jewish Council, Judas was shocked to see this turn of events and returned to the chief priests and elders with the money. Perhaps Judas had not expected that Jesus actually would be condemned. In any case, when he saw that the Lord Jesus was condemned to die, he "repented himself." He realized now the full import of his wrongdoing, but coming to the chief priests to admit this, he found no sympathy from them. Their answer is typical of the world. The world is not interested in believers. It is interested only in what it wants to do, and in us only as far as we help it do what it wants to do.

In the New Testament there are different records about the death of Judas. In one place we read he "went and hanged himself." In another place the record is that "falling down headlong, his body burst open." The hangings in those days were different from hangings today. Today when a man is hanged, he is pronounced dead, put in a coffin and buried. In those days, when a man was hanged he was left hanging until, for one reason or another, the body would practically decay. He was left as an example. In the case of Judas he went and hanged himself, and in due time his decayed body fell and burst in pieces. It is a gruesome picture, but it was the end of the man who betrayed his Lord.

Probably nowhere in literature is there any record more cynical than the action of the chief priests when they handled the money which Judas returned in his remorse. Now they were concerned about their ethics; now they were concerned about legality. They had paid this money for the betrayal and now, when the silver pieces were returned they said, "It is not lawful for to put them into the treasury." It is always a strange thing to see how people can be unscrupulous along certain lines, and so careful along other lines. After discussing the matter they used the money to buy a paupers' graveyard.

This then is the total story of the betrayal of Jesus with its ugly and tragic ending. Surrounded with the truth of the Gospel and yet enslaved with personal interest: this was Judas.

Let us beware lest we feel smug in our own righteousness. What is our thirty pieces of silver? What is it that we must have, little as it is, and for the sake of which we will actually deny the Lord? That is what Judas did.

GIVE US BARABBAS

And Jesus stood before the governor; and the governor asked him, saying, Art thou the King of the Jews? And Jesus said unto him, Thou sayest. And when he was accused of the chief priests and elders, he answered nothing. Then said Pilate unto him, Hearest thou not how many things they witness against thee? And he answered him to never a word; insomuch that the governor marvelled greatly. Now at that feast the governor was wont to release unto the people a prisoner, whom they would. And they had then a notable prisoner, called Barabbas. Therefore when they were gathered together, Pilate said unto them, Whom will ye that I release unto you? Barabbas, or Jesus which is called Christ? For he knew that for envy they had delivered him. When he was set down on the judgment seat, his wife sent unto him, saying, Have thou nothing to do with that just man: for I have suffered many things this day in a dream because of him. But the chief priests and elders persuaded the multitude that they should ask Barabbas, and destroy Jesus. The governor answered and said unto them, Whether of the twain will ye that I release unto you? They said, Barabbas. Pilate saith unto them, What shall I do then with Jesus which is called Christ? They all say unto him, Let him be crucified. And the governor said, Why, what evil hath he done? But they cried out the more, saying, Let him be crucified. When Pilate saw that he could prevail nothing, but that rather a tumult was made, he took water, and washed his hands before the multitude, saying, I am innocent of the blood of this just person: see ye to it. Then answered all the people, and said, His blood be on us, and on our children. Then released he Barabbas unto them: and when he had scourged Jesus, he delivered him to be crucified (Matthew 27:11-26).

In the crucifixion scene we naturally are fascinated by the amazing conduct of the humble, meek Jesus of Nazareth. Yet now instead of looking at the Lord Jesus Christ only, let us keep our eye on Pilate. As governor he could rule for or against Jesus of Nazareth, and he knew that ruling would decide the fate of this mild, good man. In some respects you could sympathize with Pontius Pilate. After all, Pilate did not ask for this situation. When he became governor of that particular province he didn't realize how notorious he would become because of what he did about a Galilean named Jesus. As you read through the story, you can't help but feel that he was, in many respects, a fairly good man. He had nothing personal against the Lord Jesus Christ. But when Pilate passed judgment on Jesus of Nazareth he did so in serving his own personal interests, even though his action was unjust and unfair to the prisoner.

At the feast time the governor traditionally released one of the Jewish prisoners. This was a gesture on the part of the Roman government to please the Jews. It was to improve the public image of Rome. Not believing Jesus to be guilty of any crime deserving the death penalty, Pilate thought that this was one way in which he could spare the unfortunate, condemned victim. Another prisoner, Barabbas, was a desperado. By offering the crowd the choice between these two Pilate thought that the answer would undoubtedly be "Release Jesus."

Jesus of Nazareth was known throughout Jerusalem as a man who did only good; Barabbas was a vicious man who had done only wrong. But persuaded by the chief priests to ask for the release of Barabbas, the crowd yelled, "Barabbas." No doubt Pilate was shocked. He asked them what he should do with Jesus. The crowd responded, "Crucify him."

"When Pilate saw that he could prevail nothing," and that the crowd was an unruly mob, he washed his hands of the whole affair. This was his gesture to disclaim responsibility. In effect, he said, "None of this is my responsibility." Though Pilate may have thought that this was a way out for him, the whole world today holds Pilate responsible.

There are two men in connection with the crucifixion of the Lord Jesus Christ whom no one is ever disposed to forgive. One is Judas Iscariot who betrayed Him, and the other is Pontius Pilate who condemned Him. It would seem Pilate did not mean any harm. Actually he tried to spare Him. The truth is that although he had the opportunity to free Jesus, Pilate declined to rule justly, but instead allowed the people to sway his decision by an appeal to his own political interests.

To free Jesus Christ would have been too much of a political chance for Pilate to take. It would not have been expedient. Doubtless he was sorry for Jesus, but he didn't want to take the responsibility. Here again we should beware of any smug self-righteousness in our hearts. Many men today are confronted by the Lord Jesus Christ and do not want to make any decision about Him. They are asked, "What will you do with Jesus?" and they do not want to be committed either way. "Will you accept Him or reject Him?" They do not want to do either. What we all need to realize is that we cannot turn our backs on the Lord Jesus Christ and so ignore the issue. He poses an issue before each soul. We are either for Him or against him. The man who decides against Christ Jesus is deciding against himself even as Pilate did. But we can thank God that our own salvation can be secured on such a simple basis as to decide in favor of Jesus Christ.

"Father, Forgive Them"

Then the soldiers of the governor took Jesus into the common hall, and gathered unto him the whole band of soldiers. And they stripped him, and put on him a scarlet robe. And when they had platted a crown of thorns, they put it upon his head, and a reed in his right hand: and they bowed the knee before him, and mocked him, saying, Hail, King of the Jews! And they spit upon him, and took the reed, and smote him on the head. And after that they had mocked him, they took the robe off from him, and put his own raiment on him, and led him away to crucify him. And as they came out, they found a man of Cyrene, Simon by name: him they compelled to bear his cross. And when they were come unto a place called Golgotha, that is to say, a place of a skull, They gave him vinegar to drink mingled with gall: and when he had tasted thereof, he would not drink. And they crucified him, and parted his garments, casting lots: that it might be fulfilled which was spoken by the prophet, They parted my garments among them, and upon my vesture did they cast lots. And sitting down they watched him there; And set up over his head his accusation written, THIS IS JESUS THE KING OF THE JEWS. Then were there two thieves crucified with him, one on the right hand, and another on the left (Matthew 27:27-38).

The Jewish people did not actually crucify Jesus. This was done by the Roman soldiers. As far as the soldiers are concerned, they were probably ignorant of what they were doing. On the cross Jesus prayed, "Father, forgive them, for they know not what they do." This was true of the soldiers who drove the nails into His hands. They were simply carrying out a routine task.

One way to understand verses 28-30 is to know something of barrackroom life, and of the coarse, callous conduct of men who are accustomed to danger. When such men have their sport, they carry it out in a cruel fashion. They mocked Jesus by putting upon Him a scarlet robe, an imitation robe such as a king would wear. Being a king He ought to have a crown, so the soldiers made a crown of thorns. They put a reed in His right hand, as a symbol of His authority. In cruel mockery they bowed before Him, and sarcastically they cried, "Hail, King of the Jews." This whole exhibition is a sad display of human nature.

After all this physical abuse, the Lord was so weak that He could not carry His cross. He staggered under the weight of it, and a stranger was compelled to carry it. The soldiers could call this man from the crowd and force him to do it. So Simon the Cyrene carried the cross.

Golgotha, a hill that was shaped like a skull, was called "the place of a skull." Generally speaking, we call the place of the crucifixion "Calvary" and today Calvary has become an honored and revered name among us. However, this was actually the city dump, the nuisance ground. This was the place where they put criminals to death and where they dumped all the city's refuse.

The vinegar which they gave Him to drink would help to deaden the pain. Mingled with gall, it was a combination drink that would act as a sedative. But He did not drink it. It seems possible He would not take anything to deaden the pain, because He was suffering that pain for us.

The whole crude scene has another evidence of the coarse disregard for the victim's feelings. Even as the Lord suffered the pangs of dying they were rolling dice, to see who would get His clothing. Over His head was set the inscription, "This is Jesus the King of the Jews." Mark says, "The King of the Jews"; Luke says, "This is the King of the Jews"; John says, "Jesus of Nazareth, the King of the Jews." According to Luke, it was written in three languages, Greek, Latin and Hebrew, and this would explain the variant wordings. Perhaps to many this explanation may seem quite unnecessary. But there have been men of honored station in the church who have claimed the variant readings reported in the several gospels was evidence that the Scriptures are not reliable records! The comment of Luke should be enough to guide any candid student past such unworthy flimsy conclusion.

Apparently Jesus was crucified in a routine way as a criminal among criminals of that day. On each side was another cross. To the Roman soldiers He was one of three condemned men, and He deserved no better treatment than the others. This was the suffering and this was the shame willingly endured by the Lord Jesus Christ that we might be saved.

REVILED AND RIDICULED

And they that passed by reviled him, wagging their heads, And saying, Thou that destroyest the temple, and buildest it in three days, save thyself. If thou be the Son of God, come down from the cross. Likewise also the chief priests mocking him, with the scribes and elders, said, He saved others; himself he cannot save. If he be the King of Israel, let him now come down from the cross, and we will believe him. He trusted in God; let him deliver him now, if he will have him; for he said, I am the Son of God. The thieves also, which were crucified with him, cast the same in his teeth (Matthew 27:39-44).

As we try to understand the meaning of the crucifixion of Jesus of Nazareth we do well to remember that Jesus did not have to do this. He could have escaped it easily. He would not have needed to come to Jerusalem at all. Days before this, Peter suggested to Him, "Master, be it far from thee." But He went through with this very plan anyway. Why then did it have to happen? Because we have done wrong, He wanted to save us from our sins. His love for us made Him suffer willingly. Now once again notice what further suffering He had to bear. The Roman soldiers not only crucified Him after they had shamefully mocked Him, but they also tormented and abused Him. Besides the abuse of the Romans, He also suffered cruelly at the hands of the Jews, His own people.

They mocked Him by suggesting that He save Himself. This was one thing He could not do. He had already faced this in Gethsemane. If He were going to save us, He could not save Himself. To His everlasting glory, though He were rich, He became poor for our sake that through His poverty we might be rich. He suffered that we might enjoy the mercy of Almighty God. When they threw in His teeth the words, "If thou be the Son of God, come down from the cross," we are reminded of Satan's temptation, "If thou be the Son of God, command that these stones be made bread." Why should He not exercise His strength and power to protect Himself? After all, this crucifixion is only human. But such suggestion was clearly not from God. It showed complete ignorance of His plan.

Even those at the highest level in the religious community,

the chief priests, the scribes and the elders mocked Him in His suffering. "If he be the King of Israel, let him now come down from the cross, and we will believe him." Did they know what they were saying? People say that they would believe if only God would work a private miracle for them. But they would not believe. God makes no such bargains with man. The price of salvation was the cruel death of His Son Jesus Christ, nothing less, and nothing more. The price has already been paid. Anyone who offers to come to God on the condition that something special be done is ignoring what God has already done. In all the eternal ages it will forever be the wonder of all the worshiping host in heaven that God would give His Son to die for sinners.

THREE HOURS OF DARKNESS

Now from the sixth hour there was darkness over all the land unto the ninth hour. And about the ninth hour Jesus cried with a loud voice, saying, Eli, Eli, lama sabachthani? that is to say, My God, my God, why hast thou forsaken me? Some of them that stood there, when they heard that, said, This man calleth for Elias. And straightway one of them ran, and took a sponge, and filled it with vinegar, and put it on a reed, and gave him to drink. The rest said, Let be, let us see whether Elias will come to save him. Jesus, when he had cried again with a loud voice, yielded up the ghost. And, behold, the veil of the temple was rent in twain from the top to the bottom; and the earth did quake, and the rocks rent; And the graves were opened; and many bodies of the saints which slept arose, And came out of the graves after his resurrection, and went into the holy city, and appeared unto many (Matthew 27:45-53).

The record of what happened on that awful day of the crucifixion tells of a period of darkness over the whole country. Perhaps there was an eclipse of the sun from noon until three o'clock in the afternoon. During these three hours of darkness, He was dying from the physical exhaustion of hanging on the cross.

At the end of those three dark hours, He cried out, "My God, my God, why hast thou forsaken me?" These words of the Lord in suffering and sorrow are quoted from Psalm 22. With almost His last breath, Jesus was quoting Scripture. If anyone could have thought of an original, creative statement to fit this moment, don't you think it would have been the Lord Jesus Christ? Yet in this dark hour, as He came to this crisis of His life and everything moved to its climax, He quoted Old Testament Scripture! Why? Why did He quote the Old Testament? It should make us all realize how much we are missing when we neither read nor memorize the Scriptures. When the Lord Jesus was at the very limit of human endurance, He naturally chose Old Testament language,

words and thought forms, to express His heart to His heavenly
Father. If such language could be useful to Him, how much more
could we profit by a knowledge of the Bible.

When He says, "Why hast thou forsaken me?" He is not asking
the Father to give Him understanding as much as He is reviewing
the fact that His death is because of man's sin. The result of
human sin seems to have astonished Christ Jesus Himself. "Why
hast thou forsaken me?" Such is the depth of grief in the separation due to human sin.

Some who were nearby thought He was calling for Elijah. Actually the word for "my God" in Hebrew was "Eli" and the people
misinterpreted the words. Today many people hear the Word of
God and misinterpret it. They read the Bible and find in it only
what they want to hear. They interpret whatever happens on the
basis of a false premise. The false premise here was that Jesus
was calling for Elijah. When Elijah didn't come, they would say
that it proved Jesus was a fraud. They interpreted the actual events
of the Lord Jesus Christ in terms of their own false supposition.
Because the question was wrong, any answer would also be wrong.

After Jesus gave up the ghost and died, as a deliberate yielding of His Spirit to the Father, "the veil of the temple was rent
in twain from the top to the bottom." Ordinarily a curtain would
tear from the bottom up. But this curtain tore from the top down,
symbolizing that this was something God had done.

FOLLOWERS TO THE END

Now when the centurion, and they that were with him, watching
Jesus, saw the earthquake, and those things that were done, they
feared greatly, saying, Truly this was the Son of God. And many
women were there beholding afar off, which followed Jesus from
Galilee, ministering unto him: Among which was Mary Magdalene,
and Mary the mother of James and Joses, and the mother of
Zebedee's children. When the even was come, there came a rich
man of Arimathaea, named Joseph, who also himself was Jesus'
disciple: He went to Pilate, and begged the body of Jesus. Then
Pilate commanded the body to be delivered. And when Joseph
had taken the body, he wrapped it in a clean linen cloth, And
laid it in his own new tomb, which he had hewn out in the
rock: and he rolled a great stone to the door of the sepulchre,
and departed. And there was Mary Magdalene, and the other
Mary, sitting over against the sepulchre. Now the next day, that
followed the day of the preparation, the chief priests and Pharisees came together unto Pilate, Saying, Sir, we remember that
that deceiver said, while he was yet alive, After three days I will
rise again. Command therefore that the sepulchre be made sure
until the third day, lest his disciples come by night, and steal
him away, and say unto the people, He is risen from the dead:

so the last error shall be worse than the first. Pilate said unto them, Ye have a watch: go your way, make it as sure as ye can. So they went, and made the sepulchre sure, sealing the stone, and setting a watch (Matthew 27:54-66).

The record of the crucifixion goes on to tell of other things that happened. When we read that the centurion and they that were with him "feared greatly," we are to understand that they were deeply impressed and moved by what they had seen. The chief priests, the scribes and the elders had also been witnesses of the crucifixion, but they did not seem deeply impressed. We are not told that they feared greatly. Instead they mocked Him and said, "He saved others, himself he cannot save." But when the centurion saw the earthquake and experienced the darkness, he believed. Here again we see that response. is an individual matter.

Besides the centurion, there was another company of believers at the cross. This was a group of women, among whom were Mary Magdalene, Mary the mother of Joseph and James, and the mother of Zebedee's children. To the everlasting credit of women, it must be said these were faithful. In the darkest hour they stood by.

Mary Magdalene had been a wicked woman. Seven devils had been cast out of her by the Lord, but in this hour she stood by Him. Then there was the mother of Zebedee's children. Perhaps you are inclined to belittle her because she had previously wanted a special place of honor for her two sons in the coming kingdom of the Lord. Let us not be too quick to judge one another. Just because her request for her sons could not be granted does not mean that she was not a godly woman.

Then in this dark hour another one comes forward. When the Lord Jesus seemed to have been rejected by all the world, Joseph of Arimathea came to claim the body. The chief priests, scribes, elders and even the thieves had sneered at Him; His own disciples had deserted Him. But then Joseph came: a layman, not a priest, nor a scribe, nor one of the elders, not even one of the apostles. Though he had been a believer, Joseph did not make public profession of his faith because he feared the Jews. He was a cautious man, but yet he was a disciple; and in an hour when all others forsook the Lord, this man came forward boldly.

The greatest hope for the testimony of the Gospel today is the Christian layman. Today laymen have their chance to step forward even when some church leaders seem to repudiate Jesus Christ.

During the crucifixion, the Lord Jesus Christ was in the hands of cruel, callous people. After His death on the cross, the only hands that ever touched His body were the loving hands of believing people. From this time on the body of the Lord was treated with reverence and love. Joseph wrapped the body in a clean linen cloth and put Him in his own new tomb.

Some people think that in the time of the Lord Jesus Christ, no one cared much about the Resurrection, as to whether it happened or not. But even before it took place, there was a rumor that something mysterious might happen to the body of Christ. Certain of the priests and Pharisees wanted to make very sure that there would be no pretended resurrection, so they took steps to make sure that a hoax could not be perpetrated. They were able to get a detail of soldiers placed at the tomb to see that no one would open it and take out the body.

These soldiers did their best to prevent the Resurrection. But, praise God, they were not successful. There is a 28th chapter of Matthew that will forever tell the world that no effort of man could prevent the scheduled Resurrection of Jesus Christ.

> Up from the grave He arose,
> With a mighty triumph o'er His foes.

He Is Risen

In the end of the sabbath, as it began to dawn toward the first day of the week, came Mary Magdalene and the other Mary to see the sepulchre. And, behold, there was a great earthquake: for the angel of the Lord descended from heaven, and came and rolled back the stone from the door, and sat upon it. His countenance was like lightning, and his raiment white as snow: And for fear of him the keepers did shake, and became as dead men. And the angel answered and said unto the women, Fear not ye: for I know that ye seek Jesus, which was crucified. He is not here: for he is risen, as he said. Come, see the place where the Lord lay. And go quickly, and tell his disciples that he is risen from the dead; and, behold, he goeth before you into Galilee; there shall ye see him: lo, I have told you. And they departed quickly from the sepulchre with fear and great joy; and did run to bring his disciples word. And as they went to tell his disciples, behold, Jesus met them, saying, All hail. And they came and held him by the feet, and worshipped him. Then said Jesus unto them, Be not afraid: go tell my brethren that they go into Galilee, and there shall they see me (Matthew 28:1-10).

The Resurrection of the Lord Jesus Christ was on the first day of the week, and the Jewish Sabbath is, of course, on the seventh day. By common consent Christians have called the first day of the week "the Lord's Day," and it is accepted as the Christian sabbath. We need not be too disturbed when someone tells us that the Sabbath should be the seventh day. The Jewish people had sabbath years as well as sabbath days, and their sabbath days did not always fall on the seventh day. Any day of rest was a sabbath day. The word "sabbath" comes from "seventh," but it doesn't necessarily mean the seventh day of the week; rather it refers to the proportion; in other words, one-seventh of the week. While the Jewish people observe the Sabbath day on Saturday, the Christian church, generally speaking, observes the Sabbath on Sunday. Each of them observe one day in seven as a day of rest.

"As it began to dawn." The dark night had been settling over the latter part of the Lord's ministry on earth. Events seemed to make everything darker and darker until He was put to death on the cross. Now began the dawn, not only for that particular day, but in all history because the Lord Jesus did not stay in the grave. This is the glory of the Christian Gospel. He died, yes, and was buried, yes, but He rose again, and He lives forevermore!

First at the tomb was Mary Magdalene. She was last at the cross and first at the grave. The Lord allowed this woman of the street, this woman out of whom had gone seven devils, this peculiar and special honor. She stood on guard when He died, and she was there when He arose. What a marvelous privilege!

The Bible does not tell us much about angels. These creatures of God were not like man and yet they could take on human form. Some people seem to think that only believers can see angels and consequently it is all part of their "sanctified" imagination. But in this case, the guards who weren't believers saw the angel. When they saw him, they were knocked unconscious. The angel then told the women that Jesus was risen.

The women responded "with fear and great joy" and ran to tell the disciples. Perhaps you wonder how they could have fear and great joy at the same time. In our day "fear" usually means "fright." It usually means that you are afraid of something evil. But the word "fear" can simply refer to deep, emotional feeling. It can mean a great sense of awe or reverence. These women were profoundly stirred with feelings of great reverence, and they left the tomb and ran with great joy to find the disciples.

As they went, Jesus met them. They held Him by the feet and worshiped Him. This means that they fell down before Him and clutched their arms around His legs and knees. Jesus comforted them and then reaffirmed the angel's message to tell the disciples to go to Galilee.

After the Resurrection, the Lord Jesus dealt exclusively with His disciples. He didn't go to the Roman governor. Just think what an impression He could have made on Pilate! Or He could have gone to the chief priests to rebuke them. Certainly they would have listened to a resurrected Jesus! But He didn't. They had had their chance. Our Lord went instead to the humble group of Galileans who were His disciples. Upon them rested the future course of Christianity, and to them He gave this great marvelous blessing of actually seeing Him after the Resurrection. To believe in the Lord is to qualify for more and more faith as the Lord continues to assure us of Himself.

"I AM WITH YOU ALWAY"

Now when they were going, behold, some of the watch came into the city, and shewed unto the chief priests all the things that were done. And when they were assembled with the elders, and had taken counsel, they gave large money unto the soldiers, Saying, Say ye, His disciples came by night, and stole him away while we slept. And if this come to the governor's ears, we will persuade him, and secure you. So they took the money, and did as they were taught: and this saying is commonly reported among the Jews until this day. Then the eleven disciples went away into Galilee, into a mountain where Jesus had appointed them. And when they saw him, they worshipped him: but some doubted. And Jesus came and spake unto them, saying, All power is given unto me in heaven and in earth. Go ye therefore, and teach all nations, baptizing them in the name of the Father, and of the Son, and of the Holy Ghost: Teaching them to observe all things whatsoever I have commanded you: and, lo, I am with you alway, even unto the end of the world. Amen (Matthew 28:11-20).

The Jews and Romans who lived in Jerusalem at the time of Christ were not sentimental people. They were not the type to be influenced by imagination or emotion. They definitely wanted it to be understood that the Resurrection of Jesus Christ was not to be believed. If there had been any grounds to disprove it, the whole city would have been told the facts quickly. The very fact that no serious attempt to disprove the claim of the Christians was ever made should impress us.

When the soldiers told the Jewish leaders what had happened at the tomb, they were both bribed and blackmailed to say that the disciples had come at night and stolen the body. It was an utterly ridiculous story, but the Jewish leaders were desperate enough to accept the ridiculous. Yet in spite of all the Jewish leaders did to discount the resurrection story, the early Christian church grew on the conviction that Jesus Christ who was raised from the dead and who ascended into heaven is now at the right hand of God the Father.

Even in our day, people who openly claim to be Christians doubt the Resurrection. There have always been such people and there always will be.

Even among the apostles, those who really were followers of Jesus Christ, some doubted. With all the evidence before them, they still doubted. They did not think it could be true. The gospel of Luke carefully describes the various things which Jesus Christ did in the presence of His disciples to prove that He was really alive. Yet in spite of everything, some did not believe. So don't be surprised today, if some people cannot believe. That does not change any facts at all. If the tomb was empty, it was empty. If the body ascended into heaven, it ascended into heaven. Whether we believe it or not makes a difference to us but it does not change the events as they actually happened.

"Then the eleven disciples went away into Galilee." There were just eleven now. Judas was gone.

"All power is given unto me in heaven and in earth. Go ye therefore . . ." It is easy to understand how the disciples would need power as they would go. He now has all power, and in that power He sends us out to "teach all nations." This really means to "make disciples" of all nations. The word "disciple" means "learner." This does not mean that all nations will believe, nor that everyone will be saved, but it does mean that everyone should be taught and that learners should be recruited from among all nations in the world.

"And, lo, I am with you alway, even unto the end of the world." This word "world" does not mean this globe, this earth. It means unto the end of this "age" in which we are living. Actually this gracious promise is only for the people who go. The promise was not given to such as will stay. It was given to those who go in obedience to His command.

This does not necessarily mean that we must go geographically to Africa or India. It means we are to obey and do His will. Perhaps He will tell you to go to your family and witness to them. In that case He will be with you always in that situation. Perhaps He will tell you to go to your neighbors and witness to them. In that case He will be with you in that situation. Perhaps He will tell you to go to your shop or office, but whatever He tells you, obey, and you can be assured that He will be with you alway.

And so we come to the point where the earthly career of Jesus of Nazareth ends with the risen, resurrected Lord directing all His disciples to witness for Him to the ends of the earth that men may know of Him, believe in Him, and be saved by Him to the glory of God.